LUMINESCENT THREADS

Connections to
Octavia E. Butler

D0861326

edited by
Alexandra Pierce
and Mimi Mondal

twelfth
PLANET PRESS

First published in Australia in 2017
by Twelfth Planet Press
www.twelfthplanetpress.com

Cover and text design by Cathy Larsen Design
Set in 11/15 pt Fairfield Light
Copyediting by Elizabeth Disney

National Library of Australia Cataloguing-in-Publication entry

Title: Luminescent threads : connections to Octavia E. Butler /
edited by Alexandra Pierce and Mimi Mondal ; contributors:Rasha Abdulhadi
(and 47 others)

ISBN: 9781922101440 (paperback)
ISBN: 978-1-922101-43-3 (ebk)

Subjects: Butler, Octavia, 1946-2006–Correspondence.
Authors, American-Correspondence.
Science fiction, American.
Letters.

Other Creators/Contributors:
Pierce, Alexandra, editor.
Mondal, Mimi, editor.
Abdulhadi, Rasha.

CONTENTS

SECTION 1

Your work is a river I come home to

SECTION 2

What good is [science fiction's] examination of the possible effects of science and technology, or social organisation and political direction?

SECTION 3

Love lingers in between dog-eared pages

SECTION 4

I am an Octavia E. Butler Scholar

SECTION 5

Forget talent. There is only the work

SECTION 6

I love you across oceans, across generations, across lives

SECTION 7

Science Fiction Studies Memorial

SECTION 8

An interview with Octavia Butler 'We Keep Playing the Same Record'

INTRODUCTION

Alexandra Pierce

I read two of the three books of the Xenogenesis trilogy (*Dawn* and *Adulthood Rites*) many years before I had any idea who Octavia Estelle Butler was; I'm not sure whether I was reading while she was still alive, or not. I didn't know that she was African American. I certainly didn't know how important she was to so many people. Since then, I have become much more aware of both feminist science fiction and the importance of diversity in all fiction. In both of these arenas, Octavia Butler's name crops up.

In 2015, I coedited *Letters to Tiptree* in honour of James Tiptree Jr/Alice Sheldon. In the year of her centenary, we deemed it important to recognise this woman who wrote under a man's name, who seemed to be going unrecognised in the wider science fiction community but who had had such a significant impact on that community through her fiction and her life. The response was wonderful, with many people writing letters about how important she was as an author, and as a person. It also struck a chord with readers, and we started wondering which other writers ought to be paid tribute to in a similar way. Octavia Butler seemed obvious; not because she is in danger of being forgotten, but because she was remarkable in so many ways.

Octavia Butler was a pioneering African American woman

in the science fiction literary scene, and wrote powerful, difficult, provocative and beautiful fiction. She had a personal impact on innumerable people because she attended conventions, spoke at universities, and tutored at writing workshops. As we had hoped, the responses we have had for this book in your hands have been humbling. They are personal, and political, and poetic; they are fierce and full of love. A lot like Butler's work itself.

This book is intended to capture some of the ways that people relate and connect to Butler. We have named each section with a line from a letter or essay within it, which capture the essence of what each part focuses on. In the first section, 'Your work is a river I come home to', works focus on how Butler has inspired people in a variety of ways: in their work, in their lives. In the second, which uses a line from Butler's own essay 'Positive Obsessions', authors reflect on systemic and current political issues that Butler either commented on or would have, were she still alive. 'Love lingers in between dog-eared pages' includes letters and essays whose main interest is Butler's fiction – from *Kindred* to Xenogenesis and *Fledgling* – with reactions, arguments, and reflections on that work. Next, in 'I am an Octavia E. Butler Scholar', comes letters from some of the Octavia E. Butler Scholars: Clarion and Clarion West students who received the Octavia E. Butler Memorial Scholarship, set up by the Carl Brandon Society in Butler's honour after her death. The following chapter fits neatly after the Clarion one: 'Forget talent. There is only the work'. It features writers reflecting on how Butler influenced their writing through tutoring at Clarion or otherwise. Bogi Takács expresses the sentiments of the subsequent section: 'I love you across oceans, across generations, across lives'. These are, broadly speaking, love letters. They recount ways in which Butler and her work changed something about the writers, in situations as individual as the people describing them. The book is rounded out with a memorial that appeared in *Science Fiction Studies* in 2010, highlighting Butler's many contributions to science fiction as well as examining how Butler has been discussed. And we end with Octavia Butler's own words, in an interview with Stephen W. Potts from 1996. It was important that we allow Butler to speak for herself.

In 2008, Ritch Calvin noted that by that stage, 'a veritable cottage industry seem[ed] to have grown up around [Butler's] work.' He compiled a bibliography to showcase both Butler's own work, and how much had been written by other people about her. His piece for *Utopian Studies* in their Octavia Butler Special Issue (Volume 19, Number 3) ran from page 493 to page 516 of that journal, and covered (lengthy) reviews, dissertations and theses, books and chapters of books, and journal or magazine articles. A search in JSTOR (a digital library that enables researchers to search through academic journals) for 'Octavia Butler' limited to 2009-2017, to catch the work not covered by Calvin, returns 103 hits. Not all of them are especially relevant to Butler herself: some are reviews of books about Butler, which is getting a bit meta, and some have only a passing mention of Butler in relation to others. Nonetheless, this is testament to her enduring importance – as a writer and as a person. *Luminescent Threads: Connections to Octavia Butler* is a testament to that as well. Included are many moving, personal accounts of how Octavia Butler as a person, or through her fiction, influenced people in different places and times and ways.

After reading Xenogenesis, and especially when I learned more about Butler as a person, I always meant to go to more of her work ... but other books kept getting in the way. If you don't prioritise, it's easy for that to happen. In working on this book, I have now read some of Butler's short work, and all but two of Butler's novels. I can't find *Survivor*, the book that Butler refused to allow to be reprinted; I hold out hope that one day, in a little country town second-hand bookshop or op-shop, I'll find it on the shelf for five dollars. And I also haven't read *Kindred*. Because I am scared to. Because I know it will be a harrowing experience. And I know that these are weak excuses. I will get around to reading it one day.

In reading this volume, I hope that you will be encouraged, and inspired. Encouraged to persist in writing, or whatever work you do; encouraged to keep railing against oppression and know that you are not alone. Inspired to read more work by Octavia Butler, or to re-read it, or read work by those featured here. And I hope you will share that encouragement and inspiration with those around you.

Alexandra Pierce
Melbourne
Senior Editor

INTRODUCTION

Mimi Mondal

I came to this project late, after the call for submissions had already been out for a couple of months. I was familiar with the name of Twelfth Planet Press but had never met the editors. A previous editor for the project had become inconvenienced and needed replacement. I was recommended by someone, probably on the basis that I had been the Octavia Butler Memorial Scholar at the Clarion West Writers' Workshop in 2015.

2015 was my first entry to the United States, through the West Coast, through Seattle, and it was made possible by a scholarship named after Octavia – a writer I had read only a little til then. I grew up in India, and honestly my route into speculative fiction hasn't been through science fiction and fantasy at all, but through magical realism. Most of the SFF that I tried to read as a child or teenager confused and alienated me. I did not have the words to understand or express this when I was young, but now I know why – none of those books reflected anything of the world I lived in. As the child of a barely-above-the-poverty-line family who learned her English from a bilingual dictionary and could never imagine visiting a First World country, I had no insight into the worlds in those books. I did not always understand the conflicts in their plots. I skipped large parts of intricate worldbuilding, because often the words, even when explained in a dictionary, did not carry any visual information for me. Those scientists, astronauts, spies, superheroes were probably cool, but only when 'cool' was very far away from anything I understood. I would never grow up to be those people. Those people, if they existed, probably wouldn't even be friends with someone like me. Someone like me didn't even exist in their worlds except as a number – a unit in the billions of people who died when Earth was finally hit by that superlaser.

As you read through these letters, you will find many writers whose childhoods were not very different from mine. But I grew up half a world away, and the stories of poor people, underprivileged people, minorities do not travel well. (The only Americans I had met before 2015 were those who could afford to travel to India, and those Americans usually weren't poor or non-white, so I never knew there were such people as poor Americans, and only had the vaguest, most stereotypical notion of American minorities, gleaned from Hollywood movies and TV shows, and we all know what those stereotypes are.) The only Octavia Butler story I had read before 2015 was 'Bloodchild' in some best-of anthology, in which the brief author bio did not even mention she was black. It never occurred to me that black people, especially black women, wrote stories that could speculate on the entire future of humanity. I did not imagine anyone who wasn't independently wealthy could aspire to become a professional writer at all. The first time I attended a dedicated writing workshop was Clarion West. It's probably apt that this would not have been possible if I hadn't received a scholarship named after Octavia Butler.

I started reading the submissions for this anthology through possibly one of the darkest periods of my life. When I moved to the US in 2015, I was already somewhat at the end of a tether. A right-wing religious demagogue had been elected as prime minister in India a year ago. The liberal political and artistic spaces in the country were rapidly shrinking, becoming unsustainable, as were my career prospects and even the likelihood of my physical safety in the long term. I had not come to the US officially as a refugee, but in many ways I felt like one. I never stopped standing out as a foreigner, but I found resources and communities of people that welcomed me; for the first time in my life, people who were actually glad that I had joined them; the hope of re-building a writing and professional career.

And then the 2016 US elections happened. I remember staying curled up in bed way past daytime on November 8, trying to grasp for a reason to get up and finding none, absolutely none. My landlord at the time, an otherwise extremely active and optimistic gay man in his early fifties, was lying crumpled in the other bedroom. My mother, on the other end of a cross-continental phone call, was advising me to stay indoors, in case there was backlash in the streets. Where was I going to go now? What was the point of doing anything, writing anything, believing anything? Someone like me wasn't wanted anywhere – not back at home, not even in this other country which had taken so much of my faith and love. Once again, I was back to being a number: the gunk that needed to be drained out of the swamp, denied visas to stay or work, turned back from airports, put on the other side of a wall, and made to pay for it too.

It was through this endless numbness that I walked into this project. I felt barely functional, but I took it up because I had read and loved more of Octavia's work in the meantime, because

I had never stopped feeling grateful for the scholarship, because I had to keep my brain and my hand going. I had been an editor before. Even on a really bad day when nothing else made sense, I could mechanically line-edit pages and pages of text. I did not expect this anthology to hold me together, make me cry tears of gratefulness, help me draw strength and hope, through the next few months as wave after wave of bad news kept hitting. I expected these letters to fondly reminisce about a favourite author whom some of the writers may have met, but I did not expect unrestrained conversation about politics, or avowals of continued resistance and solidarity. I expected to help create a tribute volume, something elegantly detached and intellectual that went well with the muted shades of libraries and halls of fame, but the letters in this anthology are alive, bleeding, screaming, urgent – in a way that reflects my own state of mind at these times.

I don't know if this book will age well. Throughout the editorial process, we have often asked each other this question – what if this turbulent state of the world was short-lived? What if things calmed down in the next few months, the worst predictions turned out to be false alarms – would we have worked for months to produce a book that was dated even before it hit the bookstores? It's a strange dilemma. Obviously we want readers to find relevance in our labour of love, but even if we had nothing personally to lose, we would have to be really awful human beings to wish so many people we love more fear, anxiety, trauma or outright suffering than they have already encountered. Speaking personally, there will be no one happier than me if this book is dated by the time of its launch. It will still be a perfect time capsule of all these months – all the struggle, rage, resistance and hope we generated in the face of evil; all the words that we wrote when we could find so little to take control of besides our words – and in that time capsule the spirit of Octavia Butler will live on.

Mimi Mondal
New York
Editor

SECTION ONE

YOUR WORK IS A RIVER
I COME HOME TO

Alaya Dawn Johnson

Dear Octavia,

You were indirectly responsible for me finally landing my first job. I was twenty-three, and had applied for an assistant job at a subsidiary of Book-of-the-Month Club. They called me back for an interview, and I had my first surprise: the woman who would be my boss was black. This was the first black woman I'd encountered in an editorial position since I'd started applying, and I felt an indescribable relief. Retha sat me down and I spent half the interview staring at her bookshelf and the other half remembering to make eye contact. I recognized a particular book spine and interrupted her:

'Oh my god, that's the Octavia Butler omnibus edition, isn't it?' I asked her. 'With *Kindred*?'

Retha smiled and told me that she had produced it for the Quality Paperback Book Club and worked with you to do so. I couldn't have been more in awe if she'd told me that she'd just finished producing an album with Stevie Wonder. I had read *Kindred* for the first time at thirteen, and found myself going back to it every few years. It sucked me in, though I wasn't always prepared for the gut-punch of that novel. As a light-skinned black woman, I think I was always particularly fascinated by your searing look at exactly what that means, what violent sexual history lay behind my cultural heritage and light skin.

Retha hired me. She said that the way I couldn't keep my eyes off of her bookshelf, the way I lit up when we were discussing your work, sold her on taking a risk on me. I loved Retha, and I loved that job. I harbored a hope that Retha would make good on her promise to introduce me to you sometime when you were in town. You were releasing a new book soon and I couldn't wait to devour it.

Around the same time, the British speculative fiction magazine *The Third Alternative* published my very first short story, 'Third Day Lights.' The story was well received. It went on to be included in the Hartwell and Cramer *Year's Best SF* of that year. I began to have audacious dreams of meeting you as a fellow writer.

Fledgling, your latest book, finally arrived in the office. It was weird and challenging, polyamorous sexual politics with a fifty-three-year-old black vampire child at the center. I could see it laying groundwork for further explorations of its hard questions: What's the nature of consent in relationships with lopsided power dynamics? Does the desire for progress equal a desire for power? What are the responsibilities of privilege? Shori's story was just beginning.

Then you died. I found out on the message boards of that British magazine that had published my first story. I couldn't understand what I was reading at first. You had just published the first book in what had to be a new, mind-bending Octavia Butler series. I hadn't met you yet. You couldn't have died in such an arbitrary, sudden way. But, of course, death doesn't concern itself with our unfinished masterpieces or our devastated loved ones, and least of all a young fan who had harbored the secret dream of meeting you one day. I will never forget my fury at one commenter on those message boards who responded to my post about your death. 'You have some big shoes to fill,' he wrote, a line of unthinking bullshit that I'm sure he meant as a compliment. How was I going to fill your shoes? I thought angrily. How would that even be possible? I loved and admired your work, but my own style and creative vision differed substantially. And why me? Because I was the black woman writer of science fiction that he knew about, and of course there could only be one at a time? I hated seeing you reduced like that when we should be appreciating how expansive and visionary your work was. I hated feeling squashed and pressed into a box when at that moment all I had wanted was to share my grief with other writers and readers of science fiction.

Recently, when I was reading both novels again so that I could write you this letter, I recognized a part of myself that I had only glimpsed back in the days of my first job. The figures of Alice and Dana are juxtaposed throughout *Kindred*. Alice is the supposedly pampered house slave who endures years of rape from a man who tortured and sold her husband to the brutality of a Mississippi plantation. Dana is her time-traveling descendant who is Rufus's mentor but not – at least she hopes – an object of his sexual desire. In *Fledgling*, the expected power dynamics are flipped on their heads: it is the young black vampire girl who is unquestionably dominant in her romantic relationships, who unilaterally takes and then pacifies adult blood donors with a bite that makes them beg her for more. Shori worries about consent, but when her symbionts complain about how hard it is to separate themselves from their emotional and chemical dependence on her, she takes it to mean that they're mostly happy. I wondered about that for a long time, if you had intended the contrast between what we read in that conversation and what Shori takes from it. What is consent when one partner has the unilateral ability to force the other to do whatever they want? What is consent when it can never be revoked? In *Fledgling*, it is the actions of a black vampire child that provoke these questions. In *Kindred*, it is a white slave owner whose rapid-motion journey from painful childhood to brutal adulthood forces us and Dana to recognize the tragic humanity in his cruelty.

A few months ago, I found myself waiting in the rain in Cuernavaca, Mexico for a bus back to the town where I was staying. It was nighttime, I was only wearing a thin dress that had been plenty during the heat of the day, but in the rain was plastered to my body and unbearably cold. The bus didn't come. Above me men were singing along to banda songs and catcalling women. One of them – young, attractive, drunk – came down from his rooftop apartment. He kept touching me, holding me against him. He tried to kiss me and I pushed him away. He offered to let me sleep on his couch until the bus came again in the morning. I agreed. I wish I hadn't, but I agreed. The next six hours were brutal. His roommate was much drunker than he was, and insisted on dancing with his hands sliding up my legs, pushing up my dress. A hundred times I grabbed those hands and put them back on my hips. I kept smiling, I kept redirecting the conversation, I mentioned a fictitious boyfriend, I watched and evaluated and avoided any kind of overt confrontation that I knew I would lose.

'Tell me how to conquer you,' said the one who had come down to find me on the sidewalk.

I allowed him to see a little of my disquiet. 'What do you think happens to women during conquests?'

He stared at me. He was so young, just twenty-one. Good-looking. He could tell himself later that I had asked for it. There were several moments when I was sure I had lost. When they turned off the lights, when I couldn't remove their hands, when their young, strong bodies became immovable walls. And the worst part, the part that made me start to sob when I finally got back the next day – shaking but (mostly) untouched – was that while they drunkenly debated who got to fuck a lost girl in a wet dress, I felt overwhelmed by their humanity.

And now I remember Dana, alone in the attic with nothing but a knife in her right hand, Rufus intent on raping her just like he raped her ancestor. And even at that moment she can't help but think of Rufus as a person. As the boy she knew, as the young man betrayed and corrupted by the inhumanity of his age, as the conflicted, volatile soul whose generosity she had once appreciated. Dana thinks to herself that she could even forgive him for this. The horror of that moment isn't just in Rufus's attempted rape. It is that even as he denies her humanity, Dana finds it impossible to do the same to him. After all this time managing him, taking care of him, forgiving him, painfully attempting to convince him of her humanity and that of all his slaves, she's lost. She kills him, but she has no comfort of killing a monster. She's killed her kin.

It is a particular burden to see the humanity in your oppressors. When I first read *Kindred* at thirteen, I hadn't recognized it. I had begun to get an inkling of the complexity of these questions when I read *Fledgling* for the first time. But now, more than a decade later, I understand so much more of the questions of consent and power that animate both of those novels. I still regret not having been able to meet you all those years ago, but I am grateful for what you left us. I'm grateful for the gift of your art, which has shone a healing light upon the wounds that linger from that long night.

Alaya

Sheree Renée Thomas

Dear Octavia, Octavia E. Butler, Ms. Butler, Mother of Changes,

Yours is a story that is being told again and again. Long after you left us with *Fledgling*, your final published novel, and an archive of research, *a-maz-ing* notes to yourself, drafts of old and new novels yet to be completed or explored, and stories to unfold, stories to be told – the worlds you created have now created worlds of their own.

You left an international community of readers who adore you, of grateful students like myself, and a new generation of writers and scholars – a sisterhood, a brotherhood, a new world incarnation of Earthseed whose shared love of your art inspires, indeed, commands that we persevere with vision and change.

Change is hard.

Real change that forces us up and out of our comfort zones, the growth that forces us to face hard, uncomfortable truths about the world we live in, the societies we are building together, the problems we leave to sort themselves out – or not – that kind of change is the alchemy that only the faithful can muster up and sustain. You knew this. You looked around, put on your travelin' shoes, listened, learned, and crafted the stories that needed to be told. You were the first writer I knew who took Greyhound buses across America and climbed mountains in South America, too! My discovery of your work those years ago was a revelation. After having grown up reading science fiction in which I never saw myself, I wondered why no one had told me about you. And I felt then the way some feel now after watching *Hidden Figures*, a new film about the black women mathematicians who helped John Glenn and other astronauts make the journey into space. Octavia, you were hidden from me, as much a mystery as the machinations behind Dana's time travel in *Kindred* or the ancient magic (or science!) behind your most memorable shapeshifters.

Wild Seed, a novel of competing philosophies on the power and the burden and the responsibility of creation, is itself a story of change, of a woman who could change her physical self at will, an outcast – outside woman looking deep within.

You, daughter of another bold, tenacious Octavia, wrote an astonishing excavation of motherhood, and it's one of the works that has moved me the most. Anyanwu, an African shapeshifter whose description and characterization started a fire in my mind, was both maiden and crone, a woman not unlike yourself, who defied category. She could escape the hands of time or embrace them, as she saw fit. This singular black woman, who occupied the margins of society, went on a dangerous journey to make hard, hard choices and reconcile her own spiritual truths. As a young mother who might as well have had my own daughter in my arms as I sat discussing your work in the classroom, that *Wild Seed* novel, my favorite of yours, reminded me that mothering changes you in ways that only time can see.

In your Parable novels, I saw myself again. I saw my home, my blues river city, Memphis writ in the present and in a frightening future that could come to pass. Sad to see, but it's looking more and more each day like we're in the 'future' you looked around and saw back then. And Octavia, you would be *trippin'* over what has taken place and what they say now!

I cannot tell you how many times you've been called a soothsayer, seer. Your work today is being discussed in some circles as if you were an oracle. I imagine you would shake your head at that and laugh. A conjurewoman of arts, you made your rootwork your words. You saw the signs and the symbols, called the changes before we could make the right changes ourselves. I wish we had your full, rich voice now, to add your strength to the calls for justice. I wish you had lived, even if only a few years longer, to see America elect her first black President, Barack Obama! You would have loved First Lady Michelle. We all do! I can only wonder what you might have thought of that and of the difficult, tightrope journey of their family's eight years in the White House, not too far from where you traveled when researching *Kindred.*

During that time, a young, unarmed black boy named Trayvon Martin was murdered by a vigilante. Young black queer women started a movement called Black Lives Matter in protest of the brutality and the cruel criminal injustice when Trayvon's killer was set free. And now America has elected a celebrity again. Remember how that worked out the first time? After a contentious, vitriolic campaign, the BLM movement inspired a women's march once again led and organized by young women of color. That march has spread around the world. We are in the middle of deep, ideological, world change. Your generosity, humility, clear-eyed truth-telling and grace are needed now more than ever, but you have left us more than enough tools to repair, rebuild, to reimagine. I suspect that perhaps some of those women and girls may have found the courage to speak, to write, to march, to organize because you told us we could in your imagined worlds.

And even though you didn't spend a lot of time immersed in the cult of celebrity, your work and your name have become a catalyst for so much positive change, although to some of it I can only imagine your response. Octavia, folks are out here burning candles with your Earthseed poems written on them! And remember the Church of John Coltrane? Well, I don't know if they've built a church yet but your Earthseeds have inspired a religion (I'm attaching the *Time* article so you can see that I didn't make that up! http://time.com/66536/terasem-trascendence -religion-technology/). Sisters have gathered in your name, in Memphis, Atlanta, Jackson, New Orleans, Detroit, Chicago, all up and down California, Massachusetts, DC, Philadelphia, New York, across the big waters in London and in South Africa. We've traveled from *Dark Matter*, when people were still debating if there was more than Chip Delany and you, more than a handful of black folks that wrote science fiction and fantasy, to Reynaldo and n'em's Black Speculative Arts Movement that is taking on the world. John has just published his graphic novel adaptation of *Kindred*. You would love it! Tananarive, Nalo, Nisi, Andrea, Nnedi, Nora (that's a lot of N's, lol) have been writing up a storm of stories, novels, (screen)plays and are carrying on the good, good work. Walidah and adrienne did a whole book on social justice science fiction stories. There's a ton of art and music you might find truly interesting, and so much of it evokes your words, your name. Folks have been teaching your work not just in the classroom but using it as case studies for social reform and change. I think you would be really pleased with how far your work has gone beyond the page. It is in our hearts.

And remember how you wrote so elegantly of an empath, of one whose gift had been overlooked, like so many gifts invisible in these streets? You wrote of communities wracked with pain but healed through hope, united by a belief in the impossible, a people whose shared destinies might take them to the stars. Well, that's the story we need right now. We need *Parable of the Sower* and *Parable of the Talents* to remind us how hard real change is, to remind us that it is never acceptable to give up on that change, to give up on each other. Our nation, and the world, are hurting now, and I don't want to imagine how *that* story might end. Instead, I choose to remember beginnings.

In the book where I first contemplated your name, you wrote of a family pulled through time, forced to reconcile perilous, heartbreaking choices. You, a black woman who lived the reality of what it meant to be black and woman and all the beautiful things that made you you, created worlds that centered *blueblackmagical* real girls like me. Because you dared to write yourself, you wrote us all. I am – we are – here because of you and I thank you.

It's been twelve long years since I last saw you, when we celebrated your receipt of the Langston Hughes Medal, the honor created by Ama's late father, poet Raymond Patterson, Professor Emeritus of English at CCNY. I remember this gathering the way you remember a good dream, the color and the sound and spirit of it. Ama, Andrea, Pan, Asli, dear Monica Hand, so many gathered in the auditorium to see you join the line of literary legends, Langston, Baldwin, Walker, Ellison, Lamming, Morrison, Achebe, Soyinka, black writers whose works reflect their life-long commitment to social change.

I see your work now through different eyes than when I first encountered *Kindred* in a slavery and literature class, a young mother at a small college in a river city in the South. Your work is a river I come home to. Reading it again in different seasons of my own life brings fresh revelations that flow in and out of my consciousness. I recall the militant, almost disapproving credulity

I felt that first time, reading Dana's choices on the plantation of her ancestors. I grieved for her, for the trauma she witnessed and experienced, and I wanted more, so much more for her and her relatives trapped in slavery on that Baltimore plantation with an all-too-human, flawed man, feeling powerless.

My grandparents used to call me an old soul, but now I think that was just their sweet way of saying I was nosey! As a child, I was often underfoot, pestering them about the why and the how of older days. There was a pattern I tried to figure out. Patiently they helped me work through my questions and my need for solitude. By the time I entered college and was introduced to your work, I was deeply curious about how art and literature could help us navigate our past and present, help resurrect a future. I imagined – thought I needed then – a less subversive, more overt revolution among the bondspeople Dana and her white husband, Kevin, encountered in the novel. After reading Sherley Anne Williams' *Dessa Rose*, Margaret Walker's *Jubilee*, the dark, satirical musings of Charles Johnson's *Middle Passage* where an African God was chained in the hull of a slave ship, I wanted active change, not subtlety, not nuance, but change I could hold onto, change that showed Dana and her ancestors rising up.

I imagine you might laugh now, as you did when we spoke about my naivety a few years later. I can hear the deep wine of it in the air around me. Amused at my naivety that I once thought Dana should have staged a full Shaka Zulu-Amistad uprising on that plantation in Maryland, we laughed together and discussed the importance of revisiting our work, casting new eyes on even the most challenging texts, because the work changes and we do, too. I missed the complexity, the true difficulty that was Dana's choice because I was still too young to appreciate that some resistance is neither overt, nor seen. Real change comes in the fullness of time.

Recognition is a valuable gift. Octavia, you never wanted to be worshipped, to become another idol in the long pantheon of celebrity, but adore and revere you we do. I, like so many, am forever grateful to have been changed by your work, to have had the good fortune to be in your presence, and to have met you in these crossroads called life.

May you rest in power & peace,
Sheree Renée Thomas

Karen Lord

Dear Octavia,

May I call you Octavia? I apologise. I do not know you as well as I
should. I remember when I read your work for the first time – *Wild
Seed*. The brilliance of the prose, the depth of the characters and
the creativity of the plot were undeniable. I acknowledge and
respect your genius. But … the content and the themes of that
book prick me with the acute and precise pain of bespoke thorns.
I have trodden those thorns often enough in the socioeconomic
research I have done over the past decade and continue to do to
this day. I live in a world where survival demands compromise,
and at times I cannot bear fictional narratives where the
protagonists who resemble me gain complicated resolution instead
of unalloyed triumph.

I did not have the strength to read more, and so I know
more about your books through synopses, reviews and
commentaries than through the direct experience of reading. I can
see similarities to my own work: the concerns about balance of
power, the boundaries of self, the joys and demands of community,
and the bliss and burden of empathy. However, it is not your work
that inspires me so much as the fact of your success as an author,
and the vision and determination that paved the way to that
success.

In seeking examples to shape the path of my career, I have
come to realise that I learn more from an author's life than their
literature. Within that life, the spaces and silences speak to me as

clearly as the words and deeds. Space and silence can produce visionary saints and visionary authors. Solitude is precious, offering long-burning fuel for deep thought and slow writing. It seems an unattainable dream at times, but Octavia, you managed it. You made space and found silence in the early hours of the morning, writing before the workday began. You balanced solitude with interaction, detachment with engagement. Yours was a life well curated, not in the narrow, Holmesian sense of restricting knowledge to what will fit in the cramped attic of supposed relevance, but with the pragmatic approach of one who recognises that resources are finite, time is limited and there are goals to be attained.

I do not believe that social media has made the author life more or less hectic. We all make choices; that is what curating means. History provides many examples of writers burning out on a treadmill of speaking tours, contractual obligations, and academic or other day-job demands. The introvert muse is forced to perform in an extrovert role. That is why the concept of having command over one's own life, personal and professional, is deeply meaningful to me. Being a mindful curator, knowing one's needs and pursuing a life that meets those needs, requires the freedom of radical honesty, a freedom which is rarely accorded to those assigned the caretaker or servant role in society.

You were not only famed for solitude. In January 2016, the Huntington Library made public a photo of the inside cover page of one of your commonplace books, a small part of the extensive papers that reside there.[1] Your prophetic and affirming list of goals attracted attention from all over. You claimed for yourself a future with a comfortable home in comfortable surroundings, the best of healthcare for yourself and your mother, freedom of movement from small everyday journeys to adventures in the wide world, and the resources to help poor black youngsters to writers' workshops, to college, to broader horizons. The list was bookended by the core of your mission: '**My books will be read by millions of people!**' The page was illuminated with the repeated prayer, or mantra, or fiat: '**So be it! See to it!**'

Powerful words all round, but I was most impressed by the balance displayed. You spoke for your career, yourself and your family, and blended in your desire to be a benefactor to the youth. You had concern for those who would follow you, and so you became not only a benefactor, but also a teacher and mentor. There was a time for solitude and a time for communion with others; a space for the self and inner circle, and a space for the wider community. Both inward-looking and outward-looking goals were motivated by caring.

To paraphrase Audre Lorde, caring for myself, for my community, for the next generation of writers and heroes, is not indulgence. These are acts of preservation and aspiration that push back against the untruths that dull our imaginations and narrow our horizons. A society that requires artists to suffer, workers to know their place, and people to accept their assigned stereotype or status is a society constructed on lies born of greed and fear.

Authors have written their dreams and warnings for society in all manner of ways, from Plato's Republic and Thomas More's *Utopia* to Aldous Huxley's *Brave New World*, George Orwell's *1984*, and Ursula Le Guin's 'The Ones Who Walk Away from Omelas.' Your work is part of that long-established tradition of story as sociological thought-experiment, and fictional world-building as real-life world-mending. But all these stories mean nothing if we as individuals and as a community have words but lack action, and thus fail to actualise our vision.

Octavia, your words and vision became action and actuality. You inspire me to make my ambitions and my achievements both personal and panoramic. It is practical, not indulgent, to love myself, love my neighbour as myself, and recognise that my neighbour can be anyone I choose. It is sensible, not sentimental, to realise that care must begin at the heart of me before it can expand to embrace my whole universe. Because of your words and your success, I am convinced that imagination together with determination are the most powerful engines for change that this world has ever seen. You have demonstrated that we have the gift of writing the world into being, reprogramming our reality and becoming the heroes of our own narrative.

So be it! See to it!

Respectfully yours,
A Writer

---

[1]   See http://huntingtonblogs.org/2016/01/celebrating-octavia-butler/

Nisi Shawl

My one-and-only Octavia,

I did it. You knew I would. You knew right: I wrote and sold a novel – not in that order – and it has been printed and widely read and almost universally admired. Aren't you glad? I dedicated *Everfair* to you. If only you were alive to appreciate that. But you died nearly eleven years ago.

I know you were an atheist; I know I'm a bit presumptive in addressing you as if some non-material element of Octavia Estelle Butler survives your death to be addressed. Fine. I'll continue to presume for the length of this letter. How else will I be able to write you without crying endlessly?

Even the good news makes me miss you. My success, sweet as it is, tastes slightly of ashes. Your ashes.

You were right that I'd publish a novel one day, yes. I bet you wish you weren't right about other things, though. About the callow hatred of the self-aggrandizing exclusionist US President Elect whose campaign you appear to have predicted in your Parable books, for instance. Sometimes it's nicer to be wrong.

In 2007, as soon after your fatal fall as I could bear to talk about you publicly, I organized a panel at WisCon, a feminist science fiction convention whose Guest of Honor you once were. The panel's title was 'Genre Tokenism Today: The New Octavia Butler.' Here's the description:

> After the untimely death of the great writer Octavia E.
> Butler, some have asked who will take her place. A panel of

African-descended women currently writing genre fiction addresses this question, talking about Octavia's oeuvre and their own: similarities, differences, market forces, and the pressures to model their contributions to the field on hers. How many ways is this question just plain wrong? Who has a vested interest in there being 'an Octavia,' new or old? What would a 'new Octavia' look like? How does her literary legacy affect the field today, and how might it do so in the future? And how does this legacy relate to this disturbing question? [1]

N.K. Jemisin, K. Tempest Bradford, Candra K. Gill, Nnedi Okorafor, and I started by telling our audience why each of us was in no way your replacement. Never could be. Never would want to.

But now, despite that, despite the endearment with which I opened this letter, it looks like we're all going to have to be Octavias. All of us: women, and men, and every other gender as well; African Americans, Native Americans, and every other race – all of us. At least in this sense: we're going to have to write change-the-world fiction, like you. We're also going to have to bake change-the-world cookies and ride change-the-world horses and vote in change-the-world elections. We're going to have to change the world. We're going to have to do everything we can to maintain life on this planet.

We don't have weapons but we do have numbers. And we have the memory of you, your pessimism and persistence. We have the path you were walking when you died.

Especially for science fiction authors of color, that path is easier to see now that you've walked it. Easier to see means easier to take. Also, taking it is way less lonely for people of color these days than it was when you first set out. As I said, we have numbers.

We still have obstacles, too, of course, including obstructive people, those who we would expect to be our fellow travelers. Just as when you first set out. Not everyone expects to see women on this path. Not everyone expects to see 'the blacks' or 'Mexicans' or 'Orientals' or whatever other names we are (mis) given by those we surprise with our presence.

As we've found new ways to express our differences and new terms for the variety implicit in human existence, these have been used as new names for methods of discrimination. So sometimes when we write about characters with a desire for lovers of their own gender, they react badly: they taunt us and call us faggots, dykes, etc. Sometimes when we write about characters who desire no one and nothing, or everyone and everything, they think up fresh epithets for us, like cuck. Or they repurpose old ones: slut, prude. They lampoon our work, employing heavy hands to heap supposedly humorous abuse on our heads. (I'm not laughing. Neither would you – I can hear your sigh, see you glance heavenward.) They complain that we're crowding the path, blocking their progress with our own. They want us out of their way. Either we walk the path like they do, they say, or we're gone.

What would you do in those sorts of circumstances? I'm sure you would, like most of us you've left behind, persist.

I know from glimpses others have given me of your notes and journals that you used affirmations to bootstrap yourself up from obscurity to fame and fortune, Octavia. 'I write bestselling novels ... So be it. See to it.' We're going to need affirmations as well, to get through the opposition we face, both from other writers and, more broadly, from the political climate of the incoming administration. I offer these:

'We are beautiful, and we have every right to glory in

our beauty.'

'We belong where we're going. We're getting there.'

'We have important stories to tell, and important ways of telling them.'

'We live in love.'

As I write this letter to you, I'm on a train, riding home from the last stop on my *Everfair* publicity tour. Listening to Lee Morgan, warm and cozy and connected, admiring the long pale grass lying down in the fields we run through, the white-filled hollows where water froze in the night, the dried mullein spears standing sentinel by the dully gleaming tracks, the determined flights of ducks over open bays and wide streams. In the carriage around me other passengers chat, play cards, quilt, stroke the faces of their phones, drink cranberry juice, nap, adjust their glasses, dream. The world is dear and full of life.

Empty of you, though. How I wish you were still with us on this journey.

Love,
Nisi

[1] For a full report on this panel, those reading over Octavia's shoulder should visit https://thehathorlegacy.com/genre-tokenism-today-the-new-octavia-butler-panel-report/

Moya Bailey

Dear Octavia,

This is my second letter to you in the Great Beyond. How are you? Are you glad to have escaped before your prophetic fictions became real? Have you seen that the US has indeed elected a candidate that wants to 'make America great again?' Me and my friend Summer joke that you are coming back with a spaceship to take us away. It is a joke because wherever you go, that's where you are and we can't outrun our humanity (unfortunately).

Human beings have certainly made a mess of the world, haven't we? I often wonder whether we are better together or apart. I struggle like you did over the push/pull of being connected to others and valuing solitude. I have visions of Earthseed-like communes that call forth the best of our species and yet I also like my space and not having to think about anyone's desires but my own. I once heard this tension described as the porcupine dilemma; porcupines want to huddle together for warmth but not for too long as their quills start to hurt each other so they spread out only to get cold and want to huddle again. This back and forth dance of connection versus solitude is always shifting … changing. God is change.

Is there a place for equilibrium? What I love about your work is that it answers that question by not answering it. Earthseed survived for a time but then, when destroyed, it had to take root among the stars. And even then, in your later work, we saw that fleeing to another planet presents new challenges, especially when we are no longer the dominant species. God is change and so we must always adapt and be ready for our reality to shift. Life is a constant struggle and we need not be passively accepting of change; we have the power to shape it!

I am trying to remember that we have the power to shape change in this moment. The repressive nature of the coming US presidential administration is already evident. It is going to get a lot worse before it gets better. So many of the circumstances that shape your Parable characters' lives are manifesting as our reality today. All of the rights and services we've worked so hard for are already being undermined. Because of lessons I've learned from your work I am working to build community as a way to counteract this regression.

Building community is our best chance at shaping a reality that is more in line with the world we want. The process is slow but it is work I love. Through feeding people, through gathering them together and growing our collective skills, we are trying to stave off the individualism and loneliness that consumer capitalism has cultivated. Whether it's the Patternist series, the Parables, or Lilith's Brood, you've shown us the power of small intentional communities to shape the changes they want to see. Even in *Fledgling* you provide a vision of intergenerational community and model the kinds of accountability such connections require.

It was through your work that I met Ayana Jamieson, the founder of the Octavia E. Butler Legacy Network. Ayana organized a panel of Butler scholars at the 2009 National Women's Studies Association Conference that I attended. It would be years before we reconnected and realized that your work had brought us together before. We are using your work to grow the number of people who believe in this journey. The Legacy Network is growing and includes scholars and artists who are inspired by your storytelling and are now building new genres and projects as a result. We continue to build the pattern.

This summer, 2017, we will be celebrating the opening of your papers at the Huntington Library Archives. It is in your papers that we have found even more evidence of your beautiful visions of collective living at the same time as we see your loneliness. Your profound empathy made being close to too many people hard but you wrote so eloquently about the day to day struggle of communal life. Thank you for letting us bear witness by saving so much of your writing, even the pieces that were hard to hold.

I hope you are warmed by the ever-growing community of people who have been touched – rather, changed – by your work. We don't take your gift lightly. We return to you and your work again and again and we find new insights each time we do. May these words bring comfort and assurance that though you are gone you are not forgotten; your legacy lives on.

All my love,
Moya

Tara Betts

Dear Octavia,

I am wondering what future you could write for us now. We are about to move into a new president's term, here in America, and so many people have called on one of your novels as a prophetic turn toward a supposed leader much like one of your most disturbing characters. We need your stories to get through these challenging times. We need so many factors in literature that compel us to keep thinking and imagining, especially in a world that attempts to shut down imagination, and thinking, in general. For what you were able to give us, gratitude is not a sufficient word to describe what I feel.

I often talk to one of my closest friends about what kinds of stories haven't ever been told or how I am tired of movies with black stars that recycle movies that starred white people in earlier renditions – like *About Last Night, Annie,* or *The Hand That Rocks the Cradle* as *When the Bough Breaks.* I feel audiences do need mainstream stories with black characters that are just like other, mostly white, movies, and not just heavy-handed messages that talk about the plight of black lives in America (and globally). On the other hand, why can't we have new stories and stories in places and genres where we have yet to see Black characters? If there was ever a writer that made me feel that it was acceptable to think that, it was you.

From the first time I encountered Lauren Olamina, I knew that what I had been thinking was true. There is a place for black people in the future, not as random extras, but as leaders, main characters. In *Parable of the Sower*, she is the hero. This has moved me when I've looked at your stories again and again throughout the years. When the world becomes increasingly bleak, the black women in your stories do more than survive, they lead. They are not the strong, silent figure like Michonne in *The Walking Dead*. The drama they encounter, challenge, and change is less internal than Michonne's. When I think of a Lauren or a Lilith, they are practicing types of leadership that include other people in the process of surviving. They consider people's strengths, skills, and weaknesses. They learn skills and teach others. They understand the importance of children and the importance of fighting. As they exhibit these astounding qualities in harrowing situations, they still manage to express vulnerability. When their loved ones are hurt or killed, or even if they themselves are injured, they adapt. There have been countless times when I have thought of the aphorisms and writings of Lauren Olamina that you invented on the pages that I turned and revisited. Like 'the only constant is change.' This mantra spoke so much truth to me. And I consider how Lilith moved into an unknown future with strange creatures and found a sort of community and intimacy, not just with Joseph, but with the alien Oankali, who helped her birth new children in a future where the earth was recovering from a nuclear fallout.

And we need this still, those of us who only have your books now or a rare chance to see your papers stowed in a library. We need to know that there is the possibility that we can survive, not just police brutality, gun violence, poverty, climate change, increasingly powerful narcotics, but the stresses of racism, and yes, even fear of a nuclear race that no one could ever win. We need to know that we might be able to start over and still be breathing, even when the world seems irreparable. We need to know that whatever is human in us is redeemable and able to start anew. We need to know that we can shake people awake and compel them to lead with us, not behind us or beneath us. We are built to summon some fount of inner strength, ask ourselves difficult questions, and seek out answers.

I find myself drawn to how you have characters that are indeed black, but there isn't a broad, undulating banner announcing how black they are. Their identity is key to understanding them, especially in a novel like *Kindred*, but it isn't the sum of their story. Race is not all they have to talk about, not the complete, inherent sum of a person's humanity, even though that humanity is often suppressed by racism and colonialism. You make us pay attention to both the characters and people in real, daily life. No one wants to engage with a piece of warm cardboard, and these characters are never static, even in your deceptively clear lines of prose. It makes me wonder if you ever read the Black Arts Movement poet Mari Evans when she wrote her book of essays *Clarity as Concept*. In it, she talked about being undeniably clear about what you say, but also, being undeniably clear about your creative mission. Where do you stand? How do you plan to get there? I think about that even more now that some pages of your journals are circulating on the internet. I understand the level of hermitage that you chose to live out in Seattle, if for no other reason than that you had universes to build that spoke to these larger realities that black women can, should, and do inhabit.

The truth is, there need to be more following your lead, and they are coming. I think of Nalo Hopkinson, Nisi Shawl, Sheree Renee Thomas, Nnedi Okorafor, Kiini Salaam, adrienne brown, Walidah Imarisha, and Ytasha Womack. I think of artists like

Denenge Akpem, Krista Franklin, Janelle Monae, Missy Elliott, Mendi Obadike, Nikki Mitchell, and Wangechi Mutu. I think of you and L.A. Banks possibly laughing in some celestial corner and possibly, you might be smiling, and with the slightest lisp, shaking your head and looking at us while saying 'These children...' and perhaps I am making you too Southern in two simple words, but I hope we are crafting some stories that create a new legacy that would not have been possible, a steady fount of change that Lauren Olamina would nod toward in approval.

I hope, as I write these words, that I can do more than pay tribute. I hope that I am picking up some sense of duty with each keystroke, with every arch and oval that I pen. Unfortunately, I am writing this letter years after your fall that took you too soon. I remember feeling a gust of air leave my chest as if someone punched me when I read that you were gone. So, I am clutching the books like keepsakes, and I hope the words that I write are solid bricks fit to build something that stands next to the edifice of words that you left us.

With Loving Respect,
Tara Betts

Z.M. Quỳnh

Octavia Butler – Master Cultural Translator

Dear Madame Butler,

You know as well as I do that language is ill equipped to carry the true weight and meaning of the stories and sentiments that swim around in our heads. You probably chuckled when I called you 'Madame', bringing to mind images of French aristocracy or of exotic occupations like fortune-telling – and how, at least in colloquial English, it is the chosen term of endearment for female owners of brothels.

But I am Vietnamese and when I say 'Madame' I breathe the Vietnamese word, 'Ba', from my mother's matriarchal tongue for the highest respect given to a distinguished woman. In that single title is the connotation of dignified elegance, ancestral veneration, spiritual connection, and universal respect.

These are the things that have been lost in the translation of 'Ba' to 'Madame.' Language alone fails to encompass the richness of the underlying culture. The same can be said of 'cultural translation,' which refers to the translation of cultural knowledge. Even within the confines of our shared language, English, there are cultural significances that can be magnified and misunderstood, possibly leading to injustice.

Cultural translation was something you were a master at. You had the ability to translate the cultural wholeness of a people. You were a genius not only for your ability to translate ideologies, modes of being, and the narratives, struggles, and joys of a people onto the pages of a tale but also for your ability to elevate storytelling as a vehicle of social examination and change.

You did this in *Kindred* where you were able to achieve two momentous goals: conveying the realistic cultural context of the horrors of slavery and connecting the racial tension of present-day America to that history. Now, nearly three decades later, *Kindred* is still relevant where, in the year 2017, African Americans are still disproportionately discriminated against in education, employment, police violence, and domestic and sexual abuse.

Through *Kindred*, we can see that attempting to write off the current chronic loss in America of young black males to police violence as unrelated to a history of severe racism is not only ignorant, but dangerous. By failing to confront that history, we fail to find the best solutions to address present-day injustices. Solutions such as oversight of the police force and implicit bias training are not enough because they are often executed within a vacuum that fails to consider the intersection of other issues such as poverty, educational and workforce disenfranchisement, and community stressors.

As a cultural translator and storyteller, you also posited new ways of seeing and being that carried the imprint of your essence in the same way that a sculptor's handprints trail their creations. You challenged readers to question their societies' ideologies. In *Kindred*, you resisted white America's narratives that lumped all slaves into an indistinct group, affording a comfortable distanced view – divorced from responsibility. Instead, you crafted a slave community that was culturally rich and socially strong, and then you connected them to characters that lived in the current era. By doing so, you demanded accountability of present-day society for the tyranny of that era.

Many of your stories also presented social dilemmas of

peaceful coexistence – between human societies and between humans and aliens. Your stories reflected the experiment that was America – complete with social hierarchies, power struggles, catastrophes, failures, and then solutions and triumphs. In Lilith's Brood, you explored sexuality, gender, race, and inter-species relationships, again paralleling the story of African slaves in America and the complexities of their integration into a discriminatory American society.

But cultural translation is a two-way street. It requires the sensitivity of the reader as well. Oftentimes the vestiges of colonialism and racism run deep. This is where I found myself before I ever discovered your books. At the age of four, I had fled from the civil war tearing apart Vietnam to the racialized battlefields of the Los Angeles metropolitan area.

As I was growing up, Vietnamese was initially spoken at home, English at school, and Spanish in the streets. In between all those languages was the stuff of life that wove three races of people –Vietnamese, Latinos, and African Americans–into one community. As a youth, I was ignorant to the white world outside of the enclave of the apartments and schools that defined my community.

White folks played small but critical and contradictory roles in my childhood: the accountant and his family who sponsored us from the refugee camp, the ladies from the Salvation Army and their bags of donated clothes and toys, the gang of white kindergarteners who waited for me everyday after school to beat the Vietnamese out of me, and the adults in big trucks that threw rocks at my mother and shot bullets through our front window. They were appreciated; they were feared. Apart from these few instances, however, they were mostly absent from my childhood.

Because of the racism and violence we were experiencing as

a result of American, post Vietnam War grief and frustration, my parents banned Vietnamese from our homes and our tongues. As a result, by the time I was twelve, Vietnamese was all but forgotten. We are not alone in this. African slaves were forbidden their mother tongue and their cultural practices. Native Americans still struggle to reclaim their language after generations of forced relocation and for two decades, Californians banned bilingual education affecting millions of Latino children.

What does it mean to lose the single most powerful tool of cultural translation? What does speaking only English do to the colonized brain? What does being forced to hide or forget one of the strongest characteristics of our culture imply about other aspects of our culture? What else did we hide or lose besides our language?

This is what I discovered when I graduated from high school, and attended a local university where I suddenly found myself studying alongside more white folks than I had ever encountered in my life. It was a culture shock of immense proportions and I found that my words failed me often. Even though I was fluent in English it wasn't the 'right' English.

It was not long before brown and black folks on campus found each other. Within a few weeks of my freshman year, students of color were congregating like a mushroom colony in a vast meadow. While secured in this inner circle of brownness, I was assigned to read *Things Fall Apart* by Nigerian author Chinua Achebe. It was the first book I had ever read by a person of color.

It was in the pages of Achebe's book that I came face to face with racism that came not in the form of tiny five-year old fists, rocks thrown at me, or bullets shot through the window of my house. Rather, I found it in the private confines of my own mind.

Things Fall Apart followed the life of Okonkwo, an Ibo

leader and local wrestling champion in the fictional Nigerian village of Umuofia. To my dismay, despite knowing little else in the world but the intimacies of my diverse neighborhood, I could not, for the life of me, picture Achebe's characters to be anything but white. In NIGERIA! In the continent of AFRICA!

Through every passage in Achebe's book, my mind painted only fair-skinned blue-eyed 'Africans' with blond Afros. I tried desperately to fix this. I took the image of Okonkwo in my mind – ridiculously pale-skinned – and I literally colored him, inch by inch – I brownified his skin, I blackified his hair, I Africanified his features and his life.

But it didn't work! The images in my mind would only revert to Okonkwo as a white man with a blond Afro. How was it that I, who had Vietnamese parents and an entire community of Mexican and African American friends, failed to populate the characters of Achebe's book with my own experiences? This experience was replicated in virtually every other book that I was assigned to read: *The Color Purple* by Alice Walker, *I Know Why The Caged Bird Sings* by Maya Angelou to name a few. I neither saw my own face, nor the true face of the people in the books – I only saw white faces.

I asked myself: Had I, as the colonized, the refugee, the 'other,' been trained through popular media that all that was 'American' was not me, or my parents, or my black and brown community?

Had I been brainwashed to believe that the only translation for 'America' was 'white?'

I took a step back and examined every aspect of my subconscious life – my imagination, my dreams, my 'norms,' even my sexual fantasies – and I came to the realization that if the language and images of the stories that we were exposed to consistently minimized and failed to reflect us, we would eventually find ourselves erased within our own culture and eventually in history.

It was then that I embarked upon the task of re-embedding all that had been lost in translation. This journey took me to a bookstore in search of other authors of color. That is where I picked up *Wild Seed* and, in doing so, changed my life forever.

In *Wild Seed*, you translated the Onitsha culture that I read in Achebe's book and brought it to life through Anyanwu, your Igbo heroine. In your carefully woven words, I read, studied, and ingrained into my mind the intricate nuances of culture, race, politics, and power that were liable to get lost in translation. Then I, a geeky immigrant kid with a penchant for alien invasion stories and the supernatural, promptly scoured all bookstores within bussing distance for all of your other books.

I devoured in a span of days your stories not only for their hypnotic narratives but also for the cultural translation imbued within them. I inhaled your stories like a drowning victim gulps air, finding the daily struggles of my life reflected in your heroines. Through your stories, I readjusted my subconscious cultural filter and was able to see, for the first time, a place for myself, my families, and my communities in the fabric of America.

The most precious gift your stories gave to me, however, was the vision of a future where my words and my stories had both validity and the ability to engrave the narratives of my many communities into the literary history of America and beyond. Thank you.

Respectfully,
Z.M. Quỳnh

WHAT GOOD IS [SCIENCE FICTION'S] EXAMINATION OF THE POSSIBLE EFFECTS OF SCIENCE AND TECHNOLOGY, OR SOCIAL ORGANISATION AND POLITICAL DIRECTION?

Ben H. Winters

Dear Ms. Butler,

We could have used you this year, Octavia Butler. We could have used you this year for sure.

Five decades after Dr. King, four decades since *Kindred*, eight years after the first black family moved into the White House, we've elevated a man whose vision of America is of a land that needs to be reclaimed from undesirables, meaning dark-skinned people, too-smart people, people who worship weird and non-Christian gods.

We could have used you because of what you were, a science-fiction visionary who was also a black woman, a literary minority and an American minority, possessed of second sight and third sight too. Every kind of sight.

Among those forms of special sight was certainly foresight, Ms. Butler. During our woeful new president's terrifying rise, people on Twitter (Lord knows what you would have made of Twitter!) passed around quotes from *Parable of the Talents*, stunned at your prescience, at the terrifying President Jarret, a coiffed demagogue wanting to make America great again. He runs on a platform of taking the country 'back to some magical time when everyone believed in the same God, worshipped him in the same way, and understood that their safety in the universe depended on the same religious rituals and stomping anyone who was different' (*Parable of the Talents*, 22). *Build the wall!*

You wrote about all this stuff, all this stuff that's now been dragged back out of the dark. You knew how racism still hangs over this country, shadowing all our progress, and you knew where racism comes from, where it always comes from: people making themselves the good ones by making the other people the bad ones. *Build it! Build that wall!*

Your President Jarret found success the same way that President Trump did, twenty years after you wrote the story (or twenty years before the events of the book) and in actual reality. You understood it all, Ms. Butler. You could have explained. In page after page, story after story, you displayed all the most powerful impulses and drives that move humanity, from lust and ritual to hope and love to hatred and fear. Hatred and fear might have been the most powerful of all. You showed us people in chaos, people in dire straits, people fleeing from each other or to each other, fleeing across space or fleeing fires on the road, and you showed us not just their adventures but their humanity – whether they were human or aliens or modern-day vampires. (Oh, and how beautifully, amazingly modern-day they were. That moment in *Fledgling*, where the vampire first gets off the helicopter, gets me every time.)

You knew about walls, Ms. Butler. The literal walls – the walls that encircle the gated neighborhoods of your post-apocalyptic American landscapes, the walls that divided the alien fortresses of your tales of space – and the figurative walls, the kind that people build to reinforce themselves by putting others on the outside. It was a great theme of your work, the hierarchies that people feel the need to enforce: this person better than that one, this kind of person better than that kind. Men over women, white over black, young over old. *Build those walls!*

Some people might be surprised to hear that your books had great themes at all, of course; some people might roll their eyes at the notion. That's another wall that people like to build, isn't it, between fiction with a capital-F, Fiction that Matters – and on the other hand fiction that is fun, that is genre, *just* genre, *mere* genre. Something familiar about that, isn't there? That person over there lacks inherent value, because she's black, or Chinese, or queer. This book here lacks inherent value, because it's sci-fi, or fantasy, or romance.

Funny thing, though. How you did both. Because you knew that the second division, between literature and mere books, is as phony as the first, between the right and wrong kinds of people. What *you* did, and what I admire most, and what I aspire to do every time I sit down to work, was to write genre so goddamn well – to fill up every page so beautifully with shooting and running and fighting and fucking and flying and crashing and magic and monsters – to make the books so undeniable in their entertainment value that the moral value could come right along for the ride. If you've got vampires in helicopters then nobody says boo if you're writing at the same time about God and love and death and hate, about social justice and the moral obligation of human beings. It was all there. In every book and story you proved that there is no such thing as Genre Fiction and Real Fiction, any more so than there is any such thing as the Right People and the Wrong People. There is only Bad Fiction and Good Fiction, and the good fiction is the kind that is engaged with the world, that lives in it and desires to push it forward, to wake it up and make it better.

That's the way you wrote, and it's how I try to do it, too. You were an African American woman science-fiction writer and I'm a white Jewish male mystery writer, and we're both of us writers.

You wrote from the gut and gave us visions of what's true, bubbling and shifting under the landscapes of your imagination, and I'm trying to do the same thing. A lot of us try to do the same thing. Very, very few are as good at it as you were.

Thank you, Ms. Butler.
Ben

Hoda Zaki

Dear Octavia,

I don't know how you did it. I can guess, but I don't know for certain how you were able to pick critical trends in the present and imagine how they would unfold and shape society in the future. Many years ago, in reviewing *Parable of the Sower*, I described your dystopia as one of the most significant literary accomplishments of the end of the twentieth century: it was a warning to us that society was evolving in ways that would witness a renewal of slavery, corporate domination and much drug-induced violence.

Then, you did it again! You nailed it even further in *Parable of the Talents*. There, you portrayed a detailed and nuanced dystopia that is even more compelling than the one you described in *Sower*. How on earth did you know, *in 1998*, that in U.S. politics we were going to see a rise of Christian, right-wing fundamentalism that would be interlaced with white nationalism and fascism? That there would be a U.S. presidential candidate, a demagogue, who would win his campaign based on a slogan you used: 'Make America Great'? A candidate who was intolerant and opposed to religious and racial difference? One who inflamed his followers and convinced the working poor to believe in his brand of patriotism because they longed for employment and security? *You saw all this in 1998?*

In this near future you described in *Talents*, you outlined the contours of a political movement which would harness religion to politics in order to control government. You predicted that this movement would be a coalition of the wealthy business elite with the working poor and the evangelicals, and you added to this mix a few splinter groups and violent extremists. You outlined this candidate's presidential campaign game plan that promised everything to everyone, scapegoated minorities and immigrants, and provided a narrative that told people what the electorate wanted and needed to hear. *You wrote this in 1998!* In this dismal future, we see the reemergence of chattel slavery, witch burnings, the corporatization of public education, re-education camps and the jettisoning of the rule of law. We are becoming familiar now with some of these strategies used by the new political elite.

I can only guess at the process you used to warn us. I wish you were here to tell us. We know that you worked hard at extrapolation. In addition to studying and using theories of evolution, the second law of thermodynamics, and chaos theory, you selected and followed selected social trends. You kept voluminous clippings on crime and drug use, climate change and its consequences, technology and punishment, public education, immigration policy, and science and technology and their impact on reproduction. We know now, thanks to your papers at The Huntington Library, that you kept copious notes on issues such as education. You worried about the decline in public education and literacy, fearing that poverty and the lack of education would create illiteracy and lead to a permanent underclass. You were appalled at attempts to bar immigrants from schools and medical care. You followed the impact of increasing levels of inequality and how jobs were no longer paying enough to provide basic food and shelter. You studied and thought through in a rigorous manner the implications of these tendencies you believed were significant. Author Mike Davis in his *Ecology of Fear: Los Angeles and the*

Imagination of Disaster (1998) has called your method one of 'disciplined extrapolation,' which strikes me as an accurate way of describing the process you used to develop your future societies.

While your disciplined thinking provided the scaffolding you used to construct your dystopias, there was something within you, a genius, that put all of these disparate elements together in gripping narratives that challenged the present. I know that you did not like the word 'genius' because it made invisible the effort you put into your work. But there was some special quality in you that made you able to discern key elements of the future, a quality that went beyond hard work and rigorous analysis. This genius was your gift to your readers: your ability to understand at a very deep level the levers that were shaping our society today and to share it in stories.

Your legacy is multifold. Your influence continues to unfold in literature and in film. Young science fiction authors take imaginative leaps because of your work. You are a founding influence on Afrofuturism. Your work is taken seriously, at long last, by literary critics, when your first readers and loyal fans were to be found in African American women's book clubs. Critics now use your work to understand desire, sexuality, gender, race and evolution.

Your legacy goes beyond your dystopian visions because, like all dystopian authors, you included hope in your narratives. You created characters who struggled to survive and create better worlds, who took risks and were courageous. They defied the expectations of their communities. They failed and succeeded. They embraced difference because it represented a possibility for survival. You yourself did so in your own life. I don't know how you were able to persevere for as long as you did and against such odds:

you told me once you had to chain your typewriter to your desk so that it would not be stolen. You wrote against the grain of many traditions which specified who could write science fiction. I, and legions of others, are so grateful you persisted.

Your work provides inspiration for readers who can take hope in your characters' actions and for what and who they are: characters who resemble you and me and the rest of the world, and who lead and teach and resist.

Thank you, Octavia!

Missing you still,
Hoda

Brenda Tyrrell

Dear Ms. Butler,

This morning, I awoke to find Donald Trump our President-elect. This news may initially make you LOL, as the current vernacular would have me write, because when you left the world in 2006, very few people found anything about Mr. Trump remotely presidential material. Believe me, even ten years later, the frequent reaction to the possibility of Mr. Trump succeeding in his crazy plan brought peals of laughter. Yet, here I sit, drowning in waves of shock, shame, numbness, and overwhelming grief, as our nation clings to anything that might bring us some sense of comfort. Many of my creative-writing-type friends say now is the time to write – now is the time to fight with the tools they have – their pens as their swords, their paper as their armor. In fact, even our beloved (pardon the pun) Toni Morrison said, 'We speak, we write, we do language. That is how civilizations heals.'[1] And, there can be no doubt, our civilization needs healing.

Is this why you wrote? Is this why you offered your tools – to heal our civilization? I remember reading once that you said the Parables are *not* prophetic. They couldn't be, because you would not want to live in a world like that. Well, Ms. Butler, we live in a world like that. We are living in 'The Pox' that came as a direct result of our 'infinite complacency' (to borrow from H.G. Wells). Our current dilemma mirrors Olamina's plight with President Jarret: a significant amount of our population was 'mad enough' to vote Mr. Trump into office, leaving the other portion in need of counseling just to cope with the intense emotions that follow such a devastating blow to our country – one that leaves our LGBTQ+, people of color, Latino/as, women, and a wealth of others at great risk. How do we pick up the pieces? How do we fight back? Short of moving to Mars, as Earthseed should have done in *Parable of the Trickster*, I am at a loss. So, as my friends suggest, I will write. And I will teach.

I will (and do) teach your *Parable of the Sower*, Ms. Butler. Before the election, we scoffed at the possibility of Trump as President–elect and put our faith in the inherent goodness of people. The problem with that faith is that 'inherent' goodness comes in varying degrees, from person to person, and we don't always understand (or appreciate) that difference. In that regard, the classroom seems to be more important today than before the election. In a world where colonizing Mars is becoming more real by the minute, where our political system is a shambles, and where our world is slowly (but faster than we are willing to admit) disintegrating, a class centered on *Sower* is my version of being prophetic.

As I reread parts of *Parable of the Talents*, I am at once appalled at the accuracy of what is happening in this current time and completely floored (for lack of a better word) at your power of prophecy, Ms. Butler. Nisi Shawl said you would cringe at this word but, in this case, I believe it is the most accurate word.[2] Witches, cults, slave collars, a devastated world. When words like these continually come up in class discussions about your novels, how do we then prevent the logical end to these discussions – i.e. hopelessness and fear? Well, you answer this quandary as well by saying that your endings are always hopeful. On more than one occasion, this statement has given me pause for thought and made me rethink where I stand as either a pessimistic reader or as a pessimistic instructor. I do not want my students to give up before they have even started living in this world. So, I dig deeper, I look further than the words on the pages.

I look past the rape, the gender bias, the violent deaths, the blatant racism, the slavery, and the scorched, rotted earth in your stories. I wallow in the rage, disgust, and shame (much like I do, today, as I try and process the utter disbelief of the election results). And I search for the good, the hope, that you claim comes in your novels. But I do not find it. I see no hope in the words of *Sower* or *Talents*. This despondency concerns me, of course, so I do what any rational person might do: I seek solace in my friends. One friend in particular helps me – not because of any specific advice he gives me but because he is a good man, a strong man. He believes in a more cohesive and hopeful world and I believe in him. He soothes my raw edges and that's when it hits me, Ms. Butler. I return to the pages of your Parables.

Olamina and Bankole, Harry and Zahra, Allie and Justin, Marcus and Olamina, Larkin and Olamina. Despite the horror that assaults them at every turn, they have each other and Earthseed, a higher purpose, if you will. Ironically, I think of Harlan Ellison's 'I Have No Mouth, and I Must Scream' as I contemplate the hope you believe can be found in your novels. As you may recall, Ms. Butler, Mr. Ellison also claims that his short story has 'an upbeat ending. Infinitely hopeful and positive,' despite the fact that everyone except the narrator dies a horrific death, and even he turns into a giant slug. What about that is hopeful? It is hopeful, Mr. Ellison says, because in the face of unspeakable torment, human will triumphs. Bravery and courage rise above the shock and repulsion and allow us to soar despite the tremendous odds against us. While that sounds great, today, I'm not there yet. I'm not ready to rise against Mr. Trump's apparent victory. But, with the support of my friends and my students, we will stand firm in this world that you found so hopeful.

Thank you, Ms. Butler. I think that if you could see the contagious enthusiasm and stunning acumen of my students' end-of-the-semester projects, you might also see how they match the hopeful ending that you profess your novels offer. *All that you touch / You change*, even after all of these years.

Sincerely,
Brenda Tyrrell

[1]   Ironically, Morrison is referring to her own reaction when George W. Bush was re-elected in 2004. The entire article, 'No Place for Self-Pity, No Room for Fear,' is available through *The Nation's 150th Anniversary Special Edition*, 2015, accessed February 7, 2017, https://www.thenation.com/article/150th-anniversary-issue/.

[2]   I had the pleasure of interacting with Ms. Shawl at the 2016 Wisconsin science fiction convention (WisCon). During a panel discussion on Octavia Butler's work, an audience member asked how Ms. Butler would have reacted to her work being called 'prophetic.' The above quote was Ms. Shawl's response.

Connie Samaras

Dear Octavia,

I just remembered something I never told you. Some years ago, during the first summer of the new millennium, I was sitting in my backyard with a group of friends eating the food we'd made for our afternoon barbeque. It was one of those crystal clear days in Los Angeles following a big rainstorm. As everyone chattered away, one of my friends and I started spacing out on the view: the trees around us filled with brightly colored fruit; the gleaming whites of the Hollywood sign and Griffith Observatory perched above on the surrounding hills. It was all so stunningly beautiful. Suddenly my friend turned to me and asked, 'Do you think things will get as bad as Octavia Butler describes in *Parable of the Sower?*' 'Yes,' I answered ambivalently. My friend replied, 'I think it will be worse.'

Seventeen years later, the United States is now ten days into Donald Trump's presidency of intentional lies and brutal incompetency, the most dangerous presidency in American history. A constant stream of broken news flows across screens while journalists try to push back on the tide of falsehoods and hourly script changes brought to us by the administration's hard-right reality show 'Burning Down the House.' Its host is a bullying narcissist, an overgrown trust-fund baby who talks like a privileged but not very smart ten-year old, a failed sociopathic business man who never pays a debt of any kind, a D-list TV celebrity obsessed with his ratings, a racist hate-mongering pussy grabber who, one ex-wife reports, keeps a volume of Hitler's speeches on his nightstand. But I'm not telling you anything you didn't already know.

Everyone says it now feels like we're living in science fiction times. As a result, people are suddenly reading SF en masse. George Orwell's *1984* recently rose to the top of the U.S. bestsellers list. But many are also reading and teaching your Parable series. I was happy to see that *Sower* is currently ranked #96 in Contemporary Literature and Fiction on Amazon. I hope all your books continue to migrate to the top. There's much to learn from them about surviving and resisting intolerance.

It's hard not to think about your novels every day as this ignorant demagogue propped up by a band of white supremacists, craven politicians, the greedy one-percent, and, most likely, Vladimir Putin spews populist strongman fear-driven rhetoric about restoring stolen jobs and closing borders. I don't know if I'm living in a prequel to the *Parable of the Sower* where everything is about to collapse or in the *Parable of the Talents*, the part where the religious right government turns a blind eye to the many pockets of civil war generated by heavily armed modern-day brown shirts. Then again, we could be in the prequel to *Dawn*, the part just before the planet is about to be destroyed by nuclear war. Everyone is worried. Just now a headline floated by on the computer screen: 'Sense of impending doom spreads worldwide.' And just yesterday scientists pushed the Doomsday Clock forward another thirty seconds to 2.5 minutes before midnight citing the political situation in the U.S. as a central concern. (It was good to be reminded that, at the end of the Cold War in 1991, the clock was turned back by twenty minutes.)

A few days ago I read that super-wealthy Americans are preparing for civil war and a potential apocalypse. Some of the more liberal ones are throwing money at philanthropic causes to try and stave things off but all interviewed are buying backup high security homes in other countries, with New Zealand being the most popular. Some of those homes are also being built here. For example, a former nuclear missile silo in Kansas is being converted into a fifteen-story condominium. It includes armed guards, a five-year food supply, a fish farm and hydroponic garden for when the food supply runs out, blast protection walls, and virtual windows that look out onto views selected by the owner. Reading this made me think of *Dawn's* aliens. How, in addition to rescuing the few aboveground survivors of the nuclear apocalypse, they also dug out from their posh underground shelters the military and political leaders responsible for the devastation. It's deeply satisfying to know that the Oankali will never return these purveyors of doom to Earth.

I doubt I'm the only one writing to you now to say how profound your books remain with every reading. How they never seem dated but rather illuminate the period they're being read in. Vernacular histories outplay official renditions of the past. The present converts into a shared multi-dimensional commons that can never be fully understood. And the future becomes something each of us can try to make.

As you predicted, things are getting worse by the hour as Trump grabs his magic marker and theatrically signs piles of gruesome, badly written executive orders meant to unravel the government and its system of checks and balances. Many commands haven't stuck. But some initially have, like the xenophobic directive banning travelers and immigrants (including Green-Card holders) from entering the U.S. should they come from certain Muslim-majority countries. Of course the list doesn't include those predominantly Islamic countries where the president continues to do business. In the true spirit of fascism, one of the test questions asked of the newly branded interlopers is: 'What do you think of President Trump?'

I think you nailed it years ago with the twenty-first century presidents you created for the cautionary Parable series. The image of President Jarret in *Talents* is especially uncanny. No doubt because the recombinant formula you developed to create him matches the one used to engineer Trump. What prescience to have spliced together Ronald Reagan ('Make America Great Again'), Roy Cohn (Joseph McCarthy's right hand man who later mentored Trump), and Hitler (who disappointingly never seems to go completely out of style). But Trump is not the religious leader Jarret is.

As you're aware (well, not really but sometimes it feels like you are), I've been digging around your archive at the Huntington Library for some time. I recently decided to see if I had scanned notes you might've made for leaders following Jarret in the unwritten sequels to the Parable books. And there he was, in a 2004 entry on *Parable of the Trickster*, the dangerous narcissist: 'someone who knows almost nothing except he's never wrong.'

What an incredible experience it is to access the astonishing accumulation of papers and journals you left behind. I meant to write you earlier about the letter and materials I sent you over twenty years ago. I was embarrassed when I first saw you had saved everything. Briefly, I considered trying to smuggle part of it out of the library. You'll be grateful to know that would've been impossible. Originally I was going to ask you about treatments of sexuality in your work that I never seem to see discussed. But then Hillary Clinton 'lost' the election and, like so many, I went into a panicked mourning for weeks.

Among the many things I've enjoyed about looking through

your papers are your photographs, particularly the ones of animals. No matter what the creature, bear, bat, or seal, in nearly every picture they look you back squarely in the eye.

I hope you would like the photographs I've been taking in the gardens outside the library. It's been especially fun to overlay texts from your journals on to the Huntington's vast plant collections culled from all over the world. Because I'm working with chance – using film not digital – I never know which words will be legible in the final images. What appears in the end though is always wonderfully unexpected and better than if I'd tried to prefigure it. For example, in one of the photographs I had really wanted the following fragment to come through despite the fact you had scribbled it out in your journal. In bright red ink you had written: 'Los Angeles was dying. Much of the world was changing – changing rapidly, involuntarily blundering through vast climate change.' But when the film came back I saw that the words had broken into tiny red flowers floating in the trees.

Returning to my friend's comment, will the future be worse? It certainly could be in many ways. It's already been bad enough for lots of people for some time. But then there's the massive daily resistance going on, diverse, larger and more unrelenting than has been seen for decades. From the millions of women who marched the day after Trump's inauguration to the hundreds nationwide protesting daily outside their congressperson's local office. Thousands converged on major airports as soon as the Muslim ban was enacted while judges and constitutional lawyers continue to push back on the administration's illegal actions. And although the press is being told that they 'better shut up,' as one journalist retorted: 'Good luck with that.'

There's also talk of impeachment. But if that's successful

then we're back to Jarret – our religious right, homophobic Vice President moving up a rank. In spite of this and the potential for even worse – e.g. Trump's chief strategist Steve Bannon's unshakeable belief that the world is on the brink of an inevitable cataclysmic war resulting in a new order that he alone must craft – I remain for now a critical, yet no less horrified, optimist.

I wonder how things will be by the time of your birthday next June. So many have been saying they wish you were here to shine a light on this dark time. But then I think about how frequently your characters, when it's darkest on earth, look up in awe at the stars shimmering in the night sky above.

With love and deepest respect,
Connie

Jennifer Marie Brissett

Dear Ms. Butler,

May I call you Octavia? I'm going to assume that it's okay because I think we could have been friends. (It helps me to believe that.) I know that we never really, really met. Just that one time at *Yari Yari Pamberi* at NYU in 2004 when I asked you to sign my hardcover of *Parable of the Talents* and *Dark Matter* and I spoiled it by grinning like a fool in my pure pleasure of being in your presence instead of saying anything of any intelligence whatsoever.

Did you know that my first brave act as a professional writer was to decide to publish with my very feminine name and that I did that because of you? Yes, Octavia, because you did, I did. I didn't hide behind initials, a male pseudonym, or an androgynous name. I decided that if you were brave enough then I could be, too.

Anyway, I wanted to first of all thank you for living. Seriously, thank you just for existing on the planet for a while. I'm so sorry you left so soon. I wish you were still here, though. I kinda need you now.

I'm so angry all the time. I wasn't angry like this about the science fiction world before I became a writer, but now I am. I didn't expect this feeling. I don't want this feeling. Yet here it is like a demon sitting next to me taking up time and space in my world. The racism is so strong and entrenched that it's beginning to feel impenetrable. I feel so helpless in the face of it and I feel the bitterness seeping into my soul. What do I do, Octavia? How do I deal with it? How did you deal with it? I hate the smiling grinning faces and the pretense and the 'tolerance' when I know so many black voices are being held back on purpose. And there's proof of it. The other day a report was released from the *Fireside Fiction* Company that said:

> The field of short science fiction and fantasy – at least U.S. publications, which make up the bulk of the field – is essentially not publishing black writers ... Out of 2,039 original stories published in 63 magazines in 2015, only 38 stories could be found that were written by black authors. That's just under 2%. The median number of stories by black authors in these magazines is zero, which means that more than half of all speculative fiction publications measured did not publish a single original story by a black author in the year of 2015. (Kane)

The silence from the field in the face of such damning numbers has been deafening. I personally wrote an email to the current president of SFWA and said:

> Is not your organization *The Science Fiction and Fantasy WRITERS of America*? Doesn't that mean you represent the writers in the field? Here it is (again) a clear demonstration of rampant racism in the field and you don't see that you're a part of the problem at this point?

And I went on to say:

> So maybe I should lay this out for you: if magazines in the field are actively discriminating against black writers, the results are that:
> a) Black writers are prevented from getting a start in their careers
> b) Black writers are prevented from developing bibliographies that are essential to advancing their careers, such as book

deals, etc.

c) Black writers have either turned to self-publishing or have given up altogether in the face of this discrimination

d) Black writers are being prevented from qualifying to become active members of SFWA because of this discrimination, thus losing their voice in policy decisions and nominations for awards, etc.

e) SFWA is rendered a mostly white organization.

Now, if you are comfortable with SFWA representing simply the white writers of the field, then keep doing what you are doing, which is nothing. But if your intention is to represent ALL the writers in this field, then you need to do something. And that's NOT simply a press statement or posting the report. This is now an international disgrace and the field should be ashamed of itself.

I even gave them suggestions on what they could do:

1. Talk to your members, especially the editors, to find out what is going on here.

2. Since you establish the standards for recognized 'pro' magazines in the field, maybe there should also be a standard against racial discrimination and include some means of enforcement (as in, if they are actively discriminating against black people (or anyone!) they cannot be a SFWA approved market.)

3. Begin to maintain statistics yourself on racial discrimination, or partner with organizations that have been doing this work and incorporate this information into public discussions on the health of the field.

4. DO SOMETHING!!!!!

The organization finally acknowledged the report with a blog post (by Cat Rambo) and they seem to still not understand (or care not to understand) that, to quote a comment left by Rose Fox:

> Black authors are being shut out from publication in SFWA-qualifying venues. That means they can't join SFWA and volunteer, and they're not going to be on your lists of black authors. The people your efforts are helping are those who have already beaten the odds. That does nothing to make the odds better ... SFWA needs to acknowledge that the organization and its members are suffering because a great many talented authors are being excluded by the SFWA-qualifying venues that act as gatekeepers of SFWA member-ship, and needs to lean pretty strongly on those venues until they stop shutting out people who could and should be embraced by the SF/F writing and publishing communities.

Writing by itself is difficult. With the weight of all this added to the process, I feel overwhelmed. And yes, sad.

I wasn't a writer when I met you that one time, or at least I wasn't a serious one. I had owned and operated a bookstore that had closed a few years earlier and I was in a place where I was feeling sorry for myself. I was trying not to show it. I was trying to go on with my life. But the truth was I was deeply depressed.

Writing was my refuge, my entertainment, my secret joy. I didn't think about publishing or the field or any of the stuff I think about now, only the fun and mystery of making a story in my head come to life on the page. And then you died ...

And then you died.

It was such a shock. And the shock still hasn't worn off. I was listening to *Democracy Now!* early in the morning while still lying in bed when Amy Goodman announced it. I bolted straight up and thought that I had misheard. I rushed to check all the stations and all the news sites to see if it was true. My life changed that day. I realized that playtime was over, and that I had work to do. My thoughts have focused so that now when I write it's because I have something to say.

A part of me is angry at you for leaving because now I have so many questions for you. So many, many questions that I think only you could answer. Please answer, if there is any way you can, because I really need to know …

It must have been even harder back when you started than it is today to be a writer and black and female, so I wanna know, how the hell did you find the courage to do what you did? Did you strategize to go around the obstacles in your way or did you simply bust through them? Were you ever scared or angry or discouraged? Did you feel the way I do?

Did you see all your daughters and sons following in your footsteps? Did you know that your markings on the path would guide our way? Did you know so many would reap the seeds you sowed?

Maybe you knew. It makes sense that you'd know. You saw things, I'm sure of it. I see things, too. So I guess I need to be brave like you. Maybe that's the answer to my questions: be brave.

Thank you for that.

All my love,
Jennifer Marie Brissett

Sources:

Fox, Rose. Comment on 'SFWA Statement Regarding the Fireside Fiction Company Special Report.' SFWA. 28 Feb 2017. wwwsfwa. org/2016/09/sfwa-statement-regarding-fireside-fiction-company-special-report/#comment-180950

Kane, Cecily. 'Antiblack Racism in Speculative Fiction.' Fireside Fiction. Medium, 21 Aug 2016. medium.com/fireside-fiction-company/ antiblack-racism-in-speculative-fiction7e30eff97008#.5kofm1l6e

Rambo, Cat. 'SFWA Statement Regarding the Fireside Fiction Company Special Report.' SFWA. 28 Feb 2017. www.sfwa.org/2016/09/ sfwa-statement-regarding-fireside-fiction-company-special-report/

Rebecca Holden

'Let's Dwell a Little': The Trickster within Octavia E. Butler

Essay for Octavia Butler Project

'Because the world doesn't want to be saved, for goodness sake.'
Octavia E. Butler, 'A Conversation with Octavia E. Butler'
Strange Matings, 170

There is nothing new
under the sun,
but there are new suns.

Epigraph chosen for Butler's unfinished
Parable of the Trickster (Canavan 151)

I thought about Octavia Butler quite a bit after election night 2016. She would not have been surprised by the outcome, as I was. Disappointed, yes, but far from surprised. Interestingly, I didn't think about Butler when Obama won the presidency in 2008. I think that's because Butler's fiction deals with or *in* humanity's imperfections and potential for malevolence. When I think about her Parable books, I see us – all of us – in that not too distant and less and less farfetched future: some of us rising to the top to subjugate others in the new company towns, in the new forms of slavery we seem to be moving towards, and some struggling to be heard, to survive the ensuing violence, to make 'Black Lives

Matter', to see immigrants as people. Octavia constructed fun-house mirrors in her fiction that forced her readers to confront the often harsh realities of our world and still try to move forward – Trickster that she was.

For me, Butler's fiction has always been a fiction that engendered and presaged change. Octavia published her first science fiction story in 1971 and first novel in 1976 – a time of social upheaval, a time when the Black Power and the women's liberation movements were in full swing, creating havoc in American society or at least with the status quo. The world of SF was also undergoing significant change. Despite its reputation as 'toys for boys' fiction and its apparent penchant (demonstrated by the large-breasted alien women often depicted on the covers) to exoticise women and equate femaleness with sexual availability, this genre attracted many women writers during the 1970s. Women had been writing SF – and some of it feminist – all along (Leigh Brackett, Andre Norton, C.L. Moore, Judith Merril, etc.), but feminist SF as a *recognised* genre began with feminist writers reshaping SF to their own utopian ends during Second Wave feminism. In her book *Feminism and Science Fiction*, Sarah Lefanu notes that while 'between 1953, the year of its inception, and 1967, there were no women winners of the Hugo Award, between 1968 and 1984 there were eleven' (7). Writer and critic Pamela Sargent claims that during the 1970s women in SF were coming to see themselves as a recognisable group 'with certain common characteristics regardless of their individual circumstances' and to believe that 'science fiction was a form in which the issues raised by feminism could be explored' (16). [1]

At the same time, SF was still a very white field. The very fact that Butler, a black woman, wrote SF in the early 1970s, and came to make her living as an SF author, disturbed the SF status quo. Even as late as 1990, Butler herself said that she only knew two other black science fiction writers, Steven Barnes and Samuel Delany, and while there may have been other black women writing SF, she didn't know any (Kenan 500). In 'Lost Races of Science Fiction', written in 1980, Butler speculates that the reason there are so few black SF writers is

> the same reason there were once so few women SF writers. Women found a certain lack of authenticity in a genre that postulated a universe largely populated by men, in which all the power was in male hands, and women stayed in their male-defined places. Blacks find a certain lack of authenticity in a genre which postulates a universe largely populated by whites, in which the power is in white hands, and blacks are occasional oddities. (184) [2]

In the same essay, Octavia discusses advice she heard in a creative writing class in 1965 and echoed again by an SF writer in 1979 (and presumably multiple other times). Her teacher told another student 'not to use black characters in his stories unless those characters' blackness was somehow essential to the plot' as having black characters 'drew attention from the intended subject' (181). Or as the SF writer advised in 1979, writers might substitute extraterrestrials for blacks 'so as not to dwell on matters of race' (181). In her to-the-point manner, which is one of my favorite things about her, Butler writes, 'let's do a little dwelling' (182). Butler points out that no writer who sees blacks as humans 'would have trouble creating interesting backgrounds and goals for black characters ... It is no more necessary to focus on a character's blackness than it is to focus on a woman's femininity' (182).

Octavia practiced what she preached. Her stories were never about race or gender, even though her protagonists are primarily black women and thus race, gender, and other lived realities cannot be separated from her characters' lives. SF as a genre offered Butler the freedom, similar to the freedom exploited by other women SF writers of the time, to explore the full lives of her characters. In an interview from 1979, she noted that 'As a writer of science fiction, I was free to imagine new ways of thinking about people and power, free to maneuver my characters into situations that don't exist. For example, where is there a society in which men and women are honestly considered equal? ... Where do people not despise each other because of race or religion, class or ethnic origin?' (Mixon 14).

However, unlike her white peers, Butler did not use the genre to write her own black feminist utopia, nor did she pay heed to those who told her she should 'do something more relevant to the Movement' and that what she was writing 'had nothing to do with Black people' ('A Conversation' 128). Butler was keenly aware of the struggles of black Americans, and as she said, 'Well, gee, I look Black. I didn't think it was fake ... So I figured [what I did] had something to do with Black people' ('A Conversation' 128). However, Octavia refused to be pinned down by one narrative of identity, despite what others may have tried to force on her. In an interview from 1991, Butler explains:

> I was on a little early Sunday morning TV show a while back, and the hostess was a black woman and there were two other black women writers, a poet and a playwright and me. And the hostess asked as a near final question how we felt about feminism and the other two women said they didn't think much of it, they assumed it was for white people.

I said that I thought it was just as important to have equal rights for women as it was to have equal rights for black people and so I felt myself to be very much a feminist. (Kenan 501)

At the same time, Octavia was well aware of the differences among women, and this awareness differentiates her early work from much of the other feminist SF, primarily utopias and dystopias, of the 1970s. It wasn't that she wasn't moved to write her own utopia. Based on his readings of Butler's notes and journals archived in the Huntington Library, Gerry Canavan tells us that Octavia 'longed to write utopian stories' and in her own words 'need[ed] to write them' despite the 'fact that [she didn't] believe in them – [didn't] believe humanity [was] fixable' (Canavan 121). We can see Butler's utopian moves – the separation of power from race or gender in the Patternist series; the non-hierarchical, life-revering, boundary-breaking alien Oankali from the Xenogenesis trilogy; the openness of protagonist Lauren Olamina's new Earthseed religion in the Parable books; the mutually beneficial relationship between the vampire Shori and her symbionts in *Fledgling* – that many critics want to embrace as utopia. However, the Trickster that resided within Butler's stories pushed her SF in new directions, not allowing her to write any triumphant black feminist utopia, or race to the stars, nor completely condemn humanity with any straightforward dystopia about our bleakest futures.

In her essay 'The Third Parable', SF writer Nisi Shawl discusses Octavia's difficulty writing *Parable of the Trickster*, the book that was meant to be the third book of the Parable series. As Octavia's friend, Shawl regrets never telling Butler the Trickster story from Ifa, the West African religion Shawl practices, whose 'pantheon includes Exu, one of the many sacred Tricksters found in religions around the world' (209). Shawl notes that in addition to surprises and epiphanies, Exu 'rules words and the tricks one can work with them, including telling stories. And lies' (209).

The Trickster story Shawl would have told Octavia is as follows:

> There were two farmers who loved one another as brothers and shared in everything. The fields they cultivated lay side by side, with a footpath between them. Though they had been told to make offerings to the Spirit of the Trickster, these men saw no need to do so. They were sure that their knowledge and skill were all they needed to live well.
>
> One day Exu himself came walking down the path. Recognizing the two farmers as men who had neglected to give him his due, Exu hid in the bushes and prepared to show them how wrong they had been. He painted one side of his face red and the other black. Then he emerged from the bushes and continued along the path. After Exu had gone by, the farmers called out to one another, remarking on this stranger. 'Did you see that man with the red face?' asked the first man. 'You mean the man with the black face,' said the second. 'His face was black.' The two could not agree on Exu's appearance, and began to quarrel about it, at last coming to blows. Their friendship and the prosperity of their farms were destroyed.

Shawl explains: 'The parable's farmers came to grief not because they said what they saw, but because each insisted that theirs was the one correct version' (212).

Shawl goes on to compliment Butler for calling red 'red' and black 'black,' for not shying away from the truth. I would like to go a bit further and suggest that Octavia presents us with both the black and red sides of the truth. She tricks us by giving us what sometimes seems like contradictory and multiple truths, by showing us that *the* truth is not as easy to pin down as we might think. Race was not the truth that defined her protagonists, nor was gender. Both were true, but neither truth superseded the other.

Many of the 1970s feminist SF utopias and dystopias, though tolerant of some superficial differences among women, could not be flexible enough to incorporate a variety of women and the specifics of their positions, or even the full spectrum of feminisms. These texts emphasize gender discrimination as the primary source of oppression in society – think of Ursula Le Guin's *The Left Hand of Darkness* (1969), Joanna Russ's *The Female Man* (written in 1971 and published in 1975), Suzy McKee Charnas's *Walk to the End of the World* (1974) and *Motherlines* (1974), Marge Piercy's *Woman on the Edge of Time* (1976), and Sally Miller Gearhart's *The Wanderground* (1979). The creation of these utopias depends on a rather monolithic definition of 'woman'. Racial discrimination and racism itself, the utopias imply, are problems of history and do not have a place in feminist future worlds; the racialised black woman becomes the monster effectively hidden in the attic of the past.[5] Butler, however, as my title implies, wants to 'dwell a little' in and explore that attic instead of simply moving beyond it to some utopian future. To me it is Butler's recognition, despite her utopian longings, of both the high costs of survival for African Americans and the different historical realities of people, that made it impossible for her to unambiguously 'save the world' in her SF despite her very clear impetus to do so.

By asking her readers to 'dwell a little' and at the same time refusing to write stories primarily about 'racism' or 'sexism' or any other '-ism', Butler leads us to reconsider our preconceived notions about such prejudices as well as about heroes, villains, complicity, and identity politics.[6] In this way, her work explodes previous notions of what SF can and should be and what histories or futures it can and should draw or create. Thus we see SF that draws on slave narratives, characters like Anyanwu from *Wild Seed* based on African Igbo myths, and multiple shades of African American protagonists leading humanity's futures.

It also means we might mistakenly focus on *the* truth we bring to Butler's fiction and devolve into the same argument the Trickster's farmers fall victim to. In *Kindred*, we might read the depiction of Dana's slaveholding ancestor – who attempts to rape her – as a straightforward condemnation of slavery and of Dana's impulse to save his life multiple times, or we might see Dana's marriage to a white man as an endorsement of moving beyond race. Perhaps the Oankali from the Xenogenesis trilogy are the utopian saviors of humankind who live in harmony with nature and lack humanity's fatal genetic flaw – the combination of intelligence and hierarchical tendencies – that the alien Oankali see as humanity's downfall, or maybe they are evil rapists who force pregnancy and alien sex on the humans.[7] We might want to view 'Bloodchild' (1984) as a story where the slaver Tlic force their human hosts to bear Tlic young and undergo violent, sometimes deadly childbirth or, as Octavia herself describes the story, 'as a love story between two very different beings' or 'my pregnant man story' where the man 'choos[es] pregnancy in spite of as well as because of surrounding difficulties' ('Afterword,' *Bloodchild*, 30). The alien Communities from one of Butler's last published stories,

'Amnesty' (2003) could be evil for abducting humans and causing their deaths, or as the protagonist Noah comes to understand, curious 'like human scientists experimenting with lab animals – not cruel, but very thorough' (19).

These are but a few examples; each of Butler's stories shows us many truths. Butler the author might have favored some truths over others, but the Trickster she could not keep out of those stories would say yes and no to all of them. Her SF, then, moved beyond any straightforward utopic/dystopic story of the 1970s' feminist SF as well as the so-called hard SF that had been the core of the genre for decades. A story that might seem to show us the Trickster's red face, an answer to humanity's fatal contradiction, shifts subtly to that Trickster's black face. We argue about her intentions – was Butler essentialist? Was that story about slavery? Who is the true villain? I would suggest that the more time a reader spends with Butler, the more that reader sees the ambiguities, the more unsettling and thought-provoking the stories become.

Octavia's fascination with biology, disease, and the truly alien – following the epigraph she chose for her unfinished *Parable of the Trickster* – opened SF up to 'new suns'. These new suns include not only the worlds she created, but the conversations and arguments her fiction sparks, the SF writers of color she inspires, the inclusion of myths and histories previously unwelcome in SF, and the ways her stories widened the boundaries of the genre.[8] I don't believe that Octavia set out to be a trendsetter – she wrote what she felt compelled to write and what she felt compelled to write came from her life, her world, and her convictions as a person.

Octavia tricked us all, including herself. She knew, as we all know after this past election, that 'the world doesn't want to be saved, for goodness sake' (sic; 'A Conversation' 170) but she couldn't stay away. Butler compelled herself in the same way that she compelled her readers to inhabit the worlds she created, to accept partial truths and the high price of survival as something we can or must accept, and then to dance away to search for those 'new suns', only to begin again.

1   See also Brian Attebury's *Decoding Gender in Science Fiction* in which he calls the 1970s 'the decade when women writers of sf ceased to seem exceptional' (107). See Justine Larbalestier's *Battle of the Sexes in Science Fiction* (2002) and Helen Merrick's *The Secret Feminist Cabal: A Cultural History of Science Fiction Feminisms* (2009) for alternative readings of the 'explosion' of women writers into SF. See Lisa Yaszek's *Galactic Suburbia* (2008) for more in-depth reconsiderations of women writing SF before the 1960s and *Sisters of Tomorrow* (2016), edited by Lisa Yaszek and Patrick B. Sharp, an annotated collection of SF by women from the 1920s, '30s, and '40s.

2   See Harrison – an interview from 1980 – for similar comments from Butler regarding SF.

3   Many critics applaud what they see as the potentially utopian alien Oankali, who destabilise our notions of gender, race, and other binary categories, and read the Oankali as symbiotic creatures in harmony with nature. See Zaki, Green, and Miller for a few examples of those who read Butler's fiction primarily within the utopian tradition. Donna Haraway, in her 'Cyborg Manifesto' (1985) and her 'The Biopolitics of Postmodern Bodies' (1989) celebrates Butler's fiction, and *Dawn* in particular, as while not clearly utopian, harbingers of cyborg fiction. Haraway's reading ultimately celebrates Lilith's interactions and interbreeding with the Oankali as the beginning of the other order of difference and 'the resistance to the

imperative to recreate the sacred image of the same' that Haraway sees as necessary for a feminist future. See Lisbeth Gant Stevenson's "'A New Fashion in Faith': The Parable Novels in Conversation with Actual Intentional Communities" for examples of real life incarnations of communities inspired by Butler's Earthseed religion.

4   Shawl notes that she adapted her telling of this Yoruba teaching tale from 'oral tellings and from a written version compiled by a priest of the Ifa tradition' found in Iba'se Orisa by Awo Fa'lokun Fatumnbi.

5   Women of colour appear in both Piercy's *Woman on the Edge of Time* and Charnas's *Motherlines*, but as Michele Erica Green argues, all women in these novels are seen as 'interchangeable' and their racial and ethnic differences 'seem only skin-deep' (168).

6   In an interview from 1980, Butler discussed an anthology about and by black people she had agreed to do with another writer. When the other writer sent her six stories he thought might be worth including in the anthology, Butler very explicitly stated that these stories were not about black people: 'Except for one, they were all stories about racism. I wrote back to him about something I feel very strong: racism is only one facet or aspect of black existence. A lot of white writers (and some black writers) see it as the totality of black existence' (Harrison 32).

7   I am fascinated by Thomas Foster's comments about his students' mis- or partial readings of *Dawn*; the students want to read the books as an alien invasion narrative and Foster insists that Butler's conscious references to slave narratives and alien invasion stories in the trilogy have 'the potential to disrupt any triumphal narrative of human superiority in the face of alien menace' (151). At the same time Foster acknowledges how the Xenogenesis

books emphasise that the genetic trade the Oankali insist on 'does not run in both directions' (153) and thus is 'no guarantee of genuine tolerance and equality' (153).

[8] As I have written elsewhere, Butler's SF 'readjusted readers' notions of what was a suitable topic or 'hero' in science fiction at the same time that she – black, female, and powerless in her own view – challenged the popular conception about who could be a science fiction writer' or reader ('I began' 37).

Works Cited

Attebury, Brian. *Decoding Gender in Science Fiction*. New York: Routledge, 2002. Print.

Butler, Octavia E. Afterword. 'Bloodchild'. *Bloodchild* 30–32. Print.

–. 'Amnesty.' SciFi.com, 2003. Web. 30 Jan. 2008.

–. *Bloodchild and Other Stories*. New York: Four Walls Eight Windows, 1995. Print.

–. *Fledgling*. New York: Seven Stories Press, 2005. Print.

–. 'A Conversation with Octavia E. Butler.' Holden and Shawl 128–131. Print.

–. 'Lost Races of Science Fiction.' 1980. Canavan 181–186. Print.

–. *Parable of the Sower*. New York: Four Walls Eight Windows, 1993: New York: Warner, 2000. Print.

–. *Wild Seed*. New York: Warner, 1980. Print.

–. *Xenogenesis: Dawn, Adulthood Rites, Imago*. New York: Warner, 1987, 1988, 1989. Reprint. New York: Guild America, 1989. Print.

Canavan, Gerry. *Octavia E. Butler*. Chicago: University of Illinois Press, 2016. Print.

Charnas, Suzy McKee. *Motherlines*. New York: Berkley, 1978. Print.

—. *Walk to the End of the World*. 1974. *Radical Utopias*. Print.

Foster, Thomas. '"We Get to Live, and So Do They": Octavia Butler's Contact Zones' Holden and Shawl 140-167. Print.

Gant-Britton, Lisbeth. '"A New Fashion in Faith": The Parable Novels in Conversation with Actual Intentional Communities.' Holden and Shawl 186-207. Print.

Gearhart, Sally Miller. *The Wanderground: Stories of the Hill Women*. Boston, MA: Alyson Publications, Inc., 1979.

Green, Michelle Erica. '"There Goes the Neighborhood": Octavia Butler's Demand for Diversity in Utopias.' *Utopian and Science Fiction by Women: Worlds of Difference*. Ed. Jane L. Donawerth and Carol A. Kolmerten. Syracuse, NY: Syracus UP, 1994. 166-189. Print.

Haraway, Donna. *Simians, Cyborgs, and Women: The Reinvention of Nature*. New York: Routledge, 1991. Print.

Harrison, Rosalie G. 'Sci Fi Visions: An Interview with Octavia Butler.' *Equal Opportunity Forum Magazine* 8 (1980): 30-34. Print.

Holden, Rebecca J. '"I began writing about power because I had so little": The Impact of Octavia Butler's Early Work on Feminist Science Fiction as a Whole (and on One Feminist Science Fiction Scholar in Particular).' Holden and Shawl 17-44. Print.

Holden, Rebecca J. and Nisi Shawl, eds. *Strange Matings: Science Fiction, Feminism, African American Voices, and Octavia E. Butler*. Seattle: Aqueduct Press, 2013. Print.

Kenan, Randall. 'An Interview with Octavia Butler.' *Callaloo* 14.2 (1991): 495-504. Print.

Larbalestier, Justine. *Battle of the Sexes in Science Fiction*. Middletown, CT: Wesleyan University Press, 2002. Print.

Lefanu, Sarah. *Feminism and Science Fiction*. Bloomington, IN: Indiana University Press, 1989. Print.

Le Guin, Ursula K. *The Left Hand of Darkness*. New York: Ace Publishing, 1969. Print.

Merrick, Helen. *The Secret Feminist Cabal: A Cultural History of Science Fiction Feminisms*. Seattle: Aqueduct Press, 2009. Print.

Miller, Jim. 'Post-Apocalyptic Hoping: Octavia Butler's Dystopian/Utopian Vision.' *Science Fiction Studies* 25.2 (1998): 336-360. Print.

Mixon, Veronica. 'Futurist Woman: Octavia Butler.' *Essence* 9 (April 1979): 12. Print.

Piercy, Marge. *Woman on the Edge of Time*. New York: Knopf, 1976. Print.

Radical Utopias. New York: Book-of-the-Month Club, 1990. Print.

Russ, Joanna. *The Female Man*. 1975. *Radical Utopias*. Print.

Sargent, Pamela. 'Introduction.' *Women of Wonder: The Classic Years*. New York: Harcourt Brace & Co., 1995. 1-20. Print.

Shawl, Nisi. 'The Third Parable.' Holden and Shawl 207-213. Print.

Yaszek, Lisa. *Galactic Suburbia: Recovering Women's Science Fiction*. Columbus, OH: The Ohio State University Press, 2008. Print.

Yaszek, Lisa and Patrick B. Sharp, eds. *Sisters of Tomorrow: The First Women of Science Fiction*. Middletown, CT: Wesleyan University Press, 2016. Print.

Zaki, Hoda M. 'Utopia, Dystopia, and Ideology in the Science Fiction of Octavia Butler.' *Science-Fiction Studies* 17 (1990): 239-51. Print.

Andrea Hairston

This essay by Andrea Hairston appeared in Justine Larbalestier's anthology *Daughters of Earth: Feminist Science Fiction in the Twentieth Century* in conjunction with Octavia Butler's short story 'The Evening and the Morning and the Night.' All references to 'The Evening and the Morning and the Night' are to the story as printed in *Daughters of Earth*. In that story, to quote Hairston, 'Butler thrusts her characters into an impossibly bleak, hopeless setting. A miracle drug cancer cure turns the user's children into violent, self-mutilating zombies.'

Octavia Butler – Praise Song to a Prophetic Artist

Prophets needn't offer a vision of the actual future, an answer to current problems, or even the salvation of an afterlife. With historical insight and a fluent grasp of tradition, prophets illuminate the immanent possibilities of the here and now. They shake our minds loose from the iron grip of the indicative case. By substituting *might be* or *would be* for is, prophets allow us the subjunctive flight of fancy that prefigures transformation and ushers in a brand new day.

Octavia Butler is a prophetic artist.

The World: Current Condition
Whenever I agonize about how hard it is to get anything done in this world, how even small change seems impossible; when I

whine about the backlash, the backsliding, the men and women who believe that we have long since arrived at the Promised Land and that all the 'isms' – sexism, racism, classism, heterosexism – are way behind us now in our multicultural egalitarian utopia;[1] when I turn off the TV because liberation is a jeweled thong on *Sex in the City* and bold profit junkies brag about drilling holes in the Alaskan wilderness while sending more young people to kill and die in the desert for the oil there; when I despair because choice is the thousand channels owned by the same two companies, because PR wizards have convinced us that toxic sludge really is good for us and it is environmental crackpots and feminasties who are actually to blame for declining productivity;[2] as babies all over the world are too hungry to make it to their first birthday and today's front page in the local newspaper proclaims, 'World's women worse off than ten years ago';[3] as statistics on black people and people of color indicate that, despite the flashy photogenic celebrities and multimillion dollar ghetto-chic distractions, we're still getting ground down amidst the bounty and magic of this technological wonderland ... I mean, when it looks as if the future's been mortgaged, several futures in fact, and it's getting grimmer than grim, I pick up an Octavia Butler novel or story and find hope.

What could be more entertaining than hope?

Octavia Butler declares:

> I'm a 56-year-old writer who can remember being a 10-year-old writer and who expects some day to be an 80-year-old writer. I'm comfortably asocial – a hermit living in a large city – a pessimist if I'm not careful; a student, endlessly curious; a feminist; an African American; a former Baptist; and an oil and water combination of ambition, laziness, insecurity, certainty, and drive.[4]

As a prophetic feminist artist looking back at the past, looking hard at the present, Butler foretells what might be. She is an impossibility specialist, a conjurer whose wizard words call forth our humanity in the midst of holocaust, of apocalypse wrought by our biology and culture. She never lets us forget that we are all agents of change. Reading her stories and novels challenges the inertia of our spirits. With transparent, undecorated prose, she renders the banality, brutality, and insanity of human nature and society in chilling detail. Always writing her way to characters who make something out of less than nothing, she re-envisions past devastation and invents parables of the not-too-distant future, insisting there is no *deus ex machina* coming to the rescue, no magic bullet cure for what ails us. We are the change we've been waiting for. As Beatrice Alcantara, the head of the alternative institute for treating DGD, tells Alan Chi in 'The Evening And The Morning And The Night,' [sic] 'The people of Dilg are problem solvers, Alan. Think of the problems you could solve!' (Butler, 284)

A *Brief History*

Like the heroines in her stories, Butler is one of those black women who wasn't meant to be. Finding no cultural space for her voice and vision, she changed the limitations of her historical moment and redefined black literature, SF and F, and feminist literature. She created a space not only for herself and her particular imaginative genius, but also inspired a generation of new writers, literary and social theorists, fans, and casual readers with her meditations on agency and change.

With her groundbreaking research and *Dark Matter* anthologies Sheree R. Thomas has demonstrated that writers from the African Diaspora have been creating speculative fiction since the mid-nineteenth century. Martin Delany in *Blake, Or the Huts of America* (1857 or 1859) imagined a successful slave uprising; Pauline Hopkins in *Of One Blood* (1879) envisions an African American discovering a lost African empire; in *Imperium in Imperio* (1899) by Sutton E. Griggs, a secret society of black men creates an all black nation in Texas; a white woman and black man are the only New Yorkers who survive the Earth's passage through a comet's tail in W. E. B. Du Bois' 'The Comet' (1920); and a Negro doctor can change black people to white people in three days in George S. Shulyer's *Black No More* (1931).[5]

Despite these and other speculative meditations on history and culture by black artists, from the 1920s on, science fiction has been dominated and defined in the public mind by white males – authors, critics, and readers. Until recently, publishers feared that black writers, 'black' themes, or even the appearance of black characters in a story would put off (white) SF and F readers. A character's 'blackness' distracted from the blissful sense of wonder that enveloped a good SF story. Butler recounts an anecdote in which a magazine editor told her:

> that he didn't think blacks should be included in science fiction stories because they changed the character of the stories; that if you put in a black, all of a sudden the focus in on this person. He stated that if you were going to write about some sort of racial problem, that would be absolutely the only reason he could see for including a black.[6]

In other words, to deal with universal human themes, to speculate on human possibility, writers should use characters not 'burdened' with race.

The myth that black folks weren't/ aren't SF and F writers or fans, and the realities that engendered this myth, also limited the reception and development of black SF writers from the 1920s to the present. Urging black authors to write science fiction in an essay for *Dark Matter – A Century of Speculative Fiction from the African Diaspora*, Charles R. Saunders mused on the history of black readers and writers of SF and F:

> When I wrote 'Why Blacks Don't Read Science Fiction,' [1978] I believed most blacks shunned sf and fantasy because there was little for us to identify with in the content ... A literature that offered mainstream readers an escape route into the imagination and, at its best, a window into the future could not bestow a similar experience for black and other minority readers ...
>
> At the time [late '70s], science fiction was still in the process of freeing itself from the grasp on its so-called Golden Age in the 1930s-1950s, when hard science was a king whose court was closed to blacks. And fantasy was still frozen in an amber of Celtic and Arthurian themes.[7]

Reviewing Octavia Butler's Xenogenesis series in 1989, Adele S. Newman wrote:

> It is a widespread myth that Blacks don't write or read science fiction. The myth is fed by the notion that they cannot afford to indulge in fantasy.[8]

In 1998 Jeffrey Allen Tucker, Ph.D., a Samuel Delany scholar, confessed:

> When I tell people that my most recent research has been on works of African-American Science Fiction, I often get responses that range from incredulous – 'You mean, there is

such a thing?' – to the ridiculous: 'You mean like Home-
boys in Outer Space or Dionne Warwick's Psychic Friends
Network, right?'[9]

In the utilitarian Puritan cultural landscape of the United
States, where the practice and enjoyment of art is suspect, 'escaping
into the imagination' is sinful at worst, frivolous at best; 'indulging
in fantasy' is a prerogative of the privileged, not an essential aspect
of shared humanity. In the early and mid-twentieth century, the
African American artist's major labor was to correct the damage,
the devastation of a blackface minstrel past. Blues People cut off
from history didn't dabble in the future. They left that to the white
folks and spent their precious time throwing off oppression.

In the minds of many readers, writers, and critics, the
mimetic realism of so-called literary fiction held out the best
opportunity for blacks to reclaim borrowed or stolen history, recreate a positive group identity from shared experiences, and uplift
the race. The 'serious' artistry of literary fiction allowed black
artists to battle the science fiction and fantasy of white supremacy.
The experience/story of the slave trade, colonization of Africa, and
the Jim Crow laws and violent repression in the United States
reads like an SF and F dystopic narrative. Supported by religious
apologists on the hunt for benighted souls and a pseudoscientific
doctrine of racial hierarchy, the real-life 'aliens' that violated black
bodies, twisted their histories, and despoiled the future also got to
tell their stories. This on-going struggle over representation has
circumscribed African American cultural production. 'Serious'
literature could set the record straight. Instead of the coons,
Jezebels, bucks, and mammies strutting across screen, stage, page,
or hanging in the American/world imagination, realist black

narratives could show who we *actually* were. Black artists could thereby rupture minstrel fantasies and define *authentic* black men and women.[10]

Authenticity is the problem child of pseudo-science, commodity culture, and anxious nostalgia for a mono-cultural identity. In a relentlessly multicultural, pluralistic society, authenticity and other essentialist notions of identity and community help to maintain the power status quo. Conjuring the *authentic* black character, while often a mighty attempt to free the African American image from white racist control, was/is a (racist) trap of its own. Despite shared experiences, racism doesn't magically erase differences and make all black people the same. Nor is racism the only concern or obligatory obsession of black folks. The complexity hidden by the minstrel mask, by the Harlem Renaissance's New Negro visage, or the '60s Black Revolutionary power stance would not be contained. Variations in class, gender, age, ethnicity, sexuality, etc. made a monolithic performance of race impossible. Authenticity would not save us from exploitation and oppression and in fact made self determination/ self definition more difficult. As Audre Lorde famously said, 'the master's tools will never dismantle the master's house.'[11]

Not Just Tearing Down the House
Samuel R. Delany and Octavia Butler were the first celebrated African American SF writers of the twentieth century. Very different writers, drawn by the freedom and potential of the genre, neither were simply engaged in the re-appropriation and redefinition of images of blackness. They weren't just tearing down the master's house; rather, they meditated on our humanity, on who we all might become. To the frequent challenge, 'What good is science

83

fiction to Black people?' which implicitly demanded a justification for abandoning the honorable labor of racial uplift, Butler replied:

What good is any form of literature to Black people? What good is science fiction's thinking about the present, the future, and the past? What good is its tendency to warn or to consider alternative ways of thinking and doing? What good is its examination of the possible effects of science and technology, or social organization and political direction? At its best, science fiction stimulates imagination and creativity. It gets reader and writer off the beaten track, off the narrow, narrow footpath of what 'everyone' is saying, doing, thinking – whoever 'everyone' happens to this year.

And what good is all this to Black people? [12]

As Octavia Butler declared herself a feminist and wrote her early novels – SF and F works that interrupted essentialist notions of race, class, gender, etcetera, while investigating complex humanity – radical feminists of color such as Audre Lorde, bell hooks, Cherríe Moraga, Alice Walker, Gloria Anzaldúa, Toni Morrison, Pearl Cleage, Michelle Wallace, and Maxine Hong Kingston were, to paraphrase Kingston, all learning to make their minds large, as the universe is large, with room for paradoxes.[13] These warrior women expanded the limited agenda of the male-dominated Civil Rights movement and also challenged the narrowness of (white middle-class) feminism.

Since Sojourner Truth, black women have critiqued a narrowly defined feminism that would universalize the particular experiences of one group of woman and signify the experiences of 'other' women as marginal or aberrant. Gender as a category of difference like race cannot magically confine or predict the protean identities and complex experiences of the people it purports to describe. Many feminist SF and F writers vigorously challenge the social construction of gender while discounting, repressing, or sidelining other differences.[14]

In the struggle for black liberation, gender issues (along with sexuality and class issues) were/are often viewed as side issues, distractions from the 'real' black struggle. In the late '70s and early '80s Ntozake Shange, Michelle Wallace, Alice Walker, and other black feminists were accused of being race traitors for airing dirty laundry, for challenging the sexism of black men and black culture and politics in public. Shange's play *for colored girls who have considered suicide when the rainbow is enuf*, Walker's novel, *The Color Purple*, and Wallace's critical text, *Black Macho and the Myth of the Superwoman* resulted in a storm of controversy about black male bashing that is ongoing. Interestingly, black men who harass, oppress, marginalize, and brutalize black women were/are not viewed as race traitors.[15] In fact strong black women were/are seen as pathological matriarchs, as obstacles impeding black men from attaining their manhood.[16] Feminism was/is often characterized as a white, middle class, trivial movement and not part of the 'uplift the race' agenda. Thus Butler faced a public questioning not only 'what good was science fiction to black people,' but a black nationalist agenda that questioned 'what good was feminism to black people.'

Falling Out of the Margins

Many mid-twentieth-century radical feminists of color used fantastical, speculative elements in their work as did earlier writers. For example, Lorraine Hansberry invented an African nation for *Les Blancs*, as did Alice Walker for *The Color Purple* and *Possessing the Secret of Joy*. Toni Morrison's *Beloved* is a ghost story, and Pearl Cleage's *In the Time Before the Men Came* is alternative history. Yet, no matter how anti-realist their work, these authors remained in the literary fiction bins. And although an early novel, *Kindred*, was turned down by SF presses and published by a mainstream house, Butler named herself a science fiction writer.

SF and F as a form of meta-literature poses difficulties for a feminist author riffing on, among other thing, 'black' idioms and story repertoire. An author extrapolating on a past or present social reality requires an audience fluent in that social reality, an audience aware of the characters, experiences, values, gestures, and nuances that inspire the extrapolation. Any author whose references fall outside the margins of the mainstream must struggle with the false universalism of the dominant stories, must face down publishers and critics who confuse their cultural ignorance with the author's supposed artistic failings. Critics and publishers who devalue the significance of women's experience often label works centering on women's lives as trivial, insisting that their evaluation is purely aesthetic, 'all about craft.' Authors dealing in so-called women's trivia or black particularity simply aren't good enough to know what makes a well-crafted story, a rollicking good blockbuster narrative.[17]

Octavia Butler's narratives fall out of a lot of margins (Mainstream, African American, Feminist, SF and F). However, she artfully educates her audience in the motifs she riffs on. Using black women heroines to meditate on humanity – not as the ultimate universal subjects but as particular agents of change in whose stories we might find hope – Butler decenters the presumed white male reader of SF and F, looking for geeky entertainment. She also doesn't write Doris Day Blues – tales of a middle-class housewife languishing in the suburbs, trapped in nuclear-family hell, servicing a predator-capitalist husband (whose dreams of adventure have soured in the workaday world), driving her children here, there, and everywhere, but getting nowhere herself. Rescuing women from domestic bondage, from the prison of family, from an essentialized, obligatory motherhood is/was not a trivial concern.[18] However Butler's approach to family and motherhood is from a different angle. Her heroines reinvent family and create community as a way to rescue and redefine humanity. Lynn Mortimer, the narrator in 'The Evening and the Morning and the Night' observes:

> I watched a woman work quickly, knowledgeably, with a power saw. She obviously understood the perimeters of her body, was not so dissociated as to perceive herself as trapped in something she needed to dig her way out of. What had Dilg done for these people that other hospitals did not do? (Butler, 277)

Dilg is a constructed family, a community guided by a visionary woman who works to redefine the diseased bodies of DGDs [sufferers of Duryea-Gode Disease] as productive and creative. In fact, allowing DGD sufferers access to their creativity allows them to heal. In much of her work, Butler gives a 'domestic' sensibility to the 'public' discourse of liberation and survival.

In addition to being abstract cultural constructs, Butler's characters refer to body-based beings in a cultural/historical context where the performance of identity and the nature of community have a profound impact on everyone's survival. Individual agency within a strong community network heads off annihilation. Even when family members are oppressive, Butler's heroines sacrifice themselves to save their families, their communities, their people, their species from total destruction.

They are prophets witnessing for the future.

Not Being Able To Stop

> Who was I anyway? Why should anyone pay attention to what I had to say? Did I have anything to say I was writing science fiction and fantasy for God's sake. At that time nearly all the professional science-fiction writers were white men. As much as I loved science fiction and fantasy, what was I doing? Well, whatever it was I couldn't stop. Positive obsession is about not being able to stop just because you're afraid and full of doubts. Positive obsession is dangerous. It's about not being able to stop at all.[19]

A casual search through literary, feminist, African American, and SF journals and publications reveals a staggering amount of criticism devoted to analyzing, celebrating, pondering, and fussing with Butler's work. All concur that she has had a profound impact on the SF genre and black and feminist literature. In 1995, Butler received a MacArthur 'Genius' Award, and in October 2000, she received the Lifetime Achievement Award in writing from PEN.

Starting in 1976 with *Patternmaster*, Octavia Butler has published eleven novels. *Kindred* (1979), a time traveling [sic] epic, features a twentieth-century black woman snatched into the antebellum South to save the life of her white slave master ancestor. The fantasy novel was an international best-seller and has sold 250,000 copies to date [2006] ... As mentioned earlier despite eventual popularity, Butler had difficulty finding an SF and F publisher for her decidedly non-Celtic, non-Arthurian Kindred, so it came out as mainstream fiction from Doubleday.

With *Kindred* and *Wildseed* [sic] (1980), Butler reinvented the salve narrative as speculative fiction. Her artistry has been compared to Toni Morrison's *Beloved*. Butler had heard too many voices in the black consciousness movement dismissing the efforts of previous generations as a betrayal of a hip, revolutionary present. The cavalier contempt contemporary black people displayed for the slaves who accommodated their masters to survive spurred Butler to write the present into the past. Showing what black people in the early 1800s had endured, so that folks in the twentieth century could strut their stuff, Butler restored cultural memory. The sacrifices and accommodations that characters are asked to make in "The Evening and the Morning and the Night" are similar in nature. In *Kindred* and *Wildseed*, Butler honors the clarity of vision and the mundane, backbreaking heroics that laid the ground for who black people could be today.

In the Xenogenesis trilogy of *Dawn* (1987), *Adult Rites* (1988), and *Imago* (1989), the warmongers have blown up the world and most of the people with it. The only hope for humanity is assimilation. Survivors of the nuclear holocaust must integrate on a genetic level with the alien Oankali. The Xenogenesis trilogy … explores the connection between biology and agency. The cover of *Dawn* features a white heroine as opposed to the black one found in the story. In the late '80s, a black protagonist on the face of an SF novel was still too scary.[21]

In *Parable of the Sower* (1995) and *Parable of the Talents* (2000), Butler speculates on the implications of late model capitalism. In these books, the cutthroat, commodity culture values of transnational corporations and patriarchal militarism ravish and rend asunder the human fabric of life. Extrapolating from Los Angeles in the 1990s, Butler centers on those who do not have the resources to insulate themselves from vicious urban violence and decay. The majority of the population, who cannot afford a gated community protected by thugs for hire, become homeless wanderers – not unlike the 'Okies' running from the over-farmed dustbowls and the depression-depleted cities of the 1930s. Floundering in the throes of corporate fascism, abandoned by a complicit military and an ineffectual democracy, Butler's characters reinvent community in order to rescue the future. They are led by a black woman empathy who feels the actual pain of those around her. She is an embodiment of *communitas* – the individual resonating collective identity – and the antithesis of the rugged individualist who doesn't even feel his own pain. *Parable of the Talents* won the 2000 Nebular award for best novel.

Prophetic Artist
An avid science fiction reader and dear friend told me once that Octavia Butler's work, although excellent, was unrelentingly bleak and brutal. As noted earlier, Butler herself claims to be pessimistic (if not careful) and resists any attempts by readers and critics to label her fiction utopian. So why do I find this self-proclaimed pessimist so hopeful?

Cornel West says to hope is 'to go beyond the evidence to make new possibilities based on visions that become contagious to allow us to engage in heroic actions always against the odds.'[22] In *Prophetic Thought in Postmodern Times*, West argues that post-modern prophets must be discerning, empathetic, humble, and hopeful in order to deal with the material and spiritual crises of the late twentieth century. For him, hope in the face of atrocity may be the most difficult thing to manage, but it's a necessity.

To talk about human hope is to engage in an audacious attempt to galvanize and energize, to inspire and to invigorate world-weary people. Because that is what we are. We are world-weary; we are tired ... we have given up on the capacity of human beings to do anything right. The capacity of human communities to solve any problems.

We must face that skeleton as a challenge, not a conclusion. Be honest about it. Weary, but keep alive the notion that history is incomplete, that the world is unfinished, that the future is open-ended and that what we think and what we do can make a difference.[23]

Without a shred of optimism, Octavia Butler writes stories from the last outposts of humanity that are a bridge to the future. In her work, humanity teeters at the edge of extinction, but never falls in. A motley crew of opportunistic heroes – that is, heroes who seize the moment – struggle against the odds and transform what it means to be human. Through the changes they imagine and realize, we continue. History reaches into the future. Butler has no truck with arrested development or romanticized museum humans. Her hope is hard edged.

In 'The Evening and the Morning and the Night' when the magic bullet cancer cure has caused a violent degenerative (fatal) disease, Butler, as usual, celebrates the faith and spirit of women who find themselves in impossible, horrific circumstances. Despite the extremity of the situations and their seeming powerlessness, Butler's heroines struggle to act – against or in the face of enormous loss; against the persistence of the old regime in themselves and others; against the despair and hostility that can impede change. Butler's women confront the horrific reality and their own conflicting desires and come to believe, not just in their individual moments, in their ephemeral personal freedom, but in collecting possibilities across generations. Their faith is a time-traveling, space-faring spirituality.

'The Evening and the Morning and the Night' is vintage Butler.

'What are you going to do?' he asked.

The question startled me. 'You have a choice,' I said. 'I don't. If she's right ... how could I not wind up running a retreat?'

'Do you want to?'

I swallowed. I hadn't really faced that question yet. Did I want to spend my life in something that was basically a refined DGD warn? 'No!'

'But you will.'

' ... Yes.' I thought for a moment, hunted for the right words. 'You'd do it.'

'What?'

'If the pheromone was something only men had, you would do it.' (Butler, 285)

Butler's characters value community over individual success. Or better, individual success is defined in terms of community. Her questions are: what do we do to survive? How must we change if we are not to be wiped out by the others, by ourselves? Her stories focus on those who make the compromises, those who do not have the power to determine their place in society, those who are forced to live lives defined by more powerful beings/forces. However, confronting alien invaders and thug democracies, dealing with biological imperatives – genes and pheromones that could lead to violence – there is always the possibility of community, of cultural intervention.

In 'The Evening and the Morning and the Night,' despite her genetically based bodily response, despite irrational, violent revulsion, Lynn doesn't attack Beatrice; Beatrice, who has the same powerfully negative urges, mentors Lynn, offers her a future. Dilg residents don't gouge out their eyes or mutilate their bodies. They are guided by their community 'to live and do whatever they decide is important to them. What do you have, what can you realistically hope for that's better than that?' (Butler, 285)

Butler's stories are about the dispossessed – those whose identity, subjectivity, and agency are circumscribed; whose humanity is under siege; whose extinction is a distinct possibility – yet her heroines call to the future with incredible acts of compromise and imagination.

Some critics insist that her stories, like 'Bloodchild,' are SF slavery parables; Butler denies that was her intention.[24] The disjunction between her intention and readings of her work is complex. Significant is what she's not doing – she admits to not writing the British Empire in Space, to not writing another *Star Trek*.[25] She does not investigate the frequent (but not exclusively) white male heroic fantasy of conquering the final frontiers, but instead focuses on the 'accommodations' we have to make when we strike out into the unknown and encounter difference or when it lands on our shores or drops from the sky onto our deserts and the power differential is not in our favor. Accommodation smacks of defeat, of women sacrificing their individuality for husbands and offspring, of slaves betraying the revolutionary spirit to survive. It has become difficult to imagine as heroes those who would rather stay alive as slaves then find freedom in death. How can they be our heroes if they 'agree' to being slaves? Yet Butler insists on revising our memories of this sort of terrible agreement, this sort of compromise with oppressive forces. To revise the memory is to heal a wounded past.

When a man, a captain, sacrifices himself to get the passengers and crew ashore, and goes down with his ship, freely choosing death, this is a classic heroic gesture, a cornerstone of the celebrated warrior tradition. A woman, who sacrifices herself so that the ship of life doesn't go down, who accommodates the 'enemy' so her biological children or invented family might take another breath, is not a glorious hero, but an average mom and suspect feminist. Yet Butler celebrates these black-power mothers who embody communal values and sacrifice themselves and define the future.

Unfinished Business

In 'The Evening and the Morning and the Night,' Butler thrusts her characters into an impossibly bleak, hopeless setting. A miracle drug cancer cure turns the user's children into violent, self-mutilating zombies. Inevitably digging and drifting, DGDs become alienated from their own bodies and the bodies of other people. The disease cuts DGDs off from identity and community, from the past and the future, and from the possibility of being human. Lynn Mortimer as a double DGD has no hope, no faith, no trust.

DGD transforms disparate individuals into a collective, marginal group. The disease obliterates differences – DGD is a monolithic type in the eyes of the world, yet of course differences abound.[26] Seeing her suicidal fatalism mirrored in Alan, Lynn 'takes him to bed.' And, although saving him saves her, companionship and personal pleasure do not alone offer them hope or a full sense of humanity.

Traveling to the Dilg retreat tests Lynn and Alan's identities, as well as their relationship, their position in the world. Dilg offers DGDs a life possibility, not a cure back to 'normal' again, not a happy-ever-after life in the suburbs. Rather, Dilg offers DGDs an alternative to the inevitable zombie-subhuman narrative that Alan, Lynn, and the rest of the world believe in. Still bearing the scars of their injuries, of hospital warehousing, still capable of violence, DGDs at Dilg create, invent, solve problems, and integrate themselves into human society. They do not self-destruct. Butler offers a cultural, experiential/relational cure for a genetic malfunction. Beatrice explains, 'Here we can help them channel their energies. They can create something beautiful, useful, even something worthless. But they create. They don't destroy.' (Butler, 274)

For Butler, humanity is not merely an individual or essentially biological phenomenon but is constituted in our relations to others and to ourselves. Certainly Butler is fascinated by the extent to which our personal characters and social realities are determined by our genetic makeup. However, human beings aren't biological blank slates to be written on by culture. Admitting to the urges, tendencies, pathologies, bounties of our biological makeup, Butler still insists on culture's capacity to offer us choices, interventions, and communal solutions to what is negative in our heritage and enhancements for what is wonderful. We can and do culturally enhance the ugly, destructive aspects of our nature, but Butler has faith in those cultural practices that call to our best selves. Beatrice grabs Naomi Chi's hands, before she gouges out her son's eyes, and guides her to embracing him. Later Lynn and Alan recognize when Naomi is straying and help guide her back.

Difference is terrifying.

If we are different, we might not be equal or even equivalent. Difference has been used to oppress. Lynn asks Beatrice: 'What are you saying? That the bigots are right? That we have some special gift?' (Butler, 278) A genetic basis for difference is also terrifying. Does that prove the bigots right? Does that mean we have no choice in who and what we are? Is human tragedy written in our genes? 'I won't be controlled ... by a goddamn smell!' Alan growls in defiance. Butler insists that human variability, genetic or cultural, is a resource and human agency is a given. Beatrice illuminates this for Lynn when she questions the older woman about Alan's agency:

'He never really had a chance, did he?'
She looked surprised. 'That's up to you. You can keep him or drive him away. I assure you, you can drive him away.'
'How?'
'By imagining that he doesn't have a chance.' (Butler, 286)

Butler does a careful dance around freedom, responsibility, alienation, choice, and manipulation. Her heroines rarely live for themselves alone. They are impossibility specialists, high priestesses of the God of change.

All that you touch
You Change.

All that you Change
Changes you.

The only lasting truth
is Change

God
is Change.[27]

Working in community, Butler's characters do not hold onto a past world that has been blown up or snatched away from them. They may try suicide as in 'The Evening and the Morning and the Night,' but with the support of community they go on to create a possible future.

Feminists have brilliantly critiqued 'biology as destiny', demonstrating that gender is to a large degree a cultural construct. It is biology and culture that define the roles a woman plays in her society, her family, her relationships. Although some critique Butler's work for being essentialist, she interrupts the notion of biology as destiny again and again.[28] As agents of change, her characters in 'The Evening and the Morning and the Night' work with their genetic makeup, their human community, their historical context to create new identities and fashion their destiny.

Some feminist critics, like Dorothy Allison, find the motherly sacrifices of her feminist heroines for the future of the community maddening.

> I love Octavia Butler's women even when they make me want to scream with frustration ... What drives me crazy is their attitude: the decisions they make, the things they do in order to protect their children – and the assumption that children and family come first.

> Butler's nine books are exceptional not only because she is a rarity, a black woman writing science fiction, but because she advocates motherhood as the humanizing element in society (not a notion I have ever taken too seriously).[29]

For Butler, Motherhood is defining a community, nurturing a nation. Mothers define the material and spiritual future. It is not all that women are born to do, but it is how they can choose to keep hope alive. Butler's mothers redefine the public and the private sphere and in their visionary way alter the gender relations and role possibilities. Turning their backs on the limitations of tyranny, they give birth to tomorrow. Butler does not jettison Motherhood, but carefully negotiates the space between freedom, alienation, and extinction. When facing genocide, the literal or figurative erasure of the people who have named the cosmos, nurtured your being, and offered you identity – the sacrifices of Motherhood – do not constitute a loss of individuality. The right to abortion may not be your primary issue when you face forced sterilization. Despite the deadly consequences – all children of DGD parents will be DGD – and despite human beings' ferocious sexual drive – copulating and the future be damned – Lynn defends her right to choose. She will not kill part of herself when so much is already dead.

Butler investigates the heroic significance of mothering the next generation, when you were not meant to survive. If identity is a community, a performance, a dance with the other, then a woman's *choice* to sacrifice for her children in the face of extinction is a hopefully one. Such a woman has a dream of the future, when the future seems destroyed and hopeless. The vision, the hope of a better future defined by her actions in the present, make unbearable choices bearable. If there's been a nuclear holocaust or if somebody has snatched you out of your home to work sugar cane and cotton in an alien world, if your parents took a drug that modified your genes so that violent self-mutilation and madness look inevitable, there's no going back to the past and making it present with a magical cure. When the future is the only dream you can have, you act to save it in the present.

In the Georgia Sea Islands, Gullah and Geechie black folk

tell the story/myth of Ibo Landing. On every island there is a sheltered cove where a slave ship supposedly pulled into shore and unloaded its human cargo. Walking ashore, the Ibos felt the weight of the places in their bones and souls. They looked into the faces of the white sailors and slave masters and glimpsed what was in store for them. Seeing this horror-future, they turned around and went back into the water, preferring to die rather than endure slavery. Some say they didn't drown in the waves despite being weighted down by heavy chains. They flew away to Africa or walked across the ocean to the motherland.

Octavia Butler tells stories of the people who stepped on shore, glimpsed a grim future, but couldn't walk on water or fly through the clouds. Yet despite suicidal despair, perhaps even after a failed attempt to walk their grief to the bottom of the sea, these world-weary ancestors came to believe where there is life, there is hope. They saw an alternate future beyond the salvers and inspired themselves to tell the story of the freedom-loving Ibos. The telling and retelling of this mythic defiance nourished their spirits. Speculating on a glorious past offered a bridge to a glorious future.

Butler names as heroes the world-weary ancestors who accommodated and compromised. They faced the devastation of personal dreams and hopes, of their gods and children, and yet, like the Ibos flying home, they loved freedom. With their sacrifices, they offered freedom they could only remember or imagine to the future as a precious gift. These world-weary ancestors dreamt of us, survive in us, are who we are now. Octavia Butler, a prophetic artist, an agent of change, declares history unfinished business. Rehearsing the possible in the face of catastrophe, she calls us all to action.

1   Well, perhaps there is less denial about the persistence of heterosexism. Despite *Queer Eye for the Straight Guy* and the *L Word*, the flak over gay marriage registers as a solid indication of how far we still are from a queer Promised Land.

2   See *Toxic Sludge is Good for You: Lies, Damn Lies and the Public Relations Industry* by John C. Stauber and Sheldon Rampton. Monroe Maine: Common Courage Press, 1995.

3   *Daily Hampshire Gazette*, March 4, 2005. June Zeitlin of Women's Environment and Development was quoted under the headline: 'What we see are powerful trends – growing poverty, inequality, growing militarization, and funda-mental opposition to women's right. These trends are harming millions of women worldwide.'

4   Interview with Octavia Butler, sfwa.org/members/Butler/Autobiography.html.

5   Conversation with Sheree R. Thomas, April 14, 2005. See also *Dark Matter – a Century of Speculative Fiction from the African Diaspora*, ed. Sheree R. Thomas, (New York: Warner Books, 2000).

6   Octavia Butler interview with Frances M. Beal, 'Black Women and the Science Fiction Genre,' in *Black Scholar*, vol. 17, no. 2, March/April, 1986, 18. See Samuel Delany's 'Racism in Science Fiction' in *Dark Matter* for other examples.

7   Charles R. Saunders, 'Why Blacks Should Read (And Write) Science Fiction,' *Dark Matter – a Century of Speculative Fiction from the African Diaspora* (New York: Warner Books, 2000) 398–99.

8   A review of *Dawn* and *Adulthood Rites* in *Black American Literature Forum* vol. 23, no. 2, Summer, 1989, 389–396.

9   'Studying the Works of Samuel R. Delany,' Jeffrey Allen Tucker in *Ohio University College of Arts and Science Forum* vol. 15, Spring 1998.

10 For example, Francis Ellen Watkins Harper countered negative stereotypes and sanitized plantation mythology in *Iola Leroy or Shadows Uplifted* (1892). Harper showcased middle-class African Americans working to 'uplift the

race' from poverty and oppression. This would become a dominant approach in the twentieth century. Charles Chestnut critiqued white supremacy in *The Marrow of Tradition* (1901). His thorough examination of African American experience in the context of oppression laid a literary foundation for the writers that followed. Richard Wright presented black men twisting in the noose of Jim Crow in *Uncle Tom's Children* (1938) and *Native Son* (1940) and defined black literature as urban realism. Playwrights such as Langston Hughes (*Mulatto*, 1938), Alice Childress (*Trouble in Mind*, 1955), Lorraine Hansberry (*Raisin in the Sun*, 1959), James Baldwin (*Blues for Mr. Charlie*, 1964) also worked to set the record straight.

11 Audre Lord, a black lesbian feminist poet and critical thinker, made these comments at 'The Personal and Political Panel' (Second Sex Conference, October 29, 1979).

12 Octavia Butler, *Bloodchild and Other Stories* (New York: Seven Stories Press, 1996) 134–35.

13 Maxine Hong Kingston, *The Woman Warrior* (New York: Vintage Books, 1977) 35.

14 See in this volume [*Daughters of Earth: Feminist Science Fiction in the Twentieth Century*]: 'The Conquest of Gola,' 'Created He Them,' 'The Fate of the Poseidonia.'

15 A notorious example: Clarence Thomas complained of a high-tech lynching when Anita Hill accused him of sexual harassment in the hearings on his nomination to the Supreme Court. The spectre of 'lynching' black men falsely accused of raping white women, confused the debate. The 'lynching' metaphor vilified Hill and demanded simplistic racial solidarity in support of Thomas, see *Race-ing Justice, En-gendering Power: Essays on Anita Hill, Clarence Thomas, and the Construction of Social Reality*, ed. Toni Morrison (New York: Pantheon, 1992) or 'Clarity on Clarence' in *Deals with the Devil and Other Reasons to Riot*, Pearl Cleage (New York: Ballantine Books, 1993).

16 The stereotype of the evil-tempered, ball-busting black woman with

weapons grade attitude and machine gun mouth has been anxiously performed throughout the twentieth and into the twenty-first century. In addition to artistic portrayals of pathological dominatrixes ruining black men, Daniel Patrick Moynihan justified the image with science in *The Negro Family: The Case for National Action*, (1965). Shahrazad Ali wrote *The Blackman's Guide to Understanding the Black Woman* in 1989, urging black male violence to bring black women in line. Radical black feminists, such as Pearl Cleage, who wrote *Mad at Miles: A Blackwoman's Guide to Truth*, have mounted an on-going response to Ali's and other anti-woman, anti-feminist stances in African-American public discourse, yet the stereotype remains entrenched.

17 Of course, Minstrel Shows (difference contained and controlled in ethnic/ gender caricature) are still one of America's most popular (and longest running) forms of entertainment. See *Big Mama's House* (2000), *Meet the Fockers* (2004), and *Beauty Shop* (2005). Such Minstrel Show stories can be told ad nauseum with abandon and confidence.

18 See 'Created He Them' in *Daughters of Earth: Feminist Science Fiction in the Twentieth Century.* (Middletown CT: Wesleyan University Press, 2006).

19 Octavia Butler, *Bloodchild and Other Stories* (New York: Seven Stories Press, 1996), 133.

20 Octavia Butler interview with Frances M. Beal, 'Black Women and the Science Fiction Genre,' in *Black Scholar*, vol. 17, no. 2, March/April, 1986, pp14–15.

21 Butler's book covers now feature black women as do the covers of Nalo Hopkinson's *Brown Girl in the Ring*, Sheree R Thomas' *Dark Matter*, etcetera. However we are not quite out of the woods. Ursula K. Le Guin complains of the persistence of anxiety at colored faces in SF&F. See 'A Whitewashed Earthsea: How the Sci Fi Channel Wrecked My Books.' (http://slate.msn/ com/id/2111107/) posted Dec. 16, 2004 for a discussion of how her multicultural, colored Earthsea was whitewashed for the TV audience.

Terror in the bookstore has abated or perhaps migrated to the screen.

22 In Anna D. Smith's play, *Twilight Los Angeles*, 1992.

23 Cornel West, *Prophetic Thought in Postmodern Times* (Monroe, Main: Common Courage Press, 1993), 6.

24 In a 1990 interview quoted by Elyce Rae Helford in '"Would You Really Rather Die Than Bear My Young?": The Construction of Gender, Race, and Species in Octavia E. Buter's "Bloodchild"', Butler responds to the notion that all her work explores forms of slavery and domination with: 'I know some people think that, but I don't agree, although this may depend on what you mean by "slavery". In the story "Bloodchild", for example, some people assume I'm talking about slavery when what I am really talking about is symbiosis ...' (*African American Review*, vol. 28, no. 2, Summer 1994, p256).

23 See *Bloodchild*, pp31–32 for Butler's discussion of her intentions.

26 Ethnicity is mentioned only once in the story. Discussion of Alan's heritage elegantly interrupts a reader's possible assumptions about the race/ethnicity of any of the characters.

27 Octavia Butler, *Parable of the Sower* (New York: Four Walls Eight Windows, 1993), 3.

28 See for example: Elyce Rae Helford in '"Would You Really Rather Die Than Bear My Young?": The Construction of Gender, Race, and Species in Octavia E. Butler's "Bloodchild"', *African American Review*, vol. 28, no. 2 (Summer 1994): 259–271; Michelle Erica Green, '"There Goes the Neighborhood": Octavia Butler's Demand for Diversity in Utopias', *Utopian and Science Fiction by Women: Worlds of Difference*, ed. Jane L Donawerth, Carol A Kolmerten, and Susan Gubnar, Syracuse: Syracuse University Press (1994): 166–189; Hoda M Zaki, 'Utopia, Dystopia, and Ideology in the Science Fiction of Octavia Butler,' *Science Fiction Studies* 17 (1990): 239–251.

29 Dorothy Allison, 'The Future of Female: Octavia Butler's Mother Lode,' *Reading Black Reading Feminist*, ed. Henry Louis Gates Jr (New York: Meridian, 1990) 471.

SECTION THREE

LOVE LINGERS IN BETWEEN
DOG-EARED PAGES

Jewelle Gomez

The Final Frontier

Dear Octavia,

When I first started writing, your words were a line of paving stones creating a path to a new world. We were close in age and both women of color raised by single caregivers and we both took refuge in books. But your integrated Pasadena is many miles away from Boston where I grew up poor in the 1950s and 1960s. I was raised by my Ioway great-grandmother, born into the Ioway Indian tribe, who had little formal education but was an omnivorous reader. Born in 1883, she had a lengthy worldview that outstripped her impoverished birth. She and I traded second-hand paperback books and were faithful fans of the television show *Star Trek*, never missing an episode, going over the action, plots and characters afterwards as if the show were one of her treasured daytime soap operas. Thus began my tenuous relationship to speculative fiction and to the idea that I might be a writer.

The metaphorical situations *Star Trek* used to explore racism, sexism, and classism intrigued us both. Ironically, before the growth of the Black Arts Movement, few books that I'd read explicitly expressed a social conscience that felt as relevant to our everyday lives as did that short-lived TV program.

As a teenager, when I heard the introduction read over the show's opening credits – 'Space, the final frontier ... ' – my heart always beat faster knowing we were about to step out into the unknown. This mood was in keeping with the excitement of the period into which we were launched by President John F. Kennedy.

We watched in awe the news about space shots like Russia's Sputnik or the Mercury Project which made American astronaut John Glenn the first American to orbit the Earth. Space became part of our lexicon; we all imagined a future totally different from our present.

For me, however, the message I got from watching *Star Trek* was that the final frontier was not space but the human heart. Each star ship journey was an exploration of how humans would deal with the unknown. Characters – both earthling and alien – acted out our deepest fears and desires. How they managed this brave new world revealed what was possible for those of us remaining on earth.

When I started to read speculative fiction in college fans were divided between the *Dune* novels and what I dismissively called the *Hobbit* novels. I was *Dune*, through and through. They were the only books that had amazingly powerful female characters and was located in a landscape with language that could be interpreted as other than White Anglo-Saxon Protestant.

By then I was sure I wanted to write ... but what? So I took practical courses and studied journalism. Later I became a devotee of Joanna Russ; her book *The Female Man* made feminism a real idea for me. It also raised the possibility that speculative fiction might be my genre; still I saw no people of color on any of the landscapes. Vampire movies had always fascinated me so I started to write vampire stories featuring an African American girl who escaped from slavery. To my surprise and delight Russ sent me a postcard (remember when you could just look somebody's address up in the phone book for free!) encouraging me, but others sometimes disparaged the idea of a person of color writing in such a 'trivial' genre. Then I found my first novel, *Kindred*, in a secondhand store; my world turned on its axis, suddenly bringing light to my side of the planet. After reading that book I understood there were worlds which had been hidden from me that I could legitimately explore as a lesbian/feminist of color. Your story was delivered in a naturalistic style presenting an extraordinary plot: an African American woman's unexpected ability to travel back in time to the period of slavery, where she meets her antecedents.

I was further intrigued by the marriage of the African American main character to a white man. This intensified her adventures as she straddled different cultures in both aspects of her adventure – the past and the present. My own mother was in an interracial marriage (to my stepfather) which made the story even more moving to me. I couldn't remember ever reading about that in the many books I consumed. As with any successful novel I felt like you were talking directly to me. And it was all about exploring the hearts of her characters – Dana, the heroic time traveler, and her confused husband; Rufus, the spoiled boy who grows into an unpredictable and generally cruel slave owner; the brutalized but proud slave, Alice. Your imagination became a ship carrying me not into space but back through time and inside the hearts of unforgettable characters.

For a period *Kindred* was difficult to find in the bookstores and friends kept asking to borrow my copy. But I was afraid that it would never find its way back to me so I said no. I even started putting it in a drawer when friends came over to avoid sticky fingers. Finally, to stop feeling like Scrooge, I stayed at work late one evening and photocopied the entire book (yes, I knew it was illegal) and when someone wanted to borrow it I had them fill out an index card so I could get the photocopy back for the next reader! I had a lending library of one book; I felt like I was preparing for the world of *Fahrenheit 451*.

In 1997 two professors at Clarke Atlanta University organized a conference called the African American Fantastic Imagination, the first ever featuring speculative fiction writers of color. I was invited to participate and there met Tananarive Due and Steven Barnes for the first time and reunited with Samuel R. Delany whom I'd known years before in New York City. And there you were for two whole days! I was relieved you didn't remember me from a conference a decade earlier – the awestruck writer thrusting into your hands a chapter from what was to become my vampire novel, *The Gilda Stories*!

Because we rarely get to say 'thank you' to public figures that have changed our lives I didn't want to miss my chance. So I told you about my lending library of one to express how important *Kindred* had been to me and to many other women I knew. I told you that I couldn't remember how long it took for me to photocopy the entire paperback. I did remember I regretted having to bend the paperback's spine so deeply in order to make all the words legible and I recalled looking over my shoulder anxiously and repeatedly hoping no nosey co-workers were staying late too. I felt you'd given us a treasure and it was my duty to make sure it stayed out in the world. When I started telling you the story, I could feel your shyness and hesitation. I was nervous, especially as the look of incredulity spread across your face. Then you said: 'The whole thing?' I nodded and you gave a great, booming laugh and said, 'You're kidding?!' We both laughed and I said, 'I'd do anything for a good book.'

Now that *Kindred* has become a classic taught around the world I've tried to touch what exactly about it was so important that it helped make my speculative fiction writing possible. Three things come to mind: first, portraying an interracial marriage at a time that Black Power dominated our political conversations casting a shadow over any black/white interaction. This choice made the couple in the book both vulnerable and powerful at the same time. It made me look at my own mother differently; to try to imagine what was in her heart when she'd made her decision to marry and live in a small northeastern town and the vitriol she'd faced.

Next I think I was moved by your ability to make the familiar or ordinary live in the same room with the extraordinary or completely unfamiliar. I grew up with a Native American great-grandmother who was born in 1883 and with her I watched an astronaut land on the moon. At the same time we were told in school all the Indians were dead. I appreciated the friction between known and unknown, and the energy it created in life and in writing. Between what teachers said and who I knew sat at home on our couch was a world of possibility. The tension lay in what Dana and her husband knew and didn't know about each other's role in society; the same tension lived between Dana and the slaves on the plantation, and between her and the slave owner who turns out to be her distant relative. Those incongruities struck a chord inside me.

The third aspect of the book which fascinated me is the circular nature of the story. It starts in the present, takes its main characters to the past where we discover the past's relationship to the present. As Dana tries to track down the 'end' of the story of the past – what happened to the slaves and their owners – she can't because it really has no end; the past continues through her.

I imagine others get many different things from the book but I'm grateful I get to say out loud, again, how your novel made it possible for me to cross those paving stones to reach my own work. It helped me shut out the voices of naysayers at a time when they were in the majority and imagine much more than what simply lived in front of me. It's been twenty-five years since my vampire novel was published and it's still in print – as is *Kindred* – proving that the universe was more ready for you and me than many people thought.

There's a line near the beginning of *Kindred* that I repeat to myself when I feel maybe I'm writing something no one will be able to relate to: ' ... my facts ... [T]hey're no crazier than yours.' With that in mind I hope to keep exploring our final frontier of the heart.

In sisterhood,
Jewelle

Sophia Echavarria

Dear Octavia,

I first read your work in high school. *Kindred*. Swept back and forth with Dana and her complex feelings for her white ancestry. My white ancestry. But I wasn't used to black history and science fiction (or grim fantasy) sharing the same page. It was an intersection for which I didn't even think to search. I hadn't asked for you. That was a mistake, but it was easily mended.

I met your work again in university when I was given the chance to write about any topic I wanted. I remembered *Kindred*. And then I learned about *Fledgling* and Xenogenesis (later Lilith's Brood). Your work coupled time travel and slavery, aliens and human rights. All familiar discussions now more vast and abundant when woven together. When I wrote about your work, I made the mistake of using too much summary. But so many hadn't read you. I made a lot of other mistakes, too. And those are entirely on me. But the point of this is to thank you for the things you taught me.

Initially, I wrote about *Fledgling* and the *Blade* movie franchise. The animosity that Shori and Blade received from their vampiric brethren for being Day Walkers, for being part human, reminded me so much of the racism Black people and people of color face. Personally, I was reminded of the strange and inescapable in-between of my own mixed ancestry. I related deeply to the struggle of navigating the power of privilege given to someone who is born from both the oppressed and the oppressor. And while I struggled with my place in the world, I found the answer in your work.

In constructing my senior thesis, I read and re-read Lilith's Brood looking for a central theme I could base my paper on. Dana and Shori, Akin and Jodahs. All offspring of miscegenation. This was a huge revelation for twenty-one-year-old me. But I knew it was more complicated than that. Dana did not outwardly resemble Rufus in any way. And while the white skin of the Ina sits somewhere in Shori's DNA, it is a hindrance to the sun-resistant future for which her family hoped. Akin and Jodahs offer much more physical representation of their two peoples – their bodies the site of as much indecision and turmoil as the human communities facing down extinction.

What was less complicated, even though I only came to see it much later, was the duty all of these characters felt to their predecessors who still lived in strife. This is the most important thing you have taught me. Not everything you have to say is going to be for me. Yes I am Black, and yes I am a woman, and yes we will always share those things. But I am not dark and not from a background like yours. I have more privilege because of that. And you helped teach me that. What is for me is the responsibility I have to use my privilege to advocate for others.

Dana had Rufus' ear, Shori had the council of Ina, and Jodahs had the Oankali. Their connections to these powers gave them the privilege to speak, even if they weren't always heard. So I have to speak, even if I am not always heard. This is the part of your work, your legacy, that has influenced me the most.

I do not think my existence as a mixed-race Black woman will end racism or any form of oppression. That's an easy mistake to make. What I do think is that my existence upends hierarchy, that stubborn trait the Oankali love to bring up. The trait that you yourself found to be our greatest pitfall as a species. But your work upends hierarchy, too. Who can continue to regard science fiction as a trivial medium once they've encountered the critical topics of race, gender and power you've explored with it?

Your work has set an indelible example for me. It has shown me where to start. How to listen and how to speak from the in-between I will always occupy. Your work is part of a larger compass made up of the Black women who came before me and it points out where I'm needed. My only regret is that I will never have the chance to thank you in person.

But I thank you just the same.

With great love
Sophia

Tiara Janté

Thank You for Being Fearless: A Letter to Octavia E. Butler

Dear Ms. Butler,

My experience with your work has been a journey – one I embarked on recently, but it was right on time. Through *Kindred*, I learned how to time-travel – a skill I continue to perfect to this day through my writing. Writing for me is an experience – it is a way for my brain to meditate on a particular time and place, whether real or imagined, and immerse myself into its reality; it's time-travelling. Upon reading *Kindred* for the first time, I couldn't help but wonder how long it took you to perfect your own skill of traversing time the way you did so fluidly, but I've come to realize that you understood your connection to the past, and through your gift of writing you were able to bring that past into the present – fearlessly.

It's as if the remembered experiences of your enslaved ancestors were encoded into your DNA, but not too deep where it wasn't accessible for you to reach in, grab them, then record them for the masses. Some experts have begun to refer to these passed-on memories as Post-Traumatic Slave Syndrome and Intergener-ational Trauma, yet, terminology aside, there's no doubt you've been able to expertly weave the symptoms and effects of both into *Kindred*. Your ability to traverse through timelines to illustrate the interconnectedness of all time – by proving that even generations later we are still suffering psychologically from the inhumane treatment of our forebears – is almost supernatural.

There are many debates as to what genre *Kindred* fits into, and while you categorized it once as 'grim fantasy' I'd like to believe the most suitable term would be Afrofuturism, because there is no other genre that includes elements of the neo-slave narrative, science fiction and fantasy that is so comprehensively and unapologetically Black.

Genre aside, it is my opinion that *Kindred* is one of the best literary examples of slave narratives from a Black woman's perspective. Through your words we are transported with Dana to the antebellum south to experience firsthand her mental anguish and physical torture, at the hand of a monster who fails to realize that he is a monster.

And he is a monster of the worst sort because he is able to convince himself that he is entitled to the bodies he abuses sexually – a perceived entitlement based solely on his white male existence. Through *Kindred*, we get to glimpse life through the lens of Alice – a woman who some may suggest accepted her suffering, and even ushered it in at times; however, I know better. Alice did not accept her situation – she survived it – for the sake of her children. Once the responsibility of her children was taken away from her, she owned her existence by choosing when it ended, and not letting Rufus choose it for her.

Through *Kindred*, we are exposed to the reality that while we suffer the effects of the enslavement of African people to an extent in the present, time has removed us from some of the harshness of its reality. This is the dilemma Dana faces as she is shuffled back and forth between a past of enslavement and a present that provides privilege. This is the same dilemma we as Black people face when we time travel through books like *Kindred* – we are forced to step outside our improved realities to face the horrific realities belonging to our predecessors. Sometimes it's hard to relate.

This is not to suggest that all is well for Black people in this world today – and it is not to say we as African Americans are healed, but we are healing; and through our healing we have been emboldened to do wonderful things and contribute wonderful gifts to the world, like the ones you have gifted us through your stories, Ms. Butler.

Through *Kindred* you interlaced the past with the present through words that are raw and not sugarcoated – and thankfully so. Because too often our stories and struggles as women, especially Black women, are watered down for the mental wellbeing of men like Kevin, who acknowledge the evil done by their ancestors, but fail to acknowledge the privilege they have in society as a result of that evil. Confronting that evil becomes unavoidable when reading *Kindred*, however.

Kindred is more than a slave story. It is a woman's story. It is a Black woman's story. I cannot think of a time in history when we as women haven't had to fight to own our existences outside of a man. Whether it was our white male slave masters or our black husbands, historically we as black women have had to fight to define our own separate identities within the world. Dana had to fight, Alice had to fight – and even you had to fight – to be taken seriously in a world that often refuses to recognize our contributions on account of our melanin and our gender. But you have forced the world to acknowledge our magic, and have set the standard for those who have come after you.

While you've departed from this plane of existence your stories and the affirmations you breathed into life through the pages of your notebook continue to inspire brave tales that dance on the border of real and imagined so seamlessly that one has difficulty discerning what's real and what's not. You've inspired a brave new age of black speculative fiction writers such as myself to be just as fearless as you were, when manifesting our destinies, writing down our stories, and serving them to the world.

Finally, because of you, I realize the importance of my story as a Black woman in this world, as well as the importance of our stories collectively. Like you once did, I've acknowledged my role as a storyteller. My ancestors are as much a part of me today as they were a part of the world when they were living – and just like you did, I accept the responsibilities of keeping their stories alive. And so I write – fearlessly – because you've helped pave a way for me to be able to. Thank you.

Respectfully,
Tiara Janté

K. Ceres Wright

Dear Octavia:

The first book of yours I read was *Wild Seed*. I hated it. First, I expected spaceships and laser guns and there were none. Second, your male antagonist, Doro, forced your female protagonist, Anyanwu, to marry his son, then have sex with other men and bear their children, all for the glory of Doro's legacy. Doro repeatedly threatened Anyanwu and her children if she refused his demands, and she acquiesced to protect her children.

I didn't hate everything about the book, though. I loved your writing style. Smooth and easy like Mama's homemade iced tea. But I hated the way Doro treated Anyanwu. Hated how he wielded his power over her. Hated how your words made me feel – powerless, violated, dismal. Even twelve years later, I remember.

No other book has affected me as strongly as that one, and I thought, maybe this writer was raped, or helplessly under the control of someone, and bled her hatred of feeling powerless all over the pages. I'll never know for sure. But a quote from an interview helped put the book into perspective:

> *I think really a lot of my early writing had to do with my own feelings of powerlessness, so I dealt often with power, with what it did to people, what they did with it when they got it...* (Octavia Butler, *Black Sci-Fi*, documentary by Moonlight Films)

I had the luxury of closing the book and engaging in other activities to lighten my mood. But the more I meditated on the book, the more I realized that many women don't have this means of escape. They are controlled by men, or poverty, or the need to work demeaning jobs to make ends meet. Once in a while, the news will feature a tale of an escaped sex slave kept prisoner in a basement. But how many sex slaves haven't escaped? How many are enduring their own Doros?

In 2014, the terrorist organization Boko Haram kidnapped 276 girls from a government school in Nigeria, and only a small number of them have been freed or rescued. They, too, were forced to marry and have children. Even those who were rescued had to undergo a 'deradicalization' process in a government facility, and had their freedom curtailed by a diagnosis of 'psychologically unfit.' I've read testimonies of women who were molested as children and, upon telling a trusted authority figure, were again molested. Men like Doro exist, wielding their power in similar ways.

Your Xenogenesis series is also a study of power imbalances, and explores the many facets of humanity, internal conflict, and self-identification. And with spaceships! I'm afraid I was one of those you described in another quote:

> People think, 'Oh, science fiction, Star Wars. I don't like that.' And they don't want to read what I've written because they don't like Star Wars. Then again, you get the other kind who do want to read what I've written because they like Star Wars and they think that must be what I'm doing. In both cases, they're going to be disappointed. (Interview with Joshunda Sanders, http://www.inmotionmagazine.com/ac04/obutler.html)

I had grown up on the visual elements of science fiction through *Star Trek, Star Wars, Doctor Who, Blake's 7, Tomorrow People, Space 1999*, and many others. These, of course, had starships, laser guns, and space battles in order to titillate the audience and hold their attention. Deep thinking desired, but not required. Yes, I had also read Asimov, Bradbury, Clark, and more, but no stories I read dealt with family relationships and self-identification in such a complex way as you had. And, of course, none had featured characters of color in a meaningful way. You had begun writing because you thought you could write better than a B-movie you had once watched, *Devil Girl From Mars*. And you have. Your writing is layered, complex, and conveys messages about events in the real world, especially how women and minorities are treated.

There is a campaign called the Sad Puppies, which tries to influence the Hugo Awards in order to get specific novels nominated, novels that are 'unabashed pulp action that isn't heavy-handed message fic' ('How to get Correia nominated for a Hugo,' http://monsterhunternation.com/2013/01/08/how-to-get-correia-nominated-for-a-hugo/). This group mostly comprises white men who think the literati critics too often favor female and non-white writers. Can you believe it? After decades of women and minority writers being marginalized in the speculative fiction world, now they are targeted for being too popular. But you'll be heartened to know that in 2016, many of these Sad Puppy books were voted lower than 'No Award.'

You should also know more and more Black women spec fic writers are being lauded – writers such as Tananarive Due, Nalo Hopkinson, Kinitra Jallow, Nora K. Jemisin, Nnedi Okorafor, and more. There's a movie in the theaters that tells the true story of the Black women who calculated the formulas to launch a man into orbit during the 1960s' space race. Black filmmaker Ava Duvernay will direct the science fiction classic *A Wrinkle in Time*, with a diverse cast. And this year a Black woman will be the first African American to live at the International Space Station.

With the declining cost of technology and rise in the number and types of media platforms, independent Black filmmakers and artists are producing animation films, comics, and Web shows that feature people of color in leading roles. There was even a State of Black Science Fiction convention held in Atlanta last year. Where once Black people who enjoyed science fiction, fantasy, and horror were ridiculed or, worse, thought to not even exist, they are now creating their own legacies of literary, artistic, and cinematic achievements in speculative fiction that are a far cry from *Devil Girl From Mars*.

Best of all, a producer recently acquired the rights to adapt your book, *Dawn*, into a television series. And an artist has made *Kindred* into a graphic novel. Your fans anxiously wait to see your books on the silver screen, and to see themselves reflected in your characters. Your influence on the world of speculative fiction publishing has been profound, inspiring young writers, artists, and filmmakers to change the game from shoehorning in one character of color in a cast of white male leads, to featuring Black and female main characters who call the shots.

I look forward to seeing how far your influence takes the field in my lifetime ... and in the lifetimes to come.

Sincerely,
K. Ceres Wright

Valjeanne Jeffers

Themes of Power, Family and Change
in Octavia Butler's Wild Seed

Octavia Butler was born African American and poor in 1947. At the age of seven, she lost her father, and her mother worked as a maid to support the family. From these humble beginnings, Octavia rose to become a world-renowned speculative fiction author, in a genre typically dominated by white males. Before her untimely death in 2006, she had published twelve books, was the recipient of both the Nebula and Hugo awards, and had been awarded the MacArthur Fellowship. Today, her novels are taught in classrooms, and she is considered a seminal artist who has paved the way for a renaissance of African America writers. An author who once said she chose science fiction as her writing genre because 'There are no closed doors, no walls' (Octavia Butler on Charlie Rose, June 2008), and who described science fiction as 'potentially the freest genre in existence' (Octavia Butler Interview in *The Black Scholar*, 1986, p.1), Octavia Butler chose to explore themes of feminism, race, and power disparity in her writing. Thus, themes of power, family and change are often salient in Butler's novels, and these motifs are particularly prominent in the novel *Wild Seed* (1980).

In *Wild Seed*, the fourth novel of her Patternist series, Butler tells the story of the Africans Anyanwu and Doro, two beings who cross paths in the seventeenth century. Anyanwu and Doro are both immortal: she has lived for hundreds of years, he has lived for thousands; yet they possess vastly different abilities. Anyanwu is preternaturally strong and fast, a shape shifter who can become

124

whoever or whatever she chooses, and a healer. Doro has the ability to seek out other supernatural humans; in fact, this is how he finds Anyanwu. He can also kill and possess anyone's body. Yet he, himself, cannot be killed. In contrast, Anyanwu, although a meta-human, can be killed just as any other human being. Thus, Doro's immunity to death is what creates the power differential between them.

When Doro and Anyanwu first meet, she is disguised as an old woman; she has learned to age herself over the centuries to match the aging of her kinsmen, and to avoid being attacked as a witch. Doro, in contrast, is wearing the body of his latest victim. He explains to Anyanwu that her supernatural abilities are what drew him to her, and reveals that his own power is the power to kill:

'I kill, Anyanwu. That is how I keep my youth, my strength. I can do only one thing to show you what I am, and that is kill a man and wear his body like a cloth.' He breathed deeply. 'This is not the body I was born into. It's not the tenth I've worn, nor the hundredth, nor the thousandth. Your gift seems to be a gentle one. Mine is not.' (Butler, Octavia E. *Seed to Harvest*: *Wild Seed*, *Mind of My Mind*, *Clay's Ark*, and *Patternmaster*. Open Road Media Sci-Fi & Fantasy. Kindle Edition, pp. 13-14.)

Doro convinces Anyanwu to leave her homeland in Africa, and join his New World 'seed' community of Wheatley: one of the hamlets of preternatural humans that he has gathered together in an attempt to strengthen their abilities. He persuades her to join him as his wife by using his charismatic charm, and with promises to give her sons and daughters who will be immortal, for heretofore her wondrous gifts have not been inherited by her children. But there is also a threat to her life, and the lives of her children:

'How can my sons be of value to you?' He gave her a long silent look, then spoke with that same softness. 'I may have to go to them, Anyanwu. They may be more tractable than their mother.' She could not recall ever having been threatened so gently – or so effectively. Her sons ... He had still given her no proof of the power he claimed, no proof that her children would be in danger from other than an ordinary man if she managed to escape. Yet she continued to believe him. She could not bring herself to get up while he slept and vanish into the forest. For her children's sake she had to stay with him, at least until she had proof one way or the other. (Butler, *Seed to Harvest*, pp15 and 30.)

Anyanwu journeys with Doro to America thinking that she is to be his wife. But once they arrive in Wheatley, she discovers that he has chosen to marry her to one of his favorite sons, Isaac. His human 'seeds' are those who have matured from birth under his thumb, and think of themselves as his property. Anyanwu, in contrast, is 'wild seed': an intractable being, in Doro's opinion. She is independent, and lives as she chooses. Anyanwu is, in turn, horrified to discover that Doro's people treat him as a god, denying him nothing – not even their lives. He kills and takes bodies from his family in Wheatley, as readily as he would anywhere else; especially from those who have served him, and are considered by him to be useless. To disobey Doro means death. After much pleading from Isaac, she marries Isaac, to save her life.

Doro and Anyanwu's relationship, which spans decades, is one characterised by a continued struggle for dominance, by Doro's repeated attempts to break her spirit, to bend her will to his, to make her worship and *love* him as the others do. Her power, the power to shape shift into different men, women, even animals, to heal her own body and others, offends him. In this, their relationship is the archetypical union between an abusive man and his partner. Yet it also typifies the insidious relationship between the powerful, who exert control over vulnerable individuals, and of leaders who threaten other nations, and exploit the lives and labour of those they govern.

Anyanwu grows to despise Doro as he forces her to endure humiliation after humiliation. Yet, she does not flee, even after she discovers that she is one of the few inhabitants of Wheatley who could probably escape. Her ability to become an animal is one which may enable her to escape Doro's grasp. She stays because of her love for her children and grandchildren.

When Doro first seeks Anyanwu out, she has already borne forty-seven children, over the span of centuries; her children have begot offspring of their own. She has made her kinsmen rich, and learned to disguise herself as an old woman, so that they will not accuse her of witchcraft and try to kill her. In Wheatley, she continues her roles as a mother and healer: ministering to those who fall ill, bearing children by both Doro and Isaac. Although she grows to love Isaac, this love is matched by a hatred for Doro. She bears the children that he gives her wearing a myriad of male bodies, because to refuse him means certain death; yet her love for her children, and grandchildren, does not falter.

After the deaths of Isaac and her daughter Nweke, Anyanwu discovers that Doro intends to kill her; so she becomes a dolphin and escapes. Doro finds her one hundred and fifty years later in New Orleans; again he intends to kill her, for no other reason than that she dared to escape him, that she dared to defy him and live.

However, he discovers that Anyanwu has created yet another family: this one peopled by beings like herself, just as Doro has done – people who see ghosts, people who can hear the thoughts of others, people who can re-grow damaged limbs, and those who possess other gifts. Some she has bought as slaves and freed; others are her offspring. But Butler draws a sharp contrast between Doro, as a father who exploits the members of his family, and Anyanwu as a mother who nurtures them. Doro breeds people like livestock to strengthen their paranormal abilities. He sires dozens upon dozens of children, and leaves others to care for them. Anyanwu has children, or seeks other people out to comfort, and in turn be comforted by them. She seeks to heal others, and make them whole again. Anyanwu gives as much as she can of herself to her family. She is mother, healer, nurturer and protector:

> She owned no slaves. She had bought some of the people who worked for her and recruited the others among freedmen, but those she bought, she freed. They always stayed to work for her, feeling more comfortable with her and with each other than they had ever been elsewhere. That always surprised the new ones. They were not used to being comfortable with other people. They were misfits, malcontents, troublemakers – though they did not make trouble for Anyanwu. They treated her as mother, older sister, teacher, and, when she invited it, lover ... Few of them knew how their presence comforted her. She was not Doro, breeding people as though they were cattle, though perhaps her gathering of all these special ones, these slightly strange ones would accomplish the same purpose as his breeding. She was herself, gathering family. (Butler, *Seed to Harvest*, pp. 199-201.)

In the final chapters of *Wild Seed*, Butler shows us the damage that the grasping for power can cause, but also how love, family and change can repair this damage. Butler depicts this through the transformation that takes place in Anyanwu and Doro's relationship. When Doro re-enters Anyanwu's life in New Orleans, he immediately resumes the role of an abusive partner. He disrupts her life, and her family, by bringing one of his mentally unbalanced sons, Joseph, to her plantation. Joseph causes the deaths of two of Anyanwu's children. Yet this tragedy brings the two immortals closer together, and Doro's long dormant humanity, a humanity which has slept for century after century, begins to awaken. He takes responsibility for his grievous mistake, and begins to court her once more – this time with sincerity. He treats her with a respect he has not shown in centuries. Eventually he relinquishes some of his power, and allows her to heal *him*, allows himself to love her as an equal, rather than as a possession. When Anyanwu threatens suicide to escape his killing, she finally forces Doro to behave as a human being, rather than an all-powerful entity. He realises he must have her nurturing, her love, to survive, or his *humanity*, his existence as something other than a killer, will perish. Anyanwu says:

'The human part of you is dying, Doro. It is almost dead. Isaac saw that happening, and he told me. That is part of what he said to me on the night he persuaded me to marry him. He said someday you would not feel anything at all that was human, and he said he was glad he would not live to see that day. He said I must live so that I could save the human part of you. But he was wrong. I cannot save it. It's already dead.'

'No.' He closed his eyes, tried to still his trembling.

Finally, he gave up, looked over at her. If he could only make her see. 'It isn't dead, Anyanwu. I might have thought it was myself before I found you the second time, but it isn't. It will die, though, if you leave me.' ... 'I think my son was right,' he said. 'Parts of me can die little by little. What will I be when there is nothing left but hunger and feeding?' (Butler, *Seed to Harvest*, pp. 250-251.)

Yet her love is not given without conditions: Doro must treat those less powerful than himself with humanity and empathy, as something more than possessions, or as objects to obtain a goal. He will still kill to survive, but not without forethought, and not those closest to him. Doro must become a predator with a soul.

In this, Butler is perhaps telling us that some evil will always exist in the world. It is inexorable, but man- and womankind can still flourish; we can still treat one another with humanity, and work toward common goals. This is necessary, or a society will eventually lose its soul. Oppressive cultures are toxic to both those in the highest ranks of such a society, and those at the lowest ranks who are subjugated and exploited. Butler once said, 'I know that we can do better than we have because there have been times when we have done better ... But I don't know that we will' (Octavia Butler on Charlie Rose, June 2008). Better worlds are possible, better societies are possible. They are waiting to be built, but this is humanity's choice. It will always be our choice.

Works Cited

Butler, Octavia. 'Black Scholar Interview with Octavia Butler: BLACK WOMEN AND THE SCIENCE FICTION GENRE.' *The Black Scholar*, vol. 17, no. 2, 1986, pp. 14–18. www.jstor.org/stable/41067255.

Butler, Octavia E. *Seed to Harvest: Wild Seed, Mind of My Mind, Clay's Ark,* and *Patternmaster.* Open Road Media Sci-Fi & Fantasy. Kindle Edition.

'Octavia Butler on Charlie Rose.' Part 2/2 fixed, *YouTube,* uploaded by sonic1267 November 13, 2008 https://youtu.be/W1W9CNwl2e8.

Raffaella Baccolini

Nationalism, Reproduction, and Hybridity in Octavia E. Butler's 'Bloodchild'

Elyce Rae Helford has offered one of the best-sustained analyses of Octavia E. Butler's short story, 'Bloodchild', as a metaphor for slavery and gender exploitation.[1] I find her reading stimulating and often convincing and yet somehow problematic, especially in light of the love feelings between the protagonists, Gan and T'Gatoi.[2] Butler's story, in her own words, is several things. It describes 'a love story between two very different beings' – not only in terms of species, but also in terms of power – and the nature of their relation. It is also 'a coming-of-age story in which a boy must absorb disturbing information and use it to make a decision that will affect the rest of his life. On a third level, 'Bloodchild' is [her] pregnant man story', where a man chooses pregnancy not out of misplaced competition with women or curiosity, but as an 'act of love'. Finally, it is 'a story about paying the rent', and 'it amazes' her instead that it has been read 'as a story of slavery. It isn't' (Butler, 'Afterword' 30-31).

Butler's words suggest that she intended her story to be read within the tradition of SF investigating the construction of the 'Other' and the developments that come from the encounter – one that can often turn into a clash – with other cultures, nations, groups, or species. In other words, her story can also be read as a reflection on nationalistic discourses, where gender becomes relevant because of the issue of reproduction and its control. A complex and powerful tale about reproductive choices in a coercive situation, 'Bloodchild' deals with the theme of reproduction in order to reconsider not only gender relations, but as a way to explore the hybridisation of different cultures and the power inequality that informs relations. The concern to show strategies of resistance to our cultural constructions is central to Butler's story.

In nationalistic narratives, women are often constructed as "biological reproducers of 'the nation'" (Yuval-Davis 37). From a feminist perspective, then, nationalism is seen 'as a process in which new patriarchal elites gain the power to produce the generic 'we' of the nation. The homogenising project of nationalism draws upon female bodies as the symbol of the nation to generate discourses of rape, motherhood, sexual purity, and heteronormativity' (Grewal and Kaplan).[3] Women's biological functions, then, are central to the constructions of nations and their nationalist discourses. Women's reproductive rights and their effects on the nation make women primary targets of oppression; however, some women can also become fully engaged in the role of reproducers of the nation. These themes and contradictions are often investigated by women SF writers, as shown in by now classic critical dystopias such as Katharine Burdekin's *Swastika Night* and Margaret Atwood's *The Handmaid's Tale*. Butler's 'Bloodchild' offers another example.

Set on a planet inhabited by an insect-like alien species called Tlic where a group of humans have landed to escape persecution on Earth, the story is no utopia. The alien species needs a host body to grow its eggs and the humans serve as living incubators. After a period characterised first by struggles and then by negotiations, the later generations of humans live in a protected 'Preserve', where they have been allowed to form families and raise children. However, each family must in turn offer at least one member – preferably a male, as females are needed for the reproduction of the human species – to the Tlic. Once the eggs have been implanted in the human host body, they grow to a potentially lethal larval stage and then have to be removed by a female Tlic. The birth is a gruesome procedure in which the human body is sliced open and the Tlic removes the 'grubs'. The story is narrated from Gan's perspective, a young boy who is to choose whether he will offer his body as a host for the eggs of his long-term family's friend T'Gatoi, the 'Tlic government official in charge of the Preserve' ('Bloodchild' 3).

By reversing gender roles in reproduction – the female aliens impregnate male humans – Butler defamiliarises women's biological functions, thus leaving readers uncomfortable about the accepted naturalness of birth and reproduction. Considering whether to go through the process or let his sister – who as a woman has always been expected 'to carry other lives inside her' – go through it, Gan muses about the differences between the species: 'Human young ... would someday drink at her breast, not at her veins' ('Bloodchild' 26). The comparison makes readers question the romantic notion of motherhood. The fact that Gan, along with many male and female readers, thinks it natural that women bear children and sees as unnatural the alien young that drink blood does, in effect, call into question the issue of reproduction. In Butler's story as well as in nationalist discourses, women are *constructed* as the bearers of the 'race'; but the comparison between species also shows that we are not, after all, so different. The beauty and myth of motherhood are also the products of cultural constructions. Similarly, the description of the birth process (which in one case is delayed until it becomes dangerous for the male host), though at first gruesome and horrifying, is none other than an extrapolation of a human Caesarean section: 'she opened him. His body convulsed with the first cut ... The sounds he made... I had never heard such sounds come from anything human' ('Bloodchild' 15).[4] As Michelle E. Green also argues, Butler's story is no 'feminist fantasy' (172); there is nothing in the tale that suggests that the planet or the conditions in which the humans find themselves in is anywhere near utopian. But through the common formal SF strategy of estrangement, Butler shows us that the gruesome, dangerous procedure and Gan's predicament are not so different from the risks and dilemmas that women have faced and continue to face between their freedom to choose motherhood and their right to refuse it.

Gan's reaction to what he has witnessed makes him uneasy about the hitherto accepted prospect of bearing T'Gatoi's eggs. With his discomfort, the certainties of the hegemonic discourse begin to crumble and be resisted: 'I had been told all my life that this was a good and necessary thing Tlic and Terran did together – a kind of birth. I had believed it until now. I knew birth was painful and bloody, no matter what. But this was something else, something worse' ('Bloodchild' 16-17). Faced with the risk of death and the realisation of human exploitation, Gan contemplates the choices he is left with. By refusing to be implanted and have his sister Hoa go through it, he can become selfish like his older brother Qui, who shields himself behind Gan. Alternatively, he can commit suicide with the forbidden rifle his family has hidden for protection. Or, finally, he can make T'Gatoi acknowledge the coercive nature of their relationship and, thus, enact an initial change. The last part of the story, with the intense exchange between the protagonists, shows negotiation as the first step of resistance.

Gan's first act of resistance is represented by his request that T'Gatoi ask him if he wants to go through with the procedure. Such a request is also a way for Gan to denounce the issue of human exploitation on the part of the aliens. But it becomes an opportunity for T'Gatoi to remind Gan of their history:

'Ask me, Gatoi … You use us.'

'We do. We wait long years for you and teach you and join our families to yours … You know you aren't animals to us … The animals we once used began killing most of our eggs after implantation long before your ancestors arrived … Because your people arrived, we are relearning what it means to be a healthy, thriving people. And your ancestors, fleeing from their homeworld, from their own kind who would have killed or enslaved them – they survived because of us. We saw them as people and gave them the Preserve when they still tried to kill us as worms.' ('Bloodchild' 24-25)

T'Gatoi's and Gan's positions, feelings, and actions make them mediators between their respective cultures. Because of her political role, T'Gatoi stands between the Terrans 'and the [Tlic] desperation that could so easily swallow' them ('Bloodchild' 5). Gan, for his part, is in the position to negotiate respect and dignity for his choices and his people – initially for himself, but potentially also for others in the future.

Through the request for knowledge and awareness, the acceptance of responsibility and accountability, but also the recognition of compromise and negotiation, Gan is able to break through the hegemonic power of the Tlic and open up the possibility of change. Whereas T'Gatoi maintains that 'Terrans should be protected from seeing' births, Gan counters that they should be 'shown. Shown when we're young kids, and shown more than once … [No] Terran ever sees a birth that goes right. All we see is … pain and terror and maybe death' ('Bloodchild' 28-29). At the risk of being the first public example, Gan's words plant the thought in T'Gatoi's mind, where chances were 'that it would grow, and eventually she would experiment' ('Bloodchild' 29). Traditionally linked with empowerment, hope, and change, both in dystopian and postcolonial discourses, knowledge allows Gan to move from an individual accommodation to a potentially collective action. Similarly, in Gan's choice not to become like his brother, we can see the option open to him of being responsible and accountable, a necessary precondition for any potentially radical change. Finally, in the acceptance of compromise on both T'Gatoi's and Gan's part, we see a necessary negotiation for the creation of a more just relationship. When Gan reminds her 'that there is risk … in dealing with a partner,' he also succeeds in convincing her to let him keep the forbidden rifle ('Bloodchild' 26). Conversely, Gan chooses to accept and respect his end of the deal. Though Gan's option can be read as a sign of cooptation and nominal consent, I think that it can also be interpreted as another expression of the resistance implicit in what Harriet Jacobs, in *Incidents in the Life of a Slave Girl*, called the 'ethic of compromise'.

Survival means negotiating a new ethic of compromise that, in turn, allows for a form of resistance and potential change. Resistance, then, need not be, as suggested by Homi Bhabha, exclusively 'an oppositional act of political intention nor is it the simple negation or exclusion of the 'content' of another culture' (152). Negotiation together with knowledge, awareness, and responsibility provide the necessary elements for resistance in Butler's story. Such a reading of 'Bloodchild' in the light of post-colonial theories is further justified by Butler's statement:

> In earlier science fiction there tended to be a lot of conquest: you land on another planet and you set up a colony and the

natives have their quarters some place and they come in and work for you. There was a lot of that, and it was, you know, let's do Europe and Africa and South America all over again. And I thought no, no, if we do get to another world inhabited by intelligent beings ... [we] are going to have to make some kind of deal with the locals: in effect, you're going to have to pay the rent. (Kenan 31)

'Bloodchild,' then, can be seen as exploring the issue of negotiation between different cultures, a needed act that, from a mere act of resistance, can become a strategy to negotiate and empower.

Through formal SF strategies like extrapolation, estrangement, reversal, and the reconceptualisation of the intersections between gender, reproduction, love, and exploitation, Butler finds a way to make us think, critically, about our 'natural' perceptions. Butler's open ending, with the statement by each protagonist that s/he will 'take care' of the other, and Gan's oscillation between consent and resistance, leaves readers uncomfortable ('Bloodchild' 29). As I said earlier, this is no utopia; Butler does not offer a consolatory happy ending, but leaves space open for hope and change. With its reversal, estrangement, and ambiguities, the story is also a step toward deconstructing traditional binaries – i.e., the binary between male/female, the naturalness of female reproduction, nationalist discourses or any narrative based on inclusion/exclusion, and unequal power relationships characterised by coercion and (nominal) consent. The story suggests the need to reject binaries, whether between species (Tlic vs. humans), genders (male vs. female), nations or cultures (us vs. them; west vs. east; colonisers vs. colonised). It further suggests that knowledge, compromise, and negotiation are needed to enact a change that will allow humans and aliens to reach a more just, if not certainly perfect, world.

Many years after its first publication, Butler's 'Bloodchild' offers a still timely reflection on issues of reproduction, gender, and the construction of binary thinking as foundational for the social order. The ongoing controversies over abortion and new techniques that enhance reproduction show to what extent women's reproductive choices have never ceased to be under attack. Similarly, the construction of binaries – whether between genders, races, classes, nations, or cultures – continues to result in lasting damage to us all. One of the most exclusionary and homogeneous discourses, or visions, of the nation is based on the myth of common origin or shared blood/genes (Yuval-Davis 21). Butler does away with notions of purity and origin by employing the mating between different species, which becomes a strategy for 'reciprocal' survival: the Tlic need humans to reproduce; humans need a place to live. The story shows how we need to abandon the idea of pure identity and embrace instead hybridity, which, in this case – unlike other thought experiments by Butler as in the Xenogenesis trilogy – does not imply a genetic and physical hybridisation, but nonetheless envisions in hybridity a strategy for resistance, a coexistence of differences, and an encouragement for reciprocity. And in these times, it is still a revolutionary message.

[1] Parts of this article have been re-elaborated from *Constructing Identities: Translations, Cultures, Nations.* Ed. Raffaella Baccolini and Patrick Leech. Bologna: BUP, 2008.

² Cf. also Lillvis and Weinbaum (on slavery), as well as Thibodeau and Waltonen (on exploitation).

³ Nationalisms, however, are not just patriarchal. Grewal and Kaplan suggest, for example, that some women's travel narratives express nationalist ideas about the superiority of their country and the inferiority of the colonised Other.

⁴ Butler herself makes the comparison, saying that men tend to see the story as 'a horrible case of slavery', while women simply see it as having had 'caesarians' (Kennan 30).

Works Cited

Atwood, Margaret. *The Handmaid's Tale*. Boston: Houghton Mifflin, 1986.

Bhabha, Homi K. 'Signs Taken for Wonders: Questions of Ambivalence and Authority Under a Tree Outside Delhi, May 1871.' *Critical Inquiry* 12 (1985): 144–65.

Burdekin, Katharine. *Swastika Night* [1937]. Old Westbury: The Feminist Press, 1985.

Butler, Octavia E. 'Afterword.' *Bloodchild and Other Stories*. New York: Seven Stories Press, 1996. 30–32.

'Bloodchild' [1984]. *Bloodchild and Other Stories*. New York: Seven Stories Press, 1996. 3–29.

Green, Michelle Erica. '"There goes the neighborhood": Octavia Butler's Demand for Diversity in *Utopias*.' Utopian and Science Fiction by Women. *Worlds of Difference*. Ed. Jane L. Donawerth and Carol A. Kolmerten. Liverpool: Liverpool University Press, 1994. 166–89.

Grewal, Inderpal and Caren Kaplan. 'Postcolonial Studies and Transnational Feminist Practices.' *Jouvert* 5.1 (2000). Accessed 28 April 2003. http://social.chass.ncsu.edu/jouvert/v5i1/grewal.htm

Helford, Elyce Rae. '"Would you really rather die than bear my young?" The Construction of Gender, Race, and Species in Octavia E. Butler's "Bloodchild."' *African American Review* 28.2 (1994): 259–71.

Jacobs, Harriet. *Incidents in the Life of a Slave Girl* [1861]. New York: Oxford University Press, 1988.

Kenan, Randall. 'An Interview with Octavia E. Butler' [1990]. *Conversations with Octavia Butler.* Ed. Consuela Francis. Jackson: UP of Mississippi, 2010. 27–37.

Lillvis, Kristen. 'Mama's Baby, Papa's Slavery? The Problem and Promise of Mothering in Octavia E. Butler's 'Bloodchild.' *MELUS* 39.4 (2014): 7–22.

Thibodeau, Amanda. 'Alien Bodies and a Queer Future: Sexual Revision in Octavia Butler's "Bloodchild" and James Tiptree, Jr.'s "With Delicate Mad Hands."' *Science Fiction Studies* 39 (2012): 262-82.

Waltonen, Karma. 'Loving the Other in Science Fiction by Women.' *MOSF Journal of Science Fiction* 1.3 (2016): 33–44.

Weinbaum, Alys Eve. 'The Afterlife of Slavery and the Problem of Reproductive Freedom.' *Social Text* 31.2 (2013): 49–68.

Yuval-Davis, Nira. *Gender and Nation.* London: Sage, 1997.

Tuere T.S. Ganges

Dear Octavia,

Like many, I was first introduced to your work when *Kindred* was assigned in an English class. As an aspiring African American writer, I felt blessed to read the work of a fellow sister doing her thing. I went on to enjoy other novels (and if there's ever the apocalypse, I'll be smuggling *Parable of the Sower* along with the Bible as a survival guide) but the one that I always tell people about is your last novel, *Fledgling*.

I first read *Fledgling* when I worked in the call center for a book dealer. Let me tell you, the coolest part of that job was that we were ENCOURAGED to read during our down time. My writing I had to hide in a little nook I created between the side of the computer and the wall of my cubicle; but books could be splayed about our desks with total acceptance. Of course, the books had to be from the current catalog and so when I saw a Butler title on our cart of samples, I had to strong-arm my way past co-workers to have first dibs. *Fledgling* was the one to creep me out and keep me glued to the pages so much, I didn't hear a couple of incoming calls on my line.

So, Ms Butler, one thing I've always wanted to ask you about the book is: 'Girl! What in the world?! I mean, WHY in the world did you start out with such a taboo relationship?' Oh, it didn't make me put the book down at all, but I might have thrown up in my mouth a little. The sexual relations between Wright and Renee (before we found out her name was Shori) made my skin crawl more than the idea of the wounded, amnesiac 'child' chasing down deer and eating them raw and fuzzy until I found out her true age in chapter 8. Vampirism aside, you delved into pedophilia and it's pretty disturbing.

I love how you made us wonder about Wright and his attraction to someone who looks like a pre-pubescent 11-year-old girl. Your readers can argue:

'That vampire venom addiction made Wright risk everything? It's a helluva drug!'

'Girl, please, he knew what he was doing when he pulled the car over. She didn't bite him yet. Perv.'

'She looked like a lost child on the side of the road! He was only trying to help.'

'Help himself to a lil', brown-skin thang on his lap on a dark and lonely road!' *eye roll*

You see, it wasn't easy to envision Renee/Shori playfully licking drips of blood from a grown man's neck. The common knowledge of vampires being ancient despite their physical appearance aside, we had an image of a little black girl sending an adult into ecstasy with her touch. The fact that she could just as easily have ripped his throat to shreds might have pushed the vomit back down but still, there was a shudder. And if that wasn't enough, there's the narrator's account of wrapping her little arms and legs around Wright's big, hairy, naked body to make you scream. I couldn't help but think to myself, 'I figured there would be blood and gore, but dammit, this is the horrifying part right here!'

As much as I wonder why you'd introduce your readers to such shocking subject matter, I also praise your ability for doing so in such an intriguing way. I love stories that piss you off a little and characters that aren't all good or all bad. I also love a story that has many layers.

With *Fledgling* you fleshed out so much. You took us through the motions of what it must be like to wake up and not know who or what you are. While your readers empathized with that notion, you hit us with the curveball of the possible pedophile. Through squinted eyes above our crinkled noses, we were happy to read that you explained everything! The vampire venom, the symbiotic relationship, the need for compassion from vampires to their symbionts. And then, you gave us the little bite that relaxed our confusion (like Shori does with almost every flustered human she comes in contact with) by telling us the little girl we found ourselves loving to be disgusted by was actually 53 years old. A little comfort there, and we were ready to get your take on what vampires were, the culture they lived in, and how they survived.

As each layer of story, history, or detail was revealed, I'd think about you balancing time between researching medical conditions, folklore and scientific phenomenon, and pouring this infused wisdom into the pages of this speculative, yet somewhat realistic, world. I mean, Ms. Butler, there were so many times when I thought, 'You know, that makes sense.' Like, the mirror thing. Anything you are able to see with your naked eye should be reflected in a mirror ... at least when there's no magic involved. Your regular, everyday vampire strolling by a full-length mirror should be able to see themselves and make the necessary adjustments to their clothing like everyone else. And there being a component in vampire venom that makes the person being bitten feel fantastic is more realistic than a vampire being able to hypnotize people at random so that they'll tilt their heads and say, 'C'mon, babe, have a nibble.' A vampire should have to work for that first bite and the victim should totally get something out of it like ecstasy and a few extra years added onto their lives.

I felt like your refuting that vampires are 'undead' with their ability to die and to be able to reproduce with other vampires was refreshing and respectful. It made me feel like all that vampire movie stuff had been insulting our intelligence for so damned long. *Fledgling* is the vampire book vampire lovers deserve.

I'd love to see this novel made into a movie but Hollywood would make Shori older, taller, she'd have breasts and blue eyes. That, or the sexual relationship between Wright and her would be cut out. I'll admit it: audiences will watch the blood and guts all day, but we can't handle seeing a little black girl have sex with an older white man. Hell, a lot of people can't handle the interracial thing as it is. So, I'd be surprised to hear about this story coming to the big screen. It's okay, books are usually better than film anyway.

Thank you, Octavia. Thank you for entertaining us, disturbing us, and then making sense of it all. You're missed but we're so lucky to have your writing to read and read again.

Sincerely yours,
Tuere

Cat Sparks

War is very popular these days

Dear Octavia

I grew up in suburban Sydney, in a red brick house with a view of trees and water. Kids back then had library cards, rode dragster bikes and played on bitumen with collarless dogs and other kids, unsupervised and mostly safe through long afternoons until the sun went down.

By the time adulthood beckoned, I'd survived hundreds of apocalypses, from mean girls and scraped knees, through alien invasions via the snark and sneaky smarts of *Dr Who*. I had walked far future sands and admired their protruding statues. I'd stood on lonely beaches waiting for new civilizations' dawns. Dodged tripods, heat rays and UFOs. Hoarded canned food, pilfered dusty shelves of department stores under the painted gaze of mannequins forever trapped in the fashions of a fallen era. My friends and I had hidden from hunter seeker robots, blown up their secret military bases, worshipped the fallen idols of bunker culture, tended gardens preserved like terrariums underground and under glass, explored forgotten valleys, forbidden zones, compounds, castles, and been cast away on countless tropical islands.

I'd run with the best of them: mutants, vampires, zombies, malformed beasts, through wastelands, wilderness and wilds. Relishing the fantastical anarchy permitted by childhood innocence as one of those lucky enough to have that given.

In the landscapes of pre-adulthood, good always prevailed. Not easily; friendships soured, broken arches harboured shadows. Not at first; but always in the end.

Something dangerously attractive beckoned from those burnt and barren badlands. From the permanence of bridge and tower scattered into ash and dust. The high romance of a world in ruin: broken roads and broken rules. We searched for fantasies beyond the noise, the smog and cars and suits and strictures, falling in to line and into place.

Only later did I come to comprehend the sheer pornography of post-apocalypse fiction, when you're reading it and you're white and middle-class and safe. When you think the things that happen on a page couldn't possibly happen in your life. When you think the people in the stories could have saved themselves by taking different paths – be those stories broadcast news or fiction.

When I eventually stumbled blindly into *Parable of the Talents*, your words seeded an apocalypse of the deep and personal kind, forcing me to viscerally experience slavery through the jagged power of narrative. Forced me to comprehend restriction of liberty as an act of violence in the extreme, every bit as vicious as a loaded gun pressed tight against my head.

You wrote science fiction, but the apocalypse of slavery is real and here and now: bled into the cheap fabric stitched upon my back; suffered by the girls and boys behind locked, unmarked doors. It's in the suicide nets below the windows where they made my phone; in the toxic glue that holds my shoes together.

You wrote: 'It shouldn't be so easy to nudge people toward what might be their own destruction' (*Parable of the Talents*, p169, Kindle edition).

It shouldn't be so easy to burn the world in all its rugged glory; to strip the forests, melt the ice and spike the acid seas. To render millions homeless. To stand by doing nothing as they bake or starve or freeze.

You could not know how much of our tomorrow you saw coming. I cannot know how much of your blighted vision yet awaits. But you enabled me to see my childhood as a luxury, not the birthright I once took it for.

And for that, I thank you most of all.

Cat Sparks

Joan Slonczewski

Originally presented by Joan Slonczewski, at SFRA, Cleveland, June 30, 2000 (http://biology.kenyon.edu/slonc/books/butler1.html)

'Octavia Butler's Xenogenesis Trilogy: A Biologist's Response'

Octavia E. Butler's novels share with readers her extraordinary vision of what it means to be 'other,' based on intelligent biological speculation. Her Xcnogenesis trilogy, now retitled Lilith's Brood for reissue by Warner, creates a stunning vision of abduction and seduction by an alien species. This vision is presented in terms remarkably consistent with modern molecular biology, even predicting developments that have occurred since the novels were written.

As the trilogy's first book, *Dawn*, opens, the human race has nearly destroyed itself by nuclear war – 'humanicide,' as Butler calls it – a fate that seemed all too plausible in the eighties, when the book was written, and that remains a distinct possibility if the effects of humanity on our environment are not reversed. The few humans who survive the war are rescued and captured by the Oankali, a nomadic alien species that travels through the universe seeking partner species with whom to 'trade' their own genes. The story is told from the viewpoint of Lilith Iyapo, a human woman whom the Oankali adopt into their family and try to enlist in recruiting other humans. Lilith is torn between accepting the medical enhancements and the sexual advances of her captors while trying to help other humans escape.

Unlike the vast majority of alien abduction tales, *Dawn* actually presents a biologically plausible explanation for why the Oankali need to interbreed with humans – despite their own abhorrence for the human race, which to them appears monstrous for its combination of high intelligence and self-destructive violence, the 'human contradiction.' The Oankali have evolved specialized organs and subcellular structures which manipulate their own genes to maximize fitness in their environment, a self-sustaining starship which is itself a living organism.

Paradoxically, because the Oankali are such successful genetic engineers, they tend to engineer themselves into an evolutionary dead end; losing all genetic diversity, they lose the ability to adapt to change. The only way they can recover genetic diversity is to interbreed with an entirely new species, which contributes new genetic strengths – and weaknesses.

Butler's story evokes the experience of an African woman swept into slavery in the eighteenth century. Lilith's 'Awakening' among the Oankali evokes the dehumanization of slave conditions – she is naked, has to beg for clothing, and is denied reading materials and other access to her own culture and history. The theme of slavery appears frequently in Butler's books, most notably *Kindred*, in which a Black woman travels back through time to rescue a white man who becomes her ancestor. The heroine of *Kindred* struggles with the fact that she owes her own existence as an individual to the oppressive cultural system in which Black women could bear children only by submitting to the advances of their white masters. In a remarkable update, today's descendents of master and slave can use DNA analysis to go back and confront their Jeffersonian ancestors.

In *Dawn,* Lilith faces the choice of 'trading' with the Oankali to produce half-human children, or having no family at all. Like the slaves who bore their masters' children, Lilith obtains privileges of enhanced health and security for herself and her future children, who will be genetically half Oankali. The Oankali lecture her about the superiority of their egalitarian, nonviolent lifestyle, as opposed to the hierarchical, violent tendencies of humans – just as Americans told their African slaves they were fortunate to be rescued from barbarism by their 'democratic' masters.

Like the slaves and their descendents, Lilith and her children feel enormous ambivalence about her choice. In *Adulthood Rites,* part 2 of the trilogy, Lilith's half-Oankali son chooses for a while to live apart with the human 'resisters,' those who choose sterility rather than join the Oankali. He at last convinces the Oankali to provide a new home for the resisters, where they can breed again and regenerate the human species. The home provided is the planet Mars; reshaped for habitability, to be sure, but all of humanity is outcast from their own homeland, like Native Americans forced onto a reservation. Lilith's son risks his life to allow humans to choose humanity; yet he himself returns to his own hybrid heritage among the Oankali. Throughout Butler's work, people of various ethnic and cultural backgrounds struggle to make such choices.

Lilith's ambivalence about the Oankali, and about her own genetic heritage, echoes Butler's own experience in the community of writers. For many years, Butler was one of only a few Black female writers of science fiction. Her gifts were embraced and appreciated by many fellow writers, and found success with supportive publishers. Yet for publication, she had to accept cover illustrations depicting her Black characters as Caucasian. Butler's success required denial of her own racial identity, just as some of the early women writers of science fiction had to deny their gender by writing under male pseudonyms. Thus, she shared Lilith's dilemma by accepting literary success at the cost of part of her own identity.

In the Xenogenesis books, the transformation of humanity is accomplished by alien biotechnology, performed by genetic engineers called *ooloi*, who participate in the mating of human and Oankali. Until recently, genetic crossing of unrelated animals was considered untenable from the standpoint of biology. Yet in the past decade, biologists have discovered profound sources of genetic commonality between organisms as distant as humans and fruit flies. Reproductive technology has led to chimeric combinations such as sheep and goat; and an early human embryo has been generated from the egg of a cow. Researchers of the Primate Genome Project seriously propose to introduce the chimpanzee's 'superior' disease resistance genes into human chromosomes. Thus, a science fiction writer can now propose alien interbreeding based on reasonable biological speculation; but few writers in fact develop the biological basis as soundly as Butler does.

How could a species naturally evolve a lifestyle requiring the acquisition of genes from unrelated species? In the years since *Dawn* was published, research has revealed interesting parallels to the Oankali in the population dynamics of living organisms on Earth. Microbes and plants have been shown to possess surprising capacities for 'genetic trade' with other species, even taking up naked DNA released by dead organisms and incorporating it into their own chromosomes. Our current view of bacteria is that, like the Oankali, these single-celled organisms evolve so as to keep only the limited set of genes they need for their current environment, but retain nearly endless capacity to acquire new genes, such as genes for antibiotic resistance, from DNA 'out there.' Similarly, plants in the natural environment have shown an unexpected capacity to acquire herbicide resistance genes from crop plants genetically engineered for resistance, a discouraging sign for the future of weed control.

Butler is one of few science fiction writers to explore the positive potential of 'bad' genes. Genetic variants which seem defective under current conditions may confer benefits when conditions change; for example, a rare defect in the structure of white blood cells confers immunity to AIDS. Butler's Oankali are particularly interested in human mutations that cause cancer. Cancer results from a series of mutational 'steps' in a few cells of the body, leading to loss of control of growth. Yet the genes in which these mutations occur are some of the most critical genes of the body, vital for normal processes of growth and development. Furthermore, some of the viruses which cause cancer-inducing mutations have now been developed into 'vectors' of gene therapy, used to correct or ameliorate genetic defects in human patients. Thus, in Butler's story, it makes sense that the Oankali consider cancer genes to be some of the most valuable genes for which they 'trade.'

From the Oankali embrace of human cancer genes, Butler draws a broader message, that we humans need to embrace 'otherness' in ethnicities and cultures foreign to our own, even if at first they seem to violate our own values. But how far can – or should – our embrace reach? Butler does not provide easy answers.

Which leads us to the question: Is there a downside to Butler's Oankali saviors of humanity? Do the Oankali really represent a positive solution to the problem of human 'hierarchal tendencies,' as implied by the first book, *Dawn*? Is the 'non-hierarchal' way of the Oankali an absolute improvement; or is it at once salvation and the damnation we self-destructive humans deserve?

The concluding book of the trilogy, *Imago*, depicts human-Oankali *ooloi* as the ultimate post-colonialists, consummate genetic engineers who sample the genes of all different organisms for their 'interesting taste,' rather as Americans choose to dine at ethnic restaurants. The fact that all of Earth's species will ultimately vanish, as the Oankali consume the planet, does not disturb them. A similar genetic consumerism can be seen today as biotech companies search the dwindling rainforests for rare species, storing their genes for useful pharmaceuticals before the organisms vanish. Some research programs even target indigenous human populations – ethnic groups whose rare genes might enhance the health of Americans long after their own races are gone. Such research understandably draws indignant responses from those facing extinction.

In fact, the closer one looks, the Oankali are not our opposites, but rather an extension of some of humanity's most extreme tendencies. Humans disturb and pollute our ecosystem; the Oankali will literally consume every organic molecule of it. Humans in the traditional Western Christian view consider procreation the sole function of sexuality. The Oankali – despite Butler's critical stance toward Christian religions – basically share this view.

Oankali sex with humans is depicted as at once super-orgasmic and super-procreative. Oankali-human families are expected to produce children upon children; hence the new title,

Lilith's Brood. Nowhere is there a role for non-procreative forms of sexuality, such as gay or lesbian relationships. While Butler's characters occasionally take a critical view of homophobia, it is interesting that the Oankali 'third sex,' the *ooloi*, always takes a male form to seduce a female human, but a female form to seduce a male human. To a biologist, ironically, this social dynamic seems overly conservative. Recent research (and older research recently acknowledged!) reveals that a wide array of mammals and birds, including all species of higher apes, engage in many kinds of sexually diverse relations with non-procreative functions (see Bruce Bagemihl, *Biological Exuberance*, St. Martin's Press, 1999.) One might perhaps feel disappointed by the absence of this dimension in Butler's three books depicting the Oankali.

Meanwhile, the Oankali 'gene trade,' which seems so fearsome in *Dawn*, may be less unthinkable than we suppose. Would middle-class Americans today ever actually trade away their own genes, let alone their future children, as Lilith does? One need only look to the notice boards of Ivy League colleges, where students are invited to sell their own eggs to infertile strangers; and many do so, to help pay their tuition. The recipients who buy the eggs inquire into the donors' genetic and personal backgrounds, as obsessively as the Oankali analyze Lilith. Ironically, the medical process of induced ovulation jeopardizes the future fertility of 'egg donors,' who may someday require similar services to produce children of their own. The business of egg banks and sperm banks has become totally consumerized, with recipients shopping for particular traits in pursuit of perfect offspring. The Oankali, with their alien genetic engineering, have become hauntingly familiar.

Elizabeth Stephens

Dear Octavia,

Wakefulness creeps upon me slowly, like a hunter before the kill. In the darkness, I feel my scalp, finding it hard and my head heavy. My limbs are long and lithe and as I flex my fingers and toes, I note that there are ten of each. Light filters in between my lashes finally and I catch a glimpse of the inside of my palm. It is white, unlike the back of my hand which is the color of cinnamon or milk in coffee. A brutal scar runs across it and it is this scar that reminds me: I am human.

Or am I?

What is it that makes humans human? What is it that makes me, me? Is it my skin and flesh and blood and bone? Blood spills red but beneath skin runs blue. Is humanity simply color or is there more? Perhaps I am Shori. A vampire with skin like mine whose love of her lovers surely parallels the love that I have for my mate? Her resilience and cunning, her quick intellect and honor must be traits that we humans seek to embody. But how can we, when we are an us and Shori is an other? Does fighting against the other truly unite us? Is this how we define our humanness? Us against them. Them against us. The Arab culture has a saying: me against my brother, me and my brother against my cousin, me and my brother and my cousin against our neighbor. But there is another saying: united we stand, divided we fall. Aesop wrote this, and so did World War II Allied propaganda. Do we unite as humans? How can we when we as humans kill and cut and war?

Is this me?

Can my humanity accept the other or am I bound to fear? What of love? Perhaps I am Gan, a human male impregnated by an alien species. Can I fear and love simultaneously? Can humanity allow that I care for the unknown monster growing within my body? Like Lilith to the Oankali, can I be drawn into unknown emotions, or places, or people, or worlds without resistance? Or must my humanity force me to resist and then understand before I feel the cooling balm of acceptance?

I am I.

Does humanity operate within my own body singularly or are we a collective? Are there things that bind me to human beings more so than to cats or insects? Are there things that bind me to my nationality, heritage, or race more than others? Am I the other? My mother is of African descent, my father of European. Does this make me Akin – a human 'construct' born of one human, one alien parent? Must I fear myself, or everyone else, or humanity? Why not love, rather? Because as I lay my head down onto my pillow and stare across the sheets at the body across from mine noting that we share neither race, nor heritage, nor nationality, I wonder what else matters?

We are we.

Humanity is too complex to define, but I know it when I see it. I am Lauren Olamina and can feel the emotions of others in a post-apocalyptic world ruled by greed and the vestiges of bygone religions, so I invent my own form of faith. God is Change. God is malleable. These are the tenets of Earthseed. Are these not also the tenets of humanity? If they are not, then they should be. What are we but ever-changing? When life is as fluid as water, why does our humanity compel us to cling to rigidity? Why not ride each wave? Why not understand our place and purpose as but droplets in the sea of time? If we did, we would understand that nothing matters but love, and nothing separates us.

We are nothing.

Humanity believes itself history, but history existed long before us. History existed in every rock, every microbe, every creature, every other whose life was not recorded in any script legible by us. I am Dana, traveling through time to visit the land of my ancestors in pre-Civil War Maryland. Here I see the roots of the African American history tree, whose branches and leaves continue to shake and snap, burn and grow even in my own time. My own time. Time is not my own, but owns me. I am more a slave to it than my ancestors were to their masters. The masters will all die, and because time too owns the masters they must realize that they are no better than their slaves.

We are everything.

We are all slaves, so to waste any time on creating categories among us is a waste. Rather, we must love. We must fight for one another. We must share. Because once time takes us back into its belly again, I am lost and you are lost even though we may still remain. Our thoughts, our words, our actions may linger on like the mountain that is denuded but still exists as sand. If all that you touch, you change, you must change it with love, and for the good because we are but sand waiting for the sands of time to reclaim what is theirs. I am Octavia, shy and nervous in my otherness as I approach the world armed with only curiosity and a typewriter. I bring the past to the present and aliens to earth and I bring about both the beginning and the end of the world. A sharpshooter with a pen, I cleave through history and time and space and as I give my gift to the world, I do it with love and like this, I am invincible. Not even time can touch me. I am immortal.

Love is immortal.

Love lingers in between dog-eared pages and love lives in us. Love is human. Love is everything. Love is Gan and Dana and Shori and Lauren and us and Octavia Butler. It exists to be shared. So in conclusion please allow me the honor to say, Octavia. Ms. Butler. Writer, vampire, lover, alien, daughter, author, slave, master, mother, other. Thank you for sharing your humanity with me.

Sincerely,
Elizabeth Stephens

Aurelius Raines II

A Missive From The Last Stall

Good morning, Octavia,

I am a bathroom reader. This you may already know, since this is where the majority of our conversations took place. One of the earliest negotiations I had with my new wife was whether to place a small magazine rack in the bathroom. She was against it.

Reading in the bathroom started when I was young. I would sit there, bored, and I would intuitively look for things to read. That's when I discovered the ingredient and warning labels on the cleaning supplies under the sink. I always did it without thinking. Just grab a can or bottle and read the warnings, practice sounding out the chemicals. It was never something I did consciously. I didn't even think about it until I accidently sprayed myself in the face while seeing if Scrubbing Bubbles used CFCs.

After that, I started grabbing books, magazines, newspapers. I know most people find that kind of thing weird ... maybe even gross. What kinds of things do we keep secret because we are afraid of what people are going to think?

So this is how I grew up through high school, college, jobs, marriage, children.

About the time that I was married with my first son on the way, I finally picked up one of your books. While browsing the shelves at Africa West, a bookstore where I attended a weekly open mics, I was fascinated with the covers of your books, with their stain-dark colors, deep gold titles and the pictures of the impossible brown people who had powerful, elysian countenances.

I started with the Patternist series, combing the pre-Google Internet to make sure that I was reading the books in the right order.

And this is where you challenged me. This is why I loved you, and mourn you now. As I read your books, I did what I always did with the hundreds of books I'd read until that point. I assumed that the characters were white. I am a little ashamed to admit that I was thoroughly stuck in white male default mode. Doctor, astronaut, merchant, sailor – unless the author specifically told me that the character was non-white, I assumed that any American in a story was white. So to read your stories and realize that the white actor that I picked to play a character was less Tom Cruise and more Omar Epps caused me to interrogate the way that I saw the world and the way that I marginalized myself.

Around the time that I started reading your books, I'd started a job in the customer service department of a major telecommunications company. I won't say which one, suffice it to say that they had been a monopoly in the '70s, and during the course of the '90s and the 2000s, were regaining their hegemony. Before this job, most of my work experience was in customer service. I liked helping people. Like the stories that I read, each call was a small drama, a problem where I was the hero of the story. Customers would call in crises and leave with resolution. Customer service taught me about empathy and de-escalating conflict. My favorite calls were the ones that were dripping with the 'n-word' as some customer was upset about the treatment they'd received at the hands of some 'gal'. I could put aside my outrage long enough to do my job, which was not to enlighten them, but make sure their services worked perfectly. And I did. They go low, I go high. The customer is happy and I get accolades for being able to handle the impossible.

I was excited about doing that job for this (unnamed) company. Unfortunately, I wasn't on the floor long before I realized the job description that I was given was not what I was expected to do. It was a sales job. I had a quota that I had to meet. This was the kind of job that I usually avoided. The longer I worked there the lower my morale became. Some of the things I was being asked to do seemed dishonest and unethical. I was a church boy and, even in my most heathenistic moments, I found deceiving and taking advantage of people looking for help unreasonable behavior. I wanted out.

But this job was paying me more money than I'd been paid in my entire life. The opportunities for growth were legion. The favorite story told about the CEO is how he started working in the garage, washing service vans. With me being a husband and father, walking away from this job seemed criminally irresponsible. So I put on my big-boy pants, went to my awful job, and lied to old people.

In the meantime, my bathroom breaks were becoming more and more frequent, and your books were going with me. The department bathroom was terminally beige and over-lit. It always smelled like feces. Always. There was a large handicapped stall at the end, and in that stall, I would escape. Out of my back pocket the book would come, and I would escape into a world where people who looked like me mattered. Where the world teetered on tipping points and brown hands played upon those scales. A world where we had story, history, agency, thought and mind. Where the coming of the clayarks does not mean the destruction the world, but the destruction of the systems of oppression that had become ridiculous in the face of total annihilation.

Sales goals became so unimportant.

There were brown female heroes in these pages and I lived through all of them. The survivors, gods, vampires and prophets. The world outside of the bathroom became the fiction. Even the felling of the World Trade Center buildings seemed trite compared the annihilation we'd brought upon ourselves in the Lilith's Brood series. The post-9/11 right-wing backlash made the *Parable of the Sower* seem like a wood-pulp time traveler, brought to us from the future, telling of certainties to come. (Even more so, now.)

After I finished each book I would go to the Borders near my home and pick up the new one. I had a ritual of examining the cover of the book as if it were a movie trailer and then, slowly, removing the beige and white barcode sticker from the back cover and reading the blurb and autobiography placed in each of your books from that time. (Your biography always said the same thing, freezing an image of you in my mind. I wish you had made it to become that eighty-year-old writer that you wanted to be. I always imagined them asking you for something else and you, having just birthed a book, felt put upon to write something else about your least favorite subject ... you.)

Why talk about yourself when you can talk about the worlds within yourself? Why blurb about what you see when you can project your vision into the world – even the walls of a corporate bathroom stall?

But here you were, in my hands and before my eyes, laying bare humanity's dirty little secret. Thousands of years of technology only served our need to rule each other. It was your words that made me consider that there actually might be something wrong with that. As I hid in that bathroom, my debates about returning to my cubicle seemed to be weighted with a greater import. What did it mean to spend your time this way when there was greater work to do?

In the Gospels, Jesus spends years teaching his disciples how to fix the world and, finally, gives them the command to go 'into the world and preach the gospel'. This is the call that Lauren Olamina receives, the day her home is invaded and burned to the ground. Stationary gospels are useless.

I am stationary and I wonder about how hard it was for you, trapped in the stall of your home. Yet, you found a line to the world through your writing. All of the stories you read, bringing the universe to your safe place; and the stories you sent back into the universe, all the while remaining safe.

My life had changed and I had been trying to write that change. I kept starting this story about a superhero who is made weak by his new family life. Not my most subtle metaphor. I was an awkward person who hated social situations, and I had managed to court, marry, and impregnate a woman. I felt like I was living way above my pay grade.

But Lilith was in this jungle in South America, given the job of being the matriarch for a new generation and kind of human. There had been nothing like this in the entirety of the universe, and she still had to navigate the old conventions of hierarchy and violence.

You brought all of this to me in the only place people allowed me to think. Where the conventions of male culture dictated that I have space to meditate and wonder and reevaluate. Where I could get rid of the waste of my programming and see a new world and an alternative to the toxic ceremony we call humanity.

It has been years since I read any of your books. I have put off reading *Parable of the Talents* because then, you will be truly gone. It is the only conversation that I have not had with you. I'm not sure what I am waiting for. Our new president tried to ban Muslims from entering the country today, and to hear your commentary in my head as I digest my place in this political absurdity would be a comfort.

The book is in my bag and although I have long since left that job that asked too much and too little of me, there are bathrooms everywhere.

Still Seeking Change
(and a full roll of toilet paper),
Aurelius

Jeffery Allen Tucker

Dear Octavia Butler,

Greetings. I am honored by this opportunity to address you. I have often imagined sharing with my favorite artists my thoughts about their work. In my own mind, I've had drinks with Grant Morrison, praising the brilliance of *All-Star Superman* while griping about the superfluous presence of the Joker in *Batman R.I.P.*; or I've been upgraded to a seat next to Peter Dinklage on a trans-Atlantic flight, during which he listens attentively to my explanation of why, for all the accolades he's received for *Game of Thrones*, his best performance was in *The Station Agent*. When I actually got the chance to talk to Esperanza Spalding, however, all I could muster was some clumsy statement about how much I daydream about playing fretless electric bass, to which she generously, but earnestly, replied, 'Me too!' as she returned my hastily bought two-dollar official concert postcard, which now bore her signature.

I met you in person once as well. It was at the 2003 conference on African Americans and Science Fiction at Howard University organized by Gregory Hampton. I don't recall what I said to you, but I remember the sincerity of your smile after you signed my paperback copy of *Wild Seed*; it was a high point, one of several at that event. I looked forward to seeing you again in the following month back in Rochester, NY for a series of events organized by Writers & Books, the local literary organization, which had selected *Kindred* for its annual 'If All of Rochester Read the Same Book' project. I'd had the opportunity to talk about the novel on a local multicultural affairs television program and to discuss it with readers at the black-owned bookstore near my apartment.

Unfortunately, a death in the family took me out of town, so I missed your talk and reading. But the poster announcing those events still holds a place on the wall in my office, above my laser printer. Next to the computer on which I am writing this is a copy of *Conversations with Octavia Butler* edited by the late Conseula Francis, featuring a photograph of you on the cover. There's a geometric congruency between your earrings and the pattern on your shirt, and your face expresses resolve, focus, and an orientation on the future, which is the object, the philosopher Ernst Bloch wrote, of the principle of hope.

Allow me, for the moment, to orient myself toward the 1990s, when I discovered your writing. Although I had read a lot of science fiction in high school and as an undergraduate, I decided to put all that away now that I was a doctoral student at an Ivy League university, on my way to becoming a serious literary scholar. However, your name kept coming up in readings and in conversations about identity, race, gender, intersectionality, and more. Then one day, I was talking to one of the library's security guards – because, frankly, there weren't a whole lot of other black folks to chat with on campus – who recommended that I read *Kindred*, which was one of her all-time favorite books. So I did, and I was blown away. I raved to other grad students and my professors about the novel: 'It's like H.G. Wells meets Harriet Jacobs!' Undeterred by their strange looks and the paucity of discretionary spending usually available to a graduate student, I sought out and purchased *Parable of the Sower*, the artfully designed hardback edition published by Four Walls Eight Windows.

The only book that I literally could not put down until I had read it entirely was Mary Shelley's *Frankenstein*. I put down *Sower* only once before finishing it; that's how strong its hold was.

I wrote letters (as we did back in the day) to friends – a teacher in Oregon, a seminarian in North Carolina, a dairy farmer in Vermont – encouraging them to read *Sower*. The dairy farmer did; she liked it too. I went home for the holidays, and when an uncle asked me what I was getting my doctorate in, I mentioned that I might want to study African American writers of Science Fiction. 'Oh no,' my uncle said. 'We don't do that. We leave that kinda stuff for white folks.' Of course, you and your works were proof that we have done that kind of stuff and done it well. My immersion into the topic followed; I did research on the works of Samuel R. Delany, and I got to give a lecture to a class led by Toni Morrison (!), who had invited Bernice Johnson Reagon to campus to share the process of composing a spiritual for the twenty-first century, based in part on Lauren Olamina's journal writings about Earthseed in *Sower*.

I hope the above shows how important your writing has been to me, but I also want to convey how important it has been to my students. I decided to study literature after reading 'A Defence of Poetry' (1840) in which Percy Bysshe Shelley (Mary's husband – everything is connected) writes:

> The great secret of morals is love; or a going out of our own nature, and an identification of ourselves with the beautiful which exists in thought, action, or person, not our own. A man, to be greatly good, must put himself in the place of another and of many others; the pains and pleasures of his species must become his own. The great instrument of

moral good is the imagination; and poetry administers to
the effect by acting upon the cause ... Poetry strengthens
the faculty which is the organ of the moral nature of man,
in the same manner as exercise strengthens a limb.[1]

Perhaps I was young and impressionable, but this essay provided
one of those 'A-ha!' moments: I suddenly understood what literature
was for, why it mattered. This is what I want for my students: an
'A-ha!' moment of their own. As a teacher, my job is to create the
conditions that make that possible. That's where you come in.

I teach your works as often as I can, and three of them have
a way of appearing frequently on my syllabi. I've taught 'Bloodchild'
in my course on Science Fiction several times; it's included in a
very fine anthology (a formulation I don't often use) edited by
Heather Masri entitled *Science Fiction: Stories and Contexts*.
'Bloodchild' has also been the final reading in my Introduction to
African American Literature course, which opens with works like
The Narrative of the Life of Frederick Douglass and the poetry of
Phillis Wheatley. In both courses, students often say that
'Bloodchild' is unlike anything else they've read. The story helps
me get them to think about and re-think some assumptions that
neophyte literary scholars may bring to a text. I usually make note
of your biography, but I don't make your afterword available.

In both courses, students initially interpret the story as an
example of twentieth-century African American fiction responding
to the call of nineteenth-century slave narratives. The evidence
supporting such an interpretation is plentiful: it's a first-person
narrative; the Terrans live in a 'Preserve;' Qui refers to Gan as
T'Gatoi's 'property;' etc. After a consensus has been reached that
'Bloodchild' is indeed a re-imagining of antebellum slavery in a

futuristic extra-terrestrial setting, I share your afterword, in which you deny that it's about slavery, calling it instead, among other things, 'a love story' and a story about 'paying the rent;'[2] i.e. there's a kind of symbiosis going on between Terrans and Tlic. Is the story's identity as neo-slave narrative, therefore, being determined by what we know about the author? 'Do we expect 'Bloodchild' to be about slavery,' I ask, 'because Butler's black?' Student responses to this new information tend to range from reluctant agreement with you to sheer incredulity; they still kind of think it's about slavery. 'But if the author says it's not about slavery, then it must not be about slavery,' I say. 'End of story, right?'

This usually prompts students to reflect on how much weight to give an author's comments about their own work and gives me an opening to introduce the main points of Wimsatt and Beardsley's 'The Intentional Fallacy'[3] or Barthes' 'The Death of the Author,'[4] the assertions of which are different from what many assume based on the title. It is a commonplace to say that a deceased author lives on in their works; Barthes' celebration of how meaning happens, how meanings proliferate, each time someone picks up a book and reads it, is not necessarily out of step with that sentiment. Of course, another possibility is that 'Bloodchild' is about both love and slavery, about how an exploitative relationship can be disguised, even (or especially) to those in the relationship, as a kind and loving one, or how loving someone can sometimes feel like total submission to them. Is love of any kind possible when one holds power over another, or are there always power differentials even in genuinely loving relationships? That's a lot of big ideas from one short story.

'Slavery of any kind fostered strange relationships,' reflects Dana Franklin in *Kindred*.[5] When I teach this novel in my course

on Slavery and the Twentieth Century African American Novel –
after reading Margaret Walker, Toni Morrison, Arna Bontemps,
and others – students again state that it's not what they expected
to encounter in such a course. I often hear a student say something
like 'I don't like science fiction, but I like this,' which prompts
discussion about the diversity of styles, topics, themes, and authors
within the tradition. I have also, on occasion, had students engage
in a thought experiment, one that now strikes me as somewhat
perverse: I ask each student to put themselves in Dana's place.
'What would you do, if you suddenly found yourself transported to
the antebellum South, with no sure way of how to get back?'

In discussion and in writing, student responses have been
instructive, particularly in how, as the differences between Dana
and Kevin's experiences demonstrate, one's circumstances and
options would be determined by one's subject position(s) – as your
writings illustrate, we are all, each of us, many things. Imagine the
responses to this question from an African American woman, a
white male international student from England, or an American-
born Chinese woman. As for myself, despite what Kevin tells
Dana about African American ingenuity and perseverance during
the antebellum era, and that which Dana herself displays, I don't
think I'd last long.

I have also taught *Kindred* in my Science Fiction course,
and after reading Gernsback, Heinlein, and Asimov – and even
after reading Le Guin, Delany, and Russ – students once more
express surprise at finding such a text in this course. This has led
to student-initiated discussions about whether or not Kindred is
'really' science fiction, an issue that doesn't get raised as much in
my African American Literature course, to which students bring a
different set of assumptions about the objects of study. At this

point, I cite your own statement that *Kindred* is not science fiction because there's no science in it,[6] which raises some of the same issues that 'Bloodchild' does. It also generates questions, some prompted by me but most coming from the students: What do we mean by 'science fiction'? What do we mean by 'science'? Does 'science' include the scientific method – questioning, hypothesis, experimentation, empirical observation – of which Dana seems to do quite a bit? And if science fiction is, among other things, about how human beings respond to technological change, isn't that represented in Dana's adjustment to the nineteenth century – e.g. there's no antiseptic on the Weylin plantation – as well as in Kevin's re-adjustment when he returns to the twentieth century and can't even work an electric pencil sharpener? And what do we mean by 'technology' – doesn't that include things like CPR, writing, as well as the technologies of violence applied to black bodies and psyches? Analytical questions proliferate when you bring Octavia Butler into the classroom.

Less frequently than 'Bloodchild' and *Kindred*, I have taught *Parable of the Sower*, usually in a graduate seminar on Utopia and Literature. I don't know if 'teach' is the right word. I assign the readings, but a graduate seminar is a discussion-based class, and the students are doing most of the discussing. I mention *Sower* here, however, because it exemplifies two of the course's key ideas. First, it demonstrates Lyman Tower Sargent's point that 'dystopia' and 'anti-utopia' are not synonymous.[7] *Sower* is clearly dystopian in its setting; however, it is utopian in its themes, represented by the hope for humanity's future expressed in Lauren's journal writings: 'the / Destiny of Earthseed is to take root among / the stars.'[8] Second, *Sower* is an example of a 'critical dystopia,' which Tom Moylan describes as the appropriate literary response to a world hurtling toward dystopia, which ours – afflicted by global warming, increasing wealth inequality, internecine wars and ensuing refugee crises – often seems to be doing.[9]

Critical dystopias also express a healthy ambivalence about utopianism itself. For example, Earthseed represents a principle of hope for individuals, the nation, and the species, but Lauren's aren't the only solutions in the novel; 2024's president-elect Christopher Charles Morpeth Donner wants to abolish the space program and 'has a plan for putting people back to work' that includes rolling back 'minimum wage, environmental, and worker protection laws.'[10] Perhaps because the most recent seminar on *Sower* occurred the week after the 2016 national election, my students compared Donner to our own president-elect, whose campaign included promises to 'Make America Great Again' by registering Muslims and deporting immigrants. It reminded me of the further deterioration of American society in *Parable of the Talents*, as well as your comments on that novel:

> Hunting for scapegoats is always popular in times of serious trouble. So is hunting for the great leader who will restore prosperity and stability ... Sometimes the only thing more dangerous than frightened, confused, desperate people looking for solutions is frightened, confused, desperate people finding and settling for truly bad solutions.[11]

That sounds like the psychology of a larger-than-expected – depressingly so, in fact – segment of the American electorate in 2016. I suppose Earthseed is also 'utopian' in that there's an idealism to it; however, there's also a logic and an ethics to it that makes it appealing. It's significant that Earthseed and Acorn are founded by someone with hyperempathy syndrome, a 'sharer.' I wonder if Lauren ever read 'A Defence of Poetry.'

These are just a few thoughts about my own experiences teaching your work. I should also say that I'm looking forward to a forthcoming book edited by Tarshia Stanley entitled *Approaches to Teaching the Works of Octavia Butler*, which provides detailed accounts of how your writings contribute to the pedagogical goals of instructors of various disciplines, at different types of schools, and engaging with a variety of students.

I'll close with the following: Recently, the passing of people dear to me – a brother-in-law, old friends, artists whom I've admired – has occasioned reflection on death and the feelings of loss that survivors endure. When we lost you, I felt an absence that I feared would never abate. But like your signature, your photograph, and the poster on my wall, the act of writing this letter shows me how present you still are for me and for my students. It's a presence that I will continue to cherish.

Sincerely,
Jeff Tucker

1 Percy Bysshe Shelley. 'A Defence of Poetry.' 1840. *English Romantic Writers*, ed. David Perkins. San Diego: Harcourt Brace Jovanovich, 1967. 1072–1087.
2 Octavia E. Butler. Afterword to 'Bloodchild.' *Bloodchild and Other Stories*. New York: Four Walls Eight Windows, 1995. 30–32.
3 W.K. Wimsatt, Jr. & M.C. Beardsley. 'The Intentional Fallacy.' *The Sewanee Review* 54.3 (Jul.–Sept. 1946): 468–488.
4 Roland Barthes. 'The Death of the Author.' *Image-Music–Text*. Trans. Stephen Heath. New York: Hill & Wang, 1977. 142–148.

5   Octavia E. Butler. *Kindred*. Boston: Beacon Press, 1988. 230.

6   Qtd. in Robert Crossley. Introduction to *Kindred* by Octavia E. Butler. Boston: Beacon Press, 1988. xii.

7   Lyman Tower Sargent. 'The Three Faces of Utopianism Revisited.' *Utopian Studies* 5.1 (1994), 1–37.

8   Octavia E. Butler. *Parable of the Sower*. 1993. New York: Warner/Aspect, 1995. 68.

9   Tom Moylan. 'The Critical Dystopia.' *Scraps of the Untainted Sky: Science Fiction, Utopia, Dystopia*. Boulder: Westview Press, 2000. 183–199.

10 Octavia E. Butler. *Parable of the Sower*. 1993. New York: Warner/Aspect, 1995. 24.

11 Octavia E. Butler. 'A Conversation with Octavia E. Butler.' *Parable of the Talents*. New York: Warner/Aspect, 2000. 414.

Paul Weimer

Dear Ms. Butler,

The future from which I write to you, now, is a world that is very different from that of even a year ago, and this letter is vastly different than one I would have written to you then, or back when you were alive. With climate change seeming to accelerate, and xenophobic intolerant forces on the march, your two Parable novels feel only increasingly relevant. Not only or because of their foresight – science fiction isn't really about foresight, it's about the now. You saw clearly in a day and age what I did not, and saw what might and could grow. You saw what was already here, in embryonic form. The back-to-the-golden-age right-wing President Jarret and his brutality, when I first read of him, felt like a variant on Robert A. Heinlein's *Future History* theocrat Nehemiah Scudder, or The Republic of Gilead of Atwood's *The Handmaid's Tale*. He was safely in a world that wasn't going to be, a dark vision of a parallel world. Today, I can see the nationalism of Donald John Trump, and his Vice President Michael Pence, and see that you weren't describing a parallel world, but an extension from the dark roots of the '90s into a future that could yet be. You were seeing ahead, warning us, a prophet showing us the darkness growing when you wrote the novels. You saw the dark forces a-borning that now none can deny have bloomed into a deadly flowering.

And yet, Ms. Butler, you did not only see the dark forces rising, but a way forward, a way to endure and move beyond today. Survival, I have come to realize, is important in your work. Your characters' concerns are with survival and what survival means even beyond the fact of endurance. Survival can be so much more, and your work illustrates that. Survival is an act of defiance. Survival is an act of resistance. Survival is an act of *humanity*. Even as Lauren and the community of Acorn struggle to survive some very brutal things in the two Parable novels, their survival stands as an act against what is arrayed against them. Survival is not enough, survival is not the only thing to be done, but survival is a necessary start. Not giving up is the first step to dealing with the darkness. Keeping the candle burning, no matter what. I see, now, as I write this, what I did not see when I read the novel.

I would have liked to read *Parable of the Trickster*, that projected third book in the series. Maybe you would have had a chance to return to it, and make the book work. Maybe not. I have enough relationships with writers, and have enough experience with my own writing, to understand the essential difficulty of the creative act. I cannot fault you for the books you have not written, I can only celebrate you for the books that you have written.

So, beyond the Parable stories, I am and always have been playing catch-up with your work, from the very beginning. I'm pretty sure that the first story I read of yours was 'Bloodchild', back in *Asimov's Science Fiction Magazine* in the 1980s. I read the story at an impressionable age and was disturbed, strongly, by its imagery. I didn't understand the themes of the story, then. I was more taken by the idea of a man being impregnated with alien grubs, and having it go oh-so-wrong, rather than seeing the themes of colonialism and slavery, and power dynamics, that the story truly speaks to. But at the time, the body horror of the story was what I remembered of it. And, oh, the cover of the issue! The desaturated, high key, white cover art's background contrasted with the red, insectile alien exiting a young boy (Gan, presumably) with a trail of blood in its wake. This cover art perfectly reinforced that body horror imagery invoked in your story. How did you feel about the Wayne Barlowe art paired with your story, I wonder?

To my regret, I didn't pursue reading any of your books for a number of years after my experience with 'Bloodchild'. It wasn't until the 1990s, when I really started to flower in my SF reading, when I decided to seek out award-winning and acclaimed authors, that I came across your novels. When I did, I started in a very different place in your oeuvre. I took a copy of *Wild Seed* out of a local library and devoured it. What impressed me most, and it was a highlight of my development as a reader and thinker of things genre, was the structure. How cleverly you set up Doro's story! You kept me going as a reader, trying to learn more, burrowing me like a parasite deeper into the text of the story to unlock his secrets. And all the while I was doing that you were immersing me into his long conflict and relationship with Anyanwu.

As a result, you hooked me back into reading your fiction. I started reading the rest of the Patternist novels, and branching out from there. It took me a while to finally reread 'Bloodchild' as a part of a short-story collection. A decade after the story scared me, and with several novels of yours under my belt, I finally grokked the story for all its depth and richness, and could read it for the brilliance of what it was. But by then I had changed, and you had changed me, too. I could appreciate you, now, in a way my thirteen-year-old self could not.

I am still catching up on your work, though. I'm yet to read *Fledgling*, and *Kindred* remains unread, and some of your short stories as well. I'm not yet done with my first read of your work, much less a reread of your oeuvre. As my story of my encounter with 'Bloodchild' illustrates, the genius of your work, for me, is in the second reading, in the subsequent encounter, in the re-engagement of your work. It is then, I think, that I truly understand what you are doing, what you meant to say to me, and the second reading is when I finally start deciphering the genetic code of the themes of the work.

And so, thank you, Ms. Butler. You were taken from us too soon, and I glommed onto your work far too late for my taste. Yours is a voice that we could sorely and surely use in this day and age. Your work stands more relevant than ever, and I feel that the circumstance that has kept you from creating more such work, more light in the darkness, more paths forward, is a grossly unfair commentary on life. After an *annus horribilis* of 2016 where too many lights in the darkness were extinguished, and dark forces arose, I find that the extinguishing of your abiding light a decade past is more keenly felt, now. I, and the rest of science fiction fandom, feel. We have that afterglow of your oeuvre, still radiating, as a poor, but very real substitute for you, yourself. May it continue to light our way as it can in the years to come. May its light bring new works from others to growth and fruition.

With sincere thanks,
Paul Weimer

Gerry Canavan

Disrespecting Octavia

My career as a literary scholar opened a door I never expected: it allowed me to research a book on Butler's life and work using her personal papers as my primary archive. What a privilege: I have come to know her amazing stories in much more depth through consideration of their early drafts, changed endings, and excised passages, even the nearly unrecognizable early versions (like the strange, Oankali-less early versions of the Xenogenesis series) that reveal dimensions of the work I hadn't realized were important before. I've seen what exists of the planned sequels to *Parable of the Talents* and *Fledgling* and have been tantalized by them, challenged by them, desperate to somehow cross over to one of the universes where they were finished and read the rest. I've read her letters and her journals, too, dating back to her childhood, wrestling with the weight of my responsibility to scholarship against my desire to protect her privacy, even after her death.

In my book *Modern Masters of Science Fiction: Octavia E. Butler* I refer to the immense collection of her personal papers at the Huntington Library as a gift she left for us – and it's a gift I really think we ought to use carefully and respectfully, in general accordance with what her wishes might have been, had she lived. I don't think the archive should become an opportunity for scandal-making or for grave-robbing. We shouldn't allow our desire for closer and closer contact with Butler's genius to turn us into vultures, no matter how understandable or irresistible that impulse might be.

However, in one regard I think we do need to let our

collective fidelity to Octavia go: we should absolutely publish her lost fiction, in some cases in direct defiance of her personal desire to suppress it.

The most egregious case of this defiance, even disrespect, would have to be *Survivor*. She loathed *Survivor*; she needled the people like Nisi Shawl who brought her copies to sign, even inscribing the book: 'Nisi, I wish you didn't have this one.' She was preoccupied with what she saw as *Survivor*'s original and irredeemable sin of the imagination: the goofy, *Star Trek*-y notion that species that had evolved in entirely different settings would nonetheless be able to get each other pregnant. (Even *Star Trek* had to find a way to fix that one eventually.) She thought the book was (her words) 'embarrassing'. She strenuously refused its republication, and even kept it out of the Seed to Harvest collection that anthologizes the rest of the Patternist series. Ten years after she left us, we need to have the confidence to disrespect her judgment about *Survivor*; it's time now for the estate to republish it.

Survivor may be flawed, but it is one of only twelve books from Butler's incredible mind that was published during her life; that's too big a prize to leave mouldering in university libraries and in lucky discoveries on the secondhand book market. More than that, we need *Survivor* for what it tells us about the Patternists, for the breathing room it gives us from their otherwise suffocatingly blank and miserable future – and for what it tells us about one of Octavia's great unfinished intellectual projects, the planned creation of a future-historical saga that escaped her grasp not once (with *Survivor* and unpublished 1970s stories like the original version of 'The Evening and the Morning and the Night') but, infuriatingly, twice (in *Parable of the Trickster* and its possible sequels). Without *Survivor* we lose a huge component of the creative spark that drove her fiction. Like it or not, *Survivor* is the tip we have of that very vast iceberg. I keep hoping the publication of a lost chapter from *Survivor* as a standalone story in *Unexpected Stories*, in 2014, was testing the waters for a full reissue of the book; I'm hoping still.

Of course – while I'm on the subject – I'd really like to see that early version of 'The Evening and the Morning and the Night' published in some form as well. It's a great story, having almost nothing to do the story of that name that was published in the anthology *Bloodchild* and having much more to do with *Survivor*, the story 'Bloodchild,' and with that early, Oankali-less version of the Xenogenesis books I already mentioned. The 1970s 'Evening' is about an extrasolar colony that fails; a disaster leaves a doomed crew marooned and waiting to die. There are five or six different but overlapping articulations of the story in the archive, each emphasizing different aspects of the narrative situation or taking the basic plot in a new direction; the hypertext nature of these alternative versions would make it great for online or eBook publication.

Parable of the Trickster may be a somewhat harder sell, as the book is genuinely unfinished in a way the early 'Evening' is not. She tried to sell 'Evening,' but it just never sold, while *Trickster* she began and abandoned over and over and over again, a nearly impossible number of times. Still, what's there of *Trickster* is fascinating and provocative, and gives us some glimmer of what the extension of the Parables series might have been like without closing any doors or providing any solid answers. The Parables books mean so much; on Twitter I see new people discovering the books daily, twenty years after their composition but somehow feeling even more relevant now, after the election of Donald Trump has unhappily proved them righter than we ever would have dreamed. In whatever form is practical, readable, and economically viable, I hope people are someday allowed to see these glimmers of what *Trickster* might have been.

There are other partial drafts of novels, too, some more complete than *Trickster*, some much less so. One, a personal favorite of mine – *Paraclete*, about a woman with the power to change reality with her writing – spans nearly a hundred pages before it peters out unfinished (having really only just begun). Another, *Bodhisattva* or *Spiritus*, about reincarnating immortals, would barely be publishable in its current form, but is such a fascinating *idea* I hate to leave it only to the scholars. Nor, for that matter, do I think *Doro-Jesus* – her strange unfinished Patternist novel, reimagining Christ himself as a mutant superhero – should be left a secret forever, just because she never completed it. And this is only the beginning of the screenplays, story treatments, essays, lectures, poems, fan fiction, attempts, failures, successes, and weird literary experiments all hiding in boxes at her archive. Uninterested in the economics of publishing, and caring only about the obvious literary merit of some of this material, I can imagine a fantastic volume that collects the best of her unfinished stories. Let them inspire others like they inspired her, like they have inspired me and the few others who have already found our way to the Huntington to read them. There's so much great material the estate can afford to be judicious about what is ultimately published – but, please, let people read the best of what she left behind.

And it's not just unfinished drafts, either. There is a full, completed novel in the archive, too: *Blindsight*, from the early 1980s. (There are actually *two* completed versions!) *Blindsight* is

Butler's lost thriller, a novel more in the mold of Stephen King (whom she admired and envied) than any of her other works. It tells the story of a boy born blind but with strange psychic powers, who becomes the leader of a cult-like religious movement. It was an unhappy project that taunted Butler; she kept returning to it, even as she was never able to get it right. She sent *Blindsight* to publishers multiple times, but was unable to sell it – hard to believe, given how good the draft of the book actually is and what her reputation would eventually become, but it happened. Finally she gave up and put the novel in a drawer.

When she was approached about *Blindsight* years later, after Morgan S. Brilliant found a copy in the files at Ace Books, Butler asked Brilliant to destroy the copy they had found. By that point, Octavia was done with the book, cannibalizing elements for later works like Xenogenesis and the Parables, and happy to let the rest of the idea die. 'I don't know whether there is a copy in her papers,' Brilliant once wrote me in an email, when she heard I was working on a project in the Butler archives. 'If so, I ask that you please respect her wishes regarding *Blindsight*.' I have no say in this, no connection with or control over the estate – but even so Brilliant's call to respect Butler's wishes has stuck with me. I thought about it a lot while working on the book, trying to honor it, and have thought about it a lot since. Undoubtedly, the call for deference has a certain obvious and even undeniable ethical power. But in the end I can't agree. I'd ask the literary estate to publish *Blindsight* too – give us back the black sheep of her completed novels, give us an unlucky thirteen, a baker's dozen. It's good; it's interesting; it's *an Octavia Butler novel* – people should see it.

I hope the literary estate can come to the conclusion that we actually honor Octavia's now-central place in the canon of twentieth-century literature by disrespecting her and her wishes in this respect. The literary world is filled with great writers whose last books were never burned by their heirs, like they had asked and like the heirs had promised; it happens so much it's practically a cliché. After ten years without her, I don't think we should keep that promise to Butler either. We can't afford to leave so much fascinating and vital material chained up. We owe it to Octavia now to disrespect her, and let it out.

Ruth Salvaggio

This essay originally appeared in *Black American Literature Forum,* Volume 18, Number 2 (Summer, 1984). Salvaggio argues that 'Butler's concern with racism and sexism is a conscious part of her vision.' Salvaggio focuses particularly on the various women in Butler's Patternmaster series, and the ways in which they deal with slavery, marriage, sexism and racism.

Octavia Butler and the Black Science-Fiction Heroine

A traditional complaint about science fiction is that it is a male genre, dominated by male authors who create male heroes who control distinctly masculine worlds. In the last decade, however, a number of women writers have been changing that typical scenario. Their feminine and feminist perspectives give us a different kind of science fiction, perhaps best described by Pamela Sargent's term 'Women of Wonder'.[1] In a sense, Octavia Butler's science fiction is a part of that new scenario, featuring strong female protagonists who shape the course of social events. Yet in another sense, what Butler has to offer is something very different. Her heroines are black women who inhabit racially mixed societies. Inevitably, the situations these women confront involve the dynamic interplay of race and sex in futuristic worlds. How a feminist science-fiction character responds to a male-dominated world is one thing; how Butler's black heroines respond to racist and sexist worlds is quite another.

Butler's concern with racism and sexism is a conscious part

of her vision. As she herself explains, a particularly 'insidious problem' with science fiction is that it 'has always been nearly all white, just as until recently, it's been nearly all male.'[2] Confronting this 'problem' head-on, Butler places her heroines in worlds filled with racial and sexual obstacles, forcing her characters to survive and eventually overcome these societal barriers to their independence. Sometimes her black heroines are paired with white men who challenge their abilities; sometimes they are paired with powerful black men who threaten their very autonomy and existence. And, always, the society in which they live constantly reminds them of barriers to their independence. Tracing the plight of each heroine is like following different variations on a single theme, the yearning for independence and autonomy. That Butler's women, despite all odds, achieve that autonomy makes her science fiction a fresh and different contribution to the genre, and makes Butler herself an exciting new voice in the traditional domains of science fiction, feminism, and black literature.

This article is intended to introduce Octavia Butler through her science-fiction heroines – beginning with the defiant Amber in *Patternmaster* (1976), then moving to the confused but powerful Mary in *Mind of My Mind* (1977) and the compromising Alanna in *Survivor* (1978).[3] The heroine I leave until last is one we encounter as the old woman Emma, hovering in the background of *Mind of My Mind*. She later appears as Anyanwu in Butler's most recent science-fiction novel, *Wild Seed* (1980).[4] In Anyanwu we discover the inspiring force for all of Butler's heroines. And in *Wild Seed* we discover dimensions of Butler's fictive world – not the typical feminist utopia, but a flawed world in which racially and sexually oppressed individuals negotiate their way through a variety of personal and societal barriers.

Germain Greer's term 'obstacle race' seems particularly appropriate when discussing Butler and her fiction, largely because the women discussed in both situations confront peculiarly social obstacles. Just as women artists, according to Greer, should be seen 'as members of a group having much in common, tormented by the same conflicts of motivation and the same practical difficulties, the obstacles both external and surmountable, internal and insurmountable of the race for achievement,' [5] so Butler's heroines share in this social and personal struggle for assertion and understanding.

Their particular struggle, however, is accentuated by the extraordinary mental facilities they possess: each of Butler's four science-fiction novels is built around a society of telepaths linked to each other through a mental 'pattern.' Thus when Anyanwu, the African woman in *Wild Seed*, is transported on a slave ship to colonial America, she senses the horror of slavery well before she actually witnesses its real-life horrors. Or when Mary, in *Mind of My Mind*, ultimately confronts her oppressive father, she kills him through the machinations of a gruesome mental war game. The violence that accompanies such racial and sexual conflict rarely centers on women in the way that it does in Butler's novels. Here we have females who must take the kind of action normally reserved for white, male protagonists. White males, curiously, play an important role in Butler's fiction – sometimes as enemies, sometimes as foils to the women. We might begin with a discussion of them in Butler's first novel, *Patternmaster*. There they dominate the plot until, as one female science-fiction writer describes in a different context, 'a woman appeared.' [6] Let us begin, then, with the traditional science-fiction plot, and the sudden intrusion of a woman.

It should not be surprising that *Patternmaster*, Butler's first novel, revolves around that typical science-fiction plot: it employs two of the most traditional mythic structures – the inheritance of sons and the journey motif. Rayal, the Patternmaster, is dying; his two sons, Coransee and Teray, vie for control of the Pattern. This rivalry of sons for possession of the father's empire follows the outlines of an archetypal literary construct: Coransee, the stronger and more obvious heir, is defeated by the young and inconspicuous Teray, who ultimately proves himself – despite all outward appearances – to be the righteous heir. Ostensibly, then, *Patternmaster* is a novel which presents us with a 'good-son' hero. We are glad when the honest Teray defeats his sinister sibling; we are glad that this decent young man has overcome the corruption and power lust of the older brother.

But all this is not really what *Patternmaster* is about. Before the adventures of our hero begin to unfold, our heroine appears – Amber. The circumstances of her appearance are just as curious as she is. Teray, captive in his brother's household, calls for a 'healer' to treat a woman who has been beaten by a man. Enter Amber – a Patternist with extraordinary mental abilities to mend the human body. Immediately, her strong-minded, judgmental character emerges, and before long she and Teray, both captives in Coransee's household, plot to escape.

The story of their escape, their quest for freedom, now begins to change the typical 'quest' motif that defines so much science fiction. For one thing, Teray soon realizes that he cannot physically survive their journey without Amber's healing powers – she may, in fact, be more physically powerful than Teray himself. For another, the fascinating relationship between hero and heroine overthrows all of our expectations about conventional romantic and/or sexual love. Because Teray is white and Amber black, their relationship continually reminds us of racial distinctions. And because Amber is a woman who refuses to act out traditional female roles (she will not be any man's wife, she is sexually androgynous, she is stronger and more independent than most men), their relationship continually highlights sexual and feminist issues.

Racism and sexism, then, are matters fundamental to an under-standing of both plot and character. Coransee's household, for instance, is hierarchically structured so that those who possess power necessarily abuse those who are powerless: 'Housemasters' control 'Outsiders' who control 'Mutes.' In this futuristic mental society in which people have the ability to comprehend each other's thoughts, mental understanding gives way to mind control and ultimately mental oppression. The great 'Pattern' itself – holding forth the promise of a mentally-unified culture which might use its combined intellectual powers for human advancement – instead has become the prize for Machiavellian power seekers. No wonder Butler continually uses the term 'slavery' to describe the 'mental leashes' which keep this society in its state of oppression.

Though Teray, the good son destined to inherit the Pattern, is the figure in whom we must place our trust and hope, it is Amber who most dramatically personifies independence, autonomy, and liberation. Forced, as a captive in Coransee's household, to be one of his 'women,' she nonetheless boasts, 'But I'm not one of his wives ... I'm an independent' (ch. 3).[7] Asked by Teray, whom she truly does come to love, to be his wife, she refuses, 'Because I want the same thing you want. My House. Mine' (ch. 6). Discussing with Teray her former sexual relationship with another woman, she explains, 'When I meet a woman who attracts me, I prefer women ... And when I meet a man who attracts me, I prefer men' (ch. 6). This is clearly not your typical romance heroine. This is certainly not your typical science-fiction heroine. Ironically, *Patternmaster* makes Amber out to be the perfect prize for two rival brothers. Instead, this 'golden brown woman with hair that was a cap of small, tight black curls' (ch. 3) turns out to be a model of independence and autonomy.

All ends well in *Patternmaster*. Teray and Amber, with their combined powers, defeat Coransee. And Teray, as the good son, will inherit the Pattern. But it is Amber who somehow stands out as having transcended this political war of wits. In a final exchange between Amber and Teray, she reminds him of how easily she can tip the scales of power. Teray's response is filled with respect, but tinged with fear: 'Not for the first time, he realized what a really dangerous woman she could be. If he could not make her his wife, he would be wise to make her at least an ally' (ch. 9).

All of Butler's heroines are dangerous women. Perhaps the most conspicuously dangerous is Mary who, in *Mind of My Mind*, has a tremendous potential for destruction. Perhaps the least conspicuously dangerous is Alanna who, in *Survivor*, exerts a subtle but radical influence on a foreign society which she and her parents have colonized. Mary and Alanna, both young black women, sport two very different types of feminism: Mary, a confused and disoriented child raised in the slums of twentieth-century Los Angeles, eventually becomes the leader of a mental empire; Alanna, an orphan in a futuristic Earth society, becomes a unifying force on a foreign planet inhabited by warring tribes. Mary must fight with and ultimately kill her father to achieve 'freedom'; Alanna must reject the Christian beliefs of her parents to bring peace and respectability to her new culture. Mary is forced to marry a white man in order to establish and control her mental empire; Alanna chooses to marry the leader of a non-human tribe in order to survive and establish a home on a new planet. Whereas Mary learns to control and dominate, Alanna learns to compromise and survive. In these two women, we discover that the source of female strength can foster very different kinds of feminist power – and very different kinds of human response.

Mary's appeal derives from her brute force. Even as a child, she becomes conditioned to life in a sexist and violent world. The novel opens with threats of male aggression:

> 'I was in my bedroom reading a novel when somebody came banging on the door really loud, like the police. I thought it was the police until I got up, looking out the window, and saw one of Rina's johns standing there. I wouldn't have bothered to answer, but the fool was kicking at the door like he wanted to break it in. I went to the kitchen and got one of our small cast-iron skillets – the size just big enough to hold two eggs. Then I went to the door. The stupid bastard was drunk.'

This same young girl who almost kills one of her mother's 'johns' will end up killing her father, a man who forced her to have sex with him and who tries to control her mental powers. Not surprisingly, Mary's opinion of men is filled with bitterness. When her father forces her to marry Karl Larkin, a white man, she can only smirk and reflect how much 'Karl looked like one of the bright, ambitious, bookish white guys from high school' (ch. 2). When she later questions Karl about their racial difference, her suspicions about his character prove correct: 'How do you feel about black people?' she asks him, only to hear him reply, 'You've seen my cook' (ch. 2).

Such racial differences call attention to other forms of

enslavement in *Mind of My Mind*. When Doro, Mary's father, tries to explain the nature of 'Mutes' to the old woman Emma, she snaps back: 'I know what you mean, Doro. I knew the first time I heard Mary use it. It means nigger!' (ch. 9) Unlike her father, however, Mary comes to sympathize with the people under her mental control. When she kills Doro, patriarchical domination becomes maternal caring. Having the potential for destructive power thrust upon her, Mary learns to control that power, to use it wisely and cautiously. She is Butler's study in brute feminist force.

Alanna's appeal derives from her steadfast character, from intense psychological control and determination. Unlike Mary, Alanna possesses no extraordinary mental abilities. She is Butler's study in the power of human endurance. Instead of combating violence with violence, Alanna accepts the social obstacles which a foreign society imposes on her. Her object is to learn to survive among these obstacles, to accommodate to a culture that is far from perfect.

The most potent of these obstacles is the addictive drug meklah, a drug so powerful that withdrawal from it almost always proves fatal. Forced into addiction, Alanna not only survives withdrawal but also survives as a prisoner taken by one of the warring tribes. Living among this 'Tehkohn' group, she confronts and learns to deal with even more obstacles: She proves herself to be a strong huntress (a mark of distinction in Tehkohn culture) and a loyal follower of Tehkohn customs. Ultimately, she marries the leader of the tribe and has their child.

Marriage is often a feminist issue in Butler's novels. Amber in *Patternmaster* refuses marriage; Mary in *Mind of My Mind* is forced to marry. Alanna's marriage to a non-human creature ironically turns out to be the most successful and respectable of all these marriage situations. Her joining with the Tehkohn leader at once liberates her from the enslaving Christianity of her missionary parents and the enslavement of the meklah drug. Moreover, it offers her the promise of establishing a home with people she has come to respect and love. Perhaps the most bitter irony of the novel is that the Christian earthlings, who call their new home 'Canaan,' cannot accept the marriage of their daughter into a tribe that will offer them their only hope of peaceful existence.

The Christian religion is depicted as notably racist in *Survivor*. As a young, wild black girl, Alanna is adopted by white parents and grows up in a world in which her color is always suspect. On one occasion, a Missionary suggests that Alanna would surely 'be happier with her own kind' since, after all, 'the girl isn't white' (ch. 3). When Alanna later asks her mother about this incident, she learns 'for the first time how important some Missionaries believed their own coloring to be' (ch. 3). Color, in fact, turns out to be one of the major motifs in the novel. The Kohn creatures display a variety of colors as their moods and emotions change: they are gray in sobriety, white in amusement, bright yellow in anger. Their color also indicates hierarchical structure. Only a few of them, for instance, possess the blue, a sign of honor and power. Yet these colorful, non-human creatures show none of the racial bigotry associated with the Christian Missionaries. Ironically, Alanna's parents can laughingly dismiss the fear that their 'black' daughter might mix with 'whites,' but are repulsed when that same daughter marries the honorable 'blue' Tehkohn leader.

As a strong-minded black woman, Alanna submits to a surprising number of social restraints: first to the Christian Missionary code, then to the meklah drug, and finally to imprisonment by the Tehkohn tribe. But in her submission she discovers a source of strength. She learns, as Mary had learned, about herself – and about the different roles she has had to play in order to survive. We see in her an amazing capacity to compromise. Alanna's flexibility allows her to meander around some obstacles, and make other apparent obstacles into real avenues of liberation.

This ability to compromise and survive is what characterizes Butler's most fully-developed and intriguing heroine – Anyanwu in *Wild Seed*. Though all of Butler's protagonists are black, only Anyanwu is born in Africa. Both her African origin and her feminist determination give us every reason to think of her as the ancestress of Amber, Mary, Alanna, and the host of other prominent black women in Butler's fiction. Just as *Wild Seed*, by tracing the origins of Patternist society back to seventeenth-century Africa, provides a foundation for all four of the Patternist science-fiction novels, so does Anyanwu help to explain the yearning for independence and autonomy sought by Amber, Mary, and Alanna.

Before discussing Anyanwu as the character central to Butler's fiction, let me outline briefly the structure and plot of *Wild Seed* to show just how encompassing the novel is – in terms of both the time and space its characters inhabit.

The story spans two continents and nearly two centuries. Meeting in Africa in 1690, Anyanwu and Doro – female and male who have the potential to live forever – travel via slave ship to colonial New England. There Doro, a patriarchal dictator who aspires to breed a race of superhumans such as himself, exploits Anyanwu's abilities as a healer to propagate and maintain his small but growing empire. At first taken in by Doro's mystique, Anyanwu soon comes to realize that she is principally to serve as his breeder and slave. Forced to marry one of Doro's sons, she not only must partake in his animalistic breeding experiments, but must painfully endure their often tragic consequences. After her husband's death, she escapes from the New England colony. In 1840, Doro finds her on a plantation in Louisiana. There, in very real slave territory, Anyanwu has established her own free household only to have it invaded and controlled by Doro. After several of Anyanwu's children meet their deaths because of Doro's intrusion, Anyanwu decides that her only possible escape from his oppression is her own death. When she vows to commit suicide, however, Doro realizes how much the loss of Anyanwu would mean to him. Deprived of his only immortal compatriot, he would be doomed to face eternity alone. But more than that, he would lose the only effective humanizing force in his life. Their reconciliation at the end of the novel brings to a tenuous resolution over a hundred years of intense personal conflict. The ending of this novel, however, is actually the beginning of Butler's three previous novels, since in it we discover the origins of Patternist society.

We might best understand Anyanwu by appreciating the fundamental opposition between her and Doro. Both characters, for instance, are potentially immortal, but their means for achieving this immortality are strikingly different. Doro is a vampire-like figure who must continually kill people and assume their bodies in order to live. Anyanwu is a healer; instead of killing others, she rejuvenates herself. In this sense, she is the direct prototype of Amber in *Patternmaster*. Just as Teray, in that futuristic novel, could not possibly survive without Amber's healing abilities, so the superhuman Doro immediately recognizes in Anyanwu's talents a means to secure his superrace. For all Doro's control over his life and the lives of others, he is necessarily restricted in the physical forms he can assume. True, he may invade other bodies, but the constraints of those bodies are a given. Anyanwu's powers allow far more flexibility and agility: In changing the physical construct of her own body, she can transform herself into various kinds of creatures – both human and non-human. On the slave ship, for instance, when one of Doro's sons tries to rape her, Anyanwu fantastically transforms herself into a leopard and mauls her assailant to his violent death. She also possesses the ability to change from youth to old age back to youth. She may even change her sex, and on one particular occasion when she does so, Anyanwu once again becomes a prototype of Amber – this time by virtue of her androgyny.

The very physical characteristics of Anyanwu, then, highlight her distinguishing qualities. She is flexible and dexterous, compared to Doro's stiffness and dominance. She uses prowess rather than direct, confrontational power. She heals rather than kills, and kills only by assuming a different form and only when she or her children are assaulted. In Anyanwu, we find a woman who – despite her imprisonment by a patriarchal tyrant – learns to use her abilities to survive. In this sense, she is most obviously the prototype of another of Butler's heroines Alanna in *Survivor*.

The marriage motif in Butler's novels, which I have commented on earlier, is also crystalized in Anyanwu – not only through her willingness to accept husbands forced upon her by Doro, but ultimately through her final reconciliation with Doro himself. Like both Amber and Mary, Anyanwu has a defiant attitude about marriage, and particularly like Mary in *Mind of My Mind*, she initially refuses to marry a white man whom Doro has chosen for her. Defiance, however, soon gives way to acceptance – and it is here, once again, that Anyanwu closely resembles Alanna, accepting the constraints of her world and trying to make something decent and productive out of the indecent situation in which she finds herself. Left on her own, without Doro's scheming intrusions, Anyanwu is able to produce and raise children possessed of both superior powers and tremendous human warmth. Her aim is to have children who may live with her, not die after a normal life span and leave her to her loneliness. Doro's paternal concerns revolve around his mechanical breeding experiments: He does not create children, but Frankenstein monsters. Anyanwu's maternity, however, is the main source of her being, the principal reason for her existence. As she explains, 'I could have husbands and wives and lovers into the next century and never have a child. Why should I have so many except that I want them and love them?' (ch. 13).

It is this kind of maternal generosity that will finally save Doro. Anyanwu, repulsed by Doro's inhumanity and his enslavement of the very superrace he has fathered, can all too easily kill herself. She can at least escape oppression through death. When Doro asks her why she has decided to die, Anyanwu explains her dilemma: '"It's the only way I can leave you ... Everything is temporary but you and me. You are all I have, perhaps all I would ever have.' She shook her head slowly. 'And you are an obscenity'" (ch. 14).

It is tempting to think that Doro pleads for Anyanwu to live not out of selfishness but out of love. We want to believe that, confronted with the possibility of her death, he comes to understand the most important aspect of life – human companionship. Perhaps this is so. Perhaps, however, Anyanwu decides to live not because she is suddenly convinced of Doro's humanity but because she at least sees some hope for a more humane future with him. If Anyanwu lives, she at least has the chance to save their children from Doro's oppression and save the two of them from eternal loneliness. It is the promise of human companionship that finally touches her. When Anyanwu chooses life, in spite of all the horrors which her relationship with Doro has produced and may still continue to produce, she is acting out of generosity both for their children and for him. Her decision reflects the courage and generosity that is in all of Butler's heroines.

Anyanwu is the great African ancestress. She encompasses and epitomizes defiance, acceptance, compromise, determination, and courage. Her personal goal is freedom, but given the obstacles that constantly prevent her from achieving that goal, she learns to make advancements through concessions. By finding her way through that great obstacle course, she is able to bring her best qualities – healing and loving – to a world that would otherwise be intolerable.

Butler's heroines, as I have been trying to show, can tell us much about her science fiction precisely because they are the very core of that fiction. These novels are about survival and power, about black women who must face tremendous societal constraints. We might very well expect them to be rebellious. We might expect them to reverse the typical male science-fiction stereotype and replace male tyranny with female tyranny. This does not happen. Though Butler's heroines are dangerous and powerful women, their goal is not power. They are heroines not because they conquer the world, but because they conquer the very notion of tyranny.

They are, as well, portraits of a different kind of feminism. Amber has the chance to marry the great Patternmaster; instead, she prefers her independence. Mary can easily become an awesome tyrant; instead, she matures into a caring mother. And Alanna, who possesses no extraordinary Patternist powers, learns to survive through accommodation rather than conflict. That very willingness to accommodate and compromise is what allows Anyanwu to endure over a century of oppressive patriarchy. At the end of each novel, we somehow get the impression that the victory of these women, though far from attained, is somehow pending. White men control the war, while black women fight a very different battle.

[1] Sargent has edited several volumes of this new fiction, initiated by her collection *Women of Wonder: Science Fiction Stories by Women about Women* (New York: Vintage, 1975). Two recent critical studies of female/feminist science fiction are Marleen S. Barr, ed., *Future Critical Anthology* (Bowling Green, OH: Bowling Green State Univ. Popular Press, 1981), and Tom Staicar, ed., *The Feminine Eye: Science Fiction and the Women Who Write It* (New York: Frederick Ungar, 1982). Barr's anthology contains a checklist, compiled by Roger Schlobin, of women science-fiction writers.

[2] 'Lost Races of Science Fiction,' *Transmission*, Summer 1980, pp. 17-18.

[3] For a good introduction to Butler's first three science-fiction novels, see Frances Smith Foster, 'Octavia Butler's Black Female Future Fiction,' *Extrapolation*, 23 (1982), 37-49. My own study guide to Butler, focusing on her four science-fiction novels and *Kindred*, a mainstream/fantasy novel, is forthcoming this year in *The Reader's Guide to Charnas, Butler, and Vinge*, co-authored with Marleen S. Barr and Richard Law (Starmont House).

[4] *Clay's Ark* was yet to be published at the time this manuscript was submitted (ed.'s note).

[5] *The Obstacle Race: The Fortunes of Women Painters and Their Work* (New York: Farrar, Straus & Giroux, 1979), p. 6.

[6] The term was used by Suzy McKee Charnas in her essay of that title, published in *Future Females*, pp. 103-108.

[7] Butler's four science-fiction novels to date were originally published by Doubleday, but have since appeared in paperback editions. For convenience, I refer to chapter numbers rather than page numbers when quoting from the texts.

Sandra Y. Govan

This essay originally appeared in *Black American Literature Forum*, Volume 18, Number 2 (1984). Sandra Govan powerfully explores the connections between the main female characters of the Patternmaster series – the way they deal with powerful male characters, their surroundings, and how they relate to one another. Govan also extends this ideas of 'connections' to Dana, in *Kindred*.

Connections, Links, and Extended Networks: Patterns in Octavia Butler's Science Fiction

'He was suddenly able to see the members of the Pattern not as starlike parts of light but as luminescent threads. He could see where the threads wound together into slender cords, into ropes, into great cables. He could see where they joined, where they coiled and twisted together to form a vast sphere of brilliance, a core of light that was like a sun formed of many suns. That core where all the people came together was Rayal.'[1]

Nearing Forsyth, ancestral home of all Patternists, Teray, the second most powerful son of Patternmaster Rayal and destined to become the Patternmaster, has just had an epiphany. He has recognized precisely the way in which all Patternists, the powerful psionically enhanced mutant humans of a future Earth society, are linked to each other through the Pattern. Science-fiction fans and discriminating others discovering and savoring Octavia

Butler's full canon may experience a revelation similar to Teray's. The four published novels of the Patternist saga – *Patternmaster* (1976), *Mind of My Mind* (1977), *Survivor* (1978), and *Wild Seed* (1980) – the projected *Clay's Ark* (publication scheduled for March 1984), and *Kindred* (1979), an ostensibly mainstream fiction outside the series, are all connected, and not simply by story line. To paraphrase Teray's revelation, the core at which all comes together in Butler's universe is the delineation of power. 'I began writing about power,' Butler has said, 'because I had so little.'[2] Her fascination with the politics of power encouraged her to 'imagine new ways of thinking about people and power' and gave her license to place her characters into adversarial situations which challenged their bid for control or authority in alternative speculative societies in which 'men and women [were] honestly considered equal ... where people [did] not despise each other because of race or religion, class or ethnic origin.'[3] Janice Bogstad has argued that, specifically, *Mind of My Mind* and *Patternmaster* 'can be characterized in terms of power relationships and their effects on individual existence of very normal people [whereas] *Survivor* is more about the establishment of a power equilibrium'[4]; similar modes are operative in *Wild Seed* and *Kindred*.

Power, then, is clearly at the center of Butler's novels. But illuminating that central core are the threads, cords, ropes, and cables wrapped around it. Power relationships are detailed by the pattern of conflicts animating Butler's characters; by their distinctive markings, especially those of her women; by the shaped plots and structural devices; and by the shared thematic concerns connecting all the novels.

In each of the published novels, the implicit struggle for power revolves around explicit conflicts of will and the contests of survival a heroine endures. The struggle of Anyanwu, a three-hundred-year-old Onitsha priestess of the Igbo people, against the domination of Doro, a four-thousand-year-old Nubian with the awesome power of instantaneous transmigration of his psychic essence, illustrates these tests. Doro and Anyanwu first come together in *Wild Seed*, the 'prequel' to the Patternist saga. They are seeming immortals, and each is powerful, though their respective powers, drives, and goals are different. Both are mutants. Although Doro is not a telepath, he can sense and 'track' people who have latent or nascent psychic gifts, those who are the witches or outcasts of their own kind. According to Butler, he is attracted to these people and encourages their reproduction because 'he enjoys their company and, sadly, because they provide his most satisfying kills.'[5] Within her community, Anyanwu's power is so omnipresent that several times during her 'various youths,' villagers have mistakenly accused her of witchcraft. Not a witch, Anyanwu serves and enriches her people as an oracle and, occasionally, a god.[6] Anyanwu is also a regenerative healer and a shape-shifter who can analyze and alter her skeletal, bio-chemical, and cellular structure.

Although she has lived as a powerful, feared, and respected independent woman in her community for generations, Anyanwu, to Doro, is only potentially valuable 'wild seed,' an offshoot from his well-nurtured, carefully husbanded, seed communities of mutant families. Initially, he wants her with him to add her genes to his breeding stock because her power is a factor he covets. Her longevity, her special healing abilities, and her physical strength can strengthen immeasurably 'any line he bred her into.'[7] Ironically, their destined linkage has been foreshadowed by their names: 'As though,' Anyanwu says, 'we were intended to meet.' Doro means 'the east – the direction from which the sun comes,' and Anyanwu means 'the sun' (WS, pp. 12-13). Once he has seen what Anyanwu has to contribute, Doro is determined to entice her away from her village and to one of his New World communities. He has already begun the selective breeding process in an effort to build outcasts 'into a strong new people' (WS, p. 22). Butler adds that, at this point, Doro is building his colonies to 'amuse himself. He seeks to create more benign versions of himself – the closest he can hope to come to true progeny. He assures the availability of congenial, controllable companions, and, he breeds food.'[8] Although he early lays the foundations, Doro's serious interest in race building (eventually he will found a superior race of psychically sensitive human beings bred for their prowess with telepathy, telekinesis, psychometry, and the ability to perform regenerative healing) comes later. For now, he wants to persuade Anyanwu to join him and so makes veiled threats against the safety of her many children while offering as an inducement the idea that she should be with her 'own kind' and that, someday, he will show her children 'she will never have to bury … A mother,' he says, 'should not have to watch her children grow old and die. If you live, they should live … Let me give you children who will live!' (WS, p. 26). An almost satanic manipulator, Doro has decided he must have the use of Anyanwu; when her usefulness is finished, he will kill her.

Anyanwu, however, thwarts Doro's design on her life because of her survival skills (when she takes the form of a bird or beast, he cannot track her) and her strength of will. His is the more terrible power; he kills instantaneously whenever he takes a host body. But hers is the nurturing healing power of the archetypal earth mother. Doro can maintain his life-force indefinitely by transferring from host to host; but, he will eventually be living, as a son warned, alienated and alone, with only a vestige of humanity left. Butler argues that it is not the 'changing that diminishes him; it is the need to regard humans as food. It is the fact that everyone dies and leaves him (until Anyanwu). It is the reality that no matter what he does, *he cannot die*.'[9] A century passes before Doro recognizes his vulnerability, before he knows the reason that he cannot simply take Anyanwu's life or take for granted her submission to his will. They are not, nor will they ever be, *alike*; but they do complement one another. Without Anyanwu there is no pleasure, no companionship, no one with whom to share his long life. Finally, sickened by his insensitivity, by his gross gratification of his immediate needs whatever the costs to others, Anyanwu moves to sever their linkage by taking her own life. Her resolve makes Doro reckon with a will he cannot control. Anyanwu forces him to recognize love, to reveal love; through love, she forces him to change.[10] He cannot stop killing, but he will be more selective. He will not kill her close relatives, and he will cease the casual killing of those who have served him best when their 'usefulness' has ended. Anyanwu makes Doro salvage what humanity he has remaining, and that is no small victory.

Neither the historical framing nor the extended chronological movement in *Wild Seed* are particularly new structural devices in science fiction. Butler's innovation comes with setting and character; it comes with the movement of black characters through time, coupled to travel through Africa and to locales central to the African diaspora. Science fiction as genre has seldom evoked an authentic African setting or employed non-stereotypical blacks as characters. (Robert Heinlein's *Farnham's Freehold* [1964] and Ray Bradbury's 'Way Up in the Middle of the Air' [1950] offer noteworthy examples.[11]) In a recent essay Butler exposes what has been the rule of thumb for science-fiction writers: They were (are?) told not to use 'any black characters … unless those characters' blackness was somehow essential to the plot.' The argument alleged that 'the presence of blacks … changed the focus of the story – drew attention away from the intended subject.' [12]

Doro's machinations are raceless. He will take any 'host,' black or white, young or old, male or female; yet, neither his nor Anyanwu's racial heritage is mere fluff. They are a black Adam and Eve, and those whom they beget shall themselves beget a new race. In the meantime, Butler's artfully didactic sketches of seventeenth-century West African cultural history and social anthropology (one can see the influence of Chinua Achebe's *Things Fall Apart* and hear the echoes of Aye Armah's *2000 Seasons*[13]) are important because they illustrate the longevity, continuity, and richness of African civilization; they also give us a present context, and they foreshadow the structural basis of the Patternist society to come. Anyanwu's voice has the deep intonations of the griot reciting the ancient history of the clan: 'We crossed [the Niger] long ago … Children born in that time have grown old and died. We were Ado and Idu, subject to Benin before the crossing. Then we fought with Benin and crossed the river to Onitsha to become free people, our own masters' (*WS*, p. 14). Patternists centuries removed from Anyanwu's village will find themselves repeating this cycle. The significance of the initial setting is also that we witness the repetitive brutality of the internal and external slave trade, and we see some portion of the horrors of the Middle Passage. These are icons shabbily treated in most science-fiction texts, if they appear at all.

Whether we focus on Wheatley,[14] the eighteenth-century New England 'seed' village Doro brings Anyanwu to, or the nineteenth-century ante-bellum Louisiana plantation Anyanwu creates and manages, through time shifts and the replication of each historically definite place, we ingest a wealth of historical and anthropological data which utilizes an Afro-centric point of view. The kinship networks that strengthened family ties in West African society survived the Middle Passage and are brought to the New World. Both Doro and Anyanwu use the kinship social model as each collects his/her people, black and white, into vast extended families linked by blood, by psionic ability, and by their difference from the world outside their sheltered communities. The cultural norms of the age occasionally raise the specter of racial discord within the family group; but, in the controlled environments which Doro oversees, racial prejudice is not tolerated. Genes and bloodlines are important not as they bear on race or sex but as they bear on the development of psychic identity, on the enhancement of psionic talent.

Generations later, the key to that ultimate enhancement lies in Doro's daughter Mary, the twentieth-century heroine of *Mind of My Mind*. Mary is a direct descendant of Anyanwu, now called Emma (meaning grandmother or ancestress as her private joke). Like Emma, Mary is a survivor and a fighter; like Emma, she possesses a unique potential Doro wants. And like Emma, she is a woman Doro underestimates.

Rather than using history or anthropology to tell Mary's story, Butler uses contemporary sociology. The abused child of a latent mother, Mary undergoes 'transition,' the rite of passage from the intense suffering imposed by unrestrained latent psionic ability (pre-transition telepaths cannot shield themselves against the reception of anyone else's emotional or physical pain) to 'active' adult. When she emerges from transition, she emerges in total control of the six most powerful telepaths, having linked them all in an unbreakable telepathic union. Mary is the center of their newly formed 'pattern' and is the genesis, the mother, of the new race Doro has worked toward. Mary and the members of her Pattern form a 'family,' the 'First Family.' Gradually, they move more and more people from latent to active, extending the family, creating new families, and thus building the Patternists' hierarchical structure; they save the latents suffering and anguish while augmenting the power of the Pattern. Mary's growing power forces the inevitable confrontation with Doro, her father (whom she has loved as child and lover) and now the 'grandfather' of the Patternists; she has not relished the contest of wills, but, like Emma/Anyanwu, Mary cannot passively submit and allow Doro to destroy her as he has in the past destroyed uncontrollable, errant 'experiments.' Mary and Doro are alike because they both need the life force of others for sustenance; but Doro is, in effect, a vampire, and Mary is 'a symbiont, a being living in partnership with her people. She gave them unity, they fed her, and both thrived. She was not a parasite ... And though she had great power, she was not naturally, instinctively, a killer. He was.'[15] Despite Doro's killer instinct, and knowing what his victory would do to her people, Mary survives Doro's attempt to 'take' her, and, drawing on the combined power of all her Patternists, she snares him within the Pattern and destroys him.

Mary's 'difference' – that she is the symbiont, not the vampire – is what saves her from Doro. Difference is what initially draws Doro to Anyanwu in *Wild Seed*. *Patternmaster*'s Amber is forced into a nomadic life outside the typical structure of Patternist society because she rejects a would-be suitor. Alanna, the Afro-Asian heroine of *Survivor*, has the hostile attention of three

---

separate social groups examining her, questioning her loyalties, because of her racial, social, and presumed biological differences. And an undefined 'difference' in Dana, *Kindred*'s heroine, links her to the activities of her distant ancestors – a white slave owner and the slave he rapes. Difference, adaptability, change, and survival are thematic threads connecting Butler's books as tightly as the first pattern held by Mary linked the Patternists.

Each of Butler's heroines is a strong protagonist paired with, or matched against, an equally powerful male. This juxtaposition subtly illustrates differences in feminine/masculine values, differences in approaches to or conceptions of power, differences in the capacity to recognize and exercise social or personal responsibility. In each story, a physical, psychic, or attitudinal difference associated with the heroine sets her apart from society and often places her in jeopardy; each survives because her 'difference' brings with it a greater faculty for constructive change.

Emma/Anyanwu coexisted with Doro, discovering his strength and learning how to challenge him, through her ability to adapt. In her long life, she weds many men, holds varied positions within a traditional African society, and moves fluidly from Old World to New and past to present, changing shape and relationships as circumstances warrant. Even her death is by her choice and expresses a refusal to adapt any further.

Mary, too, learns to adapt. In her pre-transition state, her survival depends on her ability to surmount the limitations of her environment. Strength of will keeps her from becoming the prostitute her mother was; bending her will to Doro's wishes keeps him from destroying her when she is vulnerable. Doro forces a marriage between Mary and one of his sons, his strongest telepath. Their union initially reinforces their differences: Mary is weak, black, and poor; her environment is riddled by chaotic, casual violence. Karl is strong, white, and wealthy; his lifestyle is orderly, restrained, and controlled. Mary and Karl clash, but unlike other telepaths whom Doro has forced together, they don't lose themselves by 'merging into each other uncontrollably,' nor do they try to kill each other to defend their individuality (*MMM*, p. 36). Until her transition, Mary compromises, and, though hostile, she copes with the forced alliance and even learns to appreciate it. After transition, Mary becomes the strongest telepath, and because of her power, she can bring mutually antagonistic people together for the first time, mitigating their natural antipathy. The 'difference' bred into her becomes her greatest asset; she adapts easily to controlling others and alters conditions for all of Doro's people, latent and active. With the creation of the Pattern, they become *her* people. Karl resists acknowledging the dramatic change in Mary's status, but she realizes early that the newly established, unbreakable Pattern 'represented power. Power that I had and that he would never have. And while that wasn't something I threw at him, ever, it wasn't something I denied either' (*MMM*, p. 187). Their forced liaison becomes a real marriage, and Karl, conscious not only of her power but also of her efforts to use it constructively to save rather than destroy, changes too. He becomes Mary's staunch supporter and ally.

    Patternmaster's Amber, a distant descendant of Emma/ Anyanwu, is an 'independent,' a migrant healer with no attachments to any particular House; thus, she is outside the semi-feudal hierarchical structure of the far future's Patternists. Though she is far more experienced, more sophisticated, and more ruthless than Teray, the novel's hero, she nevertheless joins him to escape Coransee, Teray's ambition-ridden brother, to go to Forsyth and the Patternmaster. Their journey is arduous. They must avoid other Patternists, as capture would mean return to Coransee; and they must avoid or kill Clayarks, mutated man-beasts who prey upon Patternists. Hostile environments are old for Amber. She has survived as an independent since her transition a few years after puberty. At the outset of the trek, Teray grudgingly acknowledges that it is Amber's survival skills which keep them alive. Eventually though, Amber is able to teach Teray some of her knowledge, and he proves an apt pupil. She teaches him about healing and, more importantly, about killing, quickly, like a healer, without draining all his psionic energy or the energy drawn from others he is linked to. Taking too much through the link can be fatal.

Teray and Amber are close to each other in the Pattern; they are compatible personalities. Frequently, they 'link' themselves to establish a conduit or canopy of instantaneous awareness and perception; if one senses danger, the other is immediately aware of it. The link also allows for the sharing of intimate personal thoughts and feelings, for the probing of both conscious and subconscious thoughts. Neither Amber nor Teray abuses the link's possibilities however; while it is more beneficial than a simple connection for protection, it binds neither of them. It does permit them to get to know each other – they respect each other, they grow to love each other, they conceive a child; yet, none of these facts sways Amber, a rather androgynous heroine, from her determination to establish her own House and be its master. Amber and Teray are allies at the start of their journey, and allies they will remain in a perfectly balanced complementary relationship. Patternmaster Rayal's benediction to the pair is that Amber will *'always be a better healer'* whereas Teray will always be a stronger healer; theirs is *'the right combination of abilities'* (P, p. 160).

Teray would not have survived his final battle with Coransee had he not taken heed of Amber, had he not learned from her. The heroine of *Survivor*, Alanna, does not have the same success with the Missionaries she tries to aid. Alanna's Missionaries are refugees from Earth. They are not Patternists but 'mutes' – in Patternist terms, humans without any psionic ability. They have fled an Earth virtually partitioned by Patternists as one kind of predator and Clayarks as another. They flee to their new world accompanied by Alanna, a human wild child whom they have captured, 'converted,' and adopted. Alanna's conversion to the Missionaries' theology (they believe their holy Mission is to 'preserve and to spread the sacred God-image of humankind,' to see a God figure only in the image of man[16]) is principally chameleon coloration. On Earth the orphaned girl, also psychically mute, had lived alone from the age of eight until she was fifteen by savage skill, stealth, and cunning. A hostile environment necessitated a vicious struggle for survival. Alanna fought and killed to stay alive; once among the Missionaries, though, she understood that she had to adopt their ways or be exiled back to the wild. Not surprisingly, Alanna's wilderness background has sharpened her perceptive ability and honed her instinct for potentially dangerous conflicts; she is easily the most astute member of the Missionary party.

When the Missionaries find themselves caught between the Garkohn and Tehkohn peoples (the Kohn peoples are large, fur-covered beings ranked by clans and activities according to the coloring in their fur), Alanna is the first to recognize the failings of the Missionaries' practice of cultural egoism, their refusal to learn alien ways, their refusal to accept differences. Alanna learns the language and the customs of both the Garkohn and the Tehkohn, and this enables her to become the Missionaries' emissary to the Tehkohn and permits her to enlist their aid. She is also able to expose Garkohn duplicity to the Missionaries. And, though it was not originally her intent, Alanna proves to the Missionaries that humankind may come in different shapes and textures and still be part of the human family. Outer differences pale to insignificance.

Alanna's strength is drawn from her own resources. Her wits are the product of an outsider's constant vigil. The force of her will can be measured by her determination to live, her determination to exact retribution for any wrong done to her. That had been Alanna's survival code until it was tempered by the Missionaries, and the code serves her again when she is captured by the Tehkohn, whom she lives among for two years. Alanna's status with the Tehkohn gradually changes from prisoner to partner, not because she betrays the Missionaries, but because she overcomes an immediate impulse to strike and allows herself to weigh differences, examine values, see merit, beauty, and strength in the cultural norms of others. Butler is able to establish her theme poignantly here because in *Survivor*, as in *Mind of My Mind*, the novel's point of view shifts. We move between Alanna and Diut, the Tehkohn leader, seeing what Alanna is learning and how she is being taught; in fact, we also have a sympathic omniscient narrator with our two participant narrators, enabling us to see more of the psychological spacing in the novel.

Alanna is not bound by Missionary prejudices (often directed at her because of her heritage and background), nor is she bound by Missionary traditions or conceits – all Kohn peoples are 'animals.' In fact, the Tehkohn hunt an animal related to them, but, unlike man and the great ape, they acknowledge their 'relative.' The Tehkohn have a structured society more egalitarian than the

Missionaries. Although Alanna is furless, once she has proven herself, she is accepted more easily among the Tehkohn than she had ever been among the Missionaries. When she confirms to the Verricks, her adoptive Missionary parents, that she has married and born a child by Diut, all the Missionaries, including the Verricks, reject her and, with her, the fact that crossbreeding between themselves and the Kohn is possible. They cannot tolerate the idea, and their intolerance forces them to deny fact rather than face it. At the novel's end, although Mrs. Verrick makes an effort to understand what has happened to her daughter, the Missionaries march off, seeking to start their Mission life afresh, isolated from Garkohn and Tehkohn. In doing so, they leave behind unacknowledged Garkohn-Missionary children and Alanna, who elects to remain with the Tehkohn where she is valued as a fighter, a judge, a wife, a survivor, and an individual.

Alanna's loyalty to the Missionaries rests on her sense of social responsibility and her sense of kinship, whereas in the more direct Patternist tales, social grouping is by family or house. In *Survivor*, despite dissension, the stubborn, bigoted Missionaries function as Alanna's family. Diut commands Alanna to try to make peace with the Verricks before they depart because, 'among the Kohn, a kinsman was a kinsman no matter how foolishly he behaved' (S, p. 184). She tries, but Jules Verrick's beliefs are too deeply entrenched.

Alanna's experience with the Missionaries, the energy she expends on behalf of recalcitrant kin, is roughly analogous to Dana's predicament in *Kindred*. But whereas Alanna is permitted to resolve her difficulties in a world whose order she understands, a world in which there is a support network broad enough to teach her and adopt her, Dana has no such advantages. She undergoes several harrowing experiences before she can begin to understand what has happened to her. And though she eventually comes to understand the what, she never does learn *why*.

Essentially, the plot of *Kindred* follows a twentieth-century black woman from California pulled mysteriously through time and space to early nineteenth-century Maryland, ancestral soil of her family tree. How Dana moves is undefined. An inexplicable psychic phenomenon links her life to that of a young white boy. Whenever Rufus, the child, is endangered, he can 'call' Dana to him for help. On her second rescue mission (once Dana saves a five-year-old Rufus from drowning; mere hours later, from her time reference, she saves an eight-year-old Rufus from a fire), Dana makes some startling discoveries. She finds herself in 1815 Maryland, a strange 'nigger' without 'papers' in a slave state. She discovers that Rufus is destined to become her ancestor, if he lives long enough to father the black woman who is to become Dana's great-great-grandmother. She also discovers the full ramifications of her peculiar situation – a twentieth-century black woman suddenly confronted by the chattel slavery system to find herself, like any other slave, a virtually powerless victim. She is at the mercy of white men – patrollers, overseers, or plantation owners – and white women; she has no freedom, no options, no rights any white person is bound to respect. Whatever happens to her during the time she is trapped in the past, actually happens. The whippings and beatings are painfully real, and the pain travels with her from past to present and back. She learns that, while Rufus can call her back, the catalyst which hurls her forward to her own time is the sincerity of her belief that her own life is in jeopardy. (There is a 'catch-22' with this time mechanism: The longer Dana lives on Rufus' plantation, the more she learns, empirically, about pain and suffering, and endurance despite pain. Once equipped with the knowledge that a brutal beating may not kill, her fear can no longer give impetus to her flight back to the twentieth century. She must struggle, like any other slave.) Time, for Dana, is subverted; she may lose seconds or minutes, later hours or weeks, out of her present life while time passes at its usual pace in the past.

Dana makes other discoveries as well. Try as she might, she is unable to teach the maturing Rufus enough about respect, responsibility, or compassion to prevent him from adopting the behavioral patterns of his class and race. She discovers firsthand the brutal effects of slavery on black and white alike. She learns that, to live in the past of her kin, she must find reservoirs of strength. Dana's movement through so alien a setting, yet one so palpably real, heightens the story's tension and our understanding of Dana's fear as she experiences the horror of her people's history.

Dana's problems appear all the more striking because they are cast as an anomaly in the fabric of authentic historic context, as opposed to distant, extrapolative, 'pretend' reality. Actually, however, the conflicts Dana surmounts are no more remarkable than those endured by thousands of slave women or those facing Butler's other heroines. Like all Butler's women, Dana is an outsider who must establish her own power base or personal territorial boundaries if she is not to be destroyed. Like the rest, she finds it a necessity either to adapt to the strange and unknown or to yield and die. Her survival skills and her determination to live are tested constantly. And, like Butler's other women, Dana's capacity to love and nurture is also examined (her relationship to Rufus and Alice suggests another archetypal earth mother image). A bittersweet irony tinctures her power to love. Though Anyanwu and Mary have known Doro in black and white hosts, and Mary becomes

Karl's wife, Dana's marriage to Kevin, a young white writer, must stand the test of disapproval in the present and denial in the past. Compounding the problem, while stranded in the past away from Kevin, Dana serves as both a mother figure to Rufus and, as the other half of a doppelgänger, the object of his sexual interest. Initially, she provides him only intellectual stimulation; Alice, her double, meets his physical needs. But when Alice, whom Rufus loves but cannot marry, kills herself, he transfers all of his attention to Dana, seeing her as 'the same woman' and, therefore, capable of fulfilling all his needs. Finally, Dana has the same acute sense of social responsibility that her sister heroines exhibit. Her attempts at reforming Rufus are for the good of the entire plantation, an enclosed community which is akin to the extended family structure. Like the others, too, Dana's battle is against tremendous odds, and she does not survive without paying heavy costs.

Though Butler denies that *Kindred* is in any way related to the Patternist novels,[17] one is tempted to see yet another connection binding Dana to Anyanwu, Mary, and Amber. The process by which Dana returns to Rufus remains unexplained, but the implicit suggestion is that they are linked by telepathic union; certainly they are linked by blood. Caring for family, however extended, is a theme that resonates consistently through all the novels.

To return to Teray's epiphany, the 'luminescent threads' binding Butler's books are probably far more numerous than those just cited. When looking at the novels, one invariably sees new links, new connections, new variations in the pattern. We could talk about Butler's feminist stance or about the mythic cast of her tales; we could talk about her androgynous characters, her characters as classic archetypes, or the unique status her characters have as coequal heroic partners. We could also, as Thelma S. Shinn has suggested, 'read Butler's fiction metaphorically ... turning inward to discover powers inherent in the self has sound psychological validity; so too does the unity Butler establishes between people through empathy and interdependence.' We could talk as well about Butler's sense of cultural nationalism or her brilliant adaptation of the classic slave narrative form in *Kindred* (Dana experiences slavery, witnesses brutal punishment, attempts escape, suffers betrayal and capture, experiences brutal punishment[19]) or her similar adaptation of the historical novel form for *Wild Seed*. The threads are ubiquitous. In my mind, it is signally important that we see Octavia Butler as an exceptional writer, as a strong black voice helping to forge a black presence in science fiction, and as a woman determined to weave from spangled cloth new patterns of her own design.

[1]   Octavia Butler, *Patternmaster* (1976; rpt. New York: Avon, 1979), p. 141. Subsequent references to this edition are included in the text.

[2]   Carolyn S. Davidson, 'The Science Fiction of Octavia Butler' *Sagala*, 2, No. 1 (1981), 35.

[3]   Quoted by Veronica Mixon in 'Futurist Woman: Octavia Butler,' *Essence*, 9 (Apr. 1979), 12.

[4]   'Octavia E. Butler and Power Relationships,' *Janus*, 4, No. 4 (Winter 1978-79), 28–29.

[5]   Letter to Sandra Y. Govan, 16 Jan. 1984.

[6]   Despite the accusations of the villagers, Butler maintains that Anyanwu is not a witch among her people. 'The Igbo were as harsh in their treatment of witches as Europeans of the time. Anyanwu fought the charge of witchcraft, 'knowing' that a witch was one who worked evil magic. She had done no evil

with her abilities.' Butler adds that 'Anyanwu is partly based on the Onitsha legend of Atagbusi, a shape-shifter much honored by her people because she used her abilities to help them' (Letter to Govan, 16 Jan. 1984). Butler used Richard Henderson's *The King in Every Man* as source material for *Wild Seed*.

7   *Wild Seed* (1980; rpt. New York: Timescape, 1981), p. 26. Subsequent references to this edition, designated WS, are included in the text.

8   Letter to Govan, 16 Jan. 1984.

9   Ibid.

10 'This novel,' writes Michael Bishop in his review of *Wild Seed* (Foundation, No. 21 [1981], p. 86), 'is one of the oddest love stories you are ever likely to read; it treats effectively of the enduring human conflicts between duty and desire, conscience and expediency.'

11 Both present black characters in what seems to be vicious racist caricature; Heinlein's novel is particularly offensive.

12 'Lost Races of Science Fiction,' *Transmission*, Summer 1980, pp. 17–18. In another essay Butler notes: 'Science fiction has long treated people who might or might not exist – extraterrestrials. Unfortunately, however, many of the same science fiction writers who started us thinking about the possibility of extraterrestrial life did nothing to make us think about here-at-home human variation – women, blacks, Indians, Asians, Hispanics, etc. In science fiction of not too many years ago, such people either did not exist, exited only occasionally as oddities, or existed as stereotypes' ('Future Forum,' *Future Life*, No. 17 [1980], p. 60).

13 In an unpublished interview given to Margaret O'Connor of the University of North Carolina-Chapel Hill in Nov.–Dec. 1981, Butler observed that '*Wild Seed* was almost entirely library research ... an earlier reading of the novels of Chinua Achebe ignited my interest in the Igbo people.' While Butler makes no mention of Armah, what I hear must be the reverberation of a shared sensitivity to the use of the collective voice in African oral history. Butler has also indicated that she made use of Iris Andreski's *Old*

Wives Tales and Henderson's *The King in Every Man* (Letter to Govan, 16 Jan. 1984).

[14] The reference is clearly to Phillis Wheatley; O'Connor makes the same observation in her essay on Butler to be included in the initial volume of *The Dictionary of Literary Biography – Afro-American Writers* series.

[15] *Mind of My Mind* (1977; rpt. New York: Avon, 1978), p. 217. Subsequent references to this edition, designated MMM, are cited in the text.

[16] *Survivor* (New York: Signet, 1979), p. 28. Subsequent references to this edition are cited in the text.

[17] See her interview with Margaret O'Connor.

[18] 'Science Fiction as Metaphor: Octavia Butler's Ironic Transformations,' paper delivered at The Southwest/Texas Chapters of the Popular Culture and American Culture Conference, Lubbock, TX, 27 Oct. 1983, p. 5.

[19] For this idea I am indebted to Helen Houston of Tennessee State University. During a telephone conversation Professor Houston pointed out *Kindred*'s structural similarity to the traditional slave narrative. The slave first experiences slavery by telling of its effects on others; then the slave witnesses white brutality, attempts escape, is betrayed and captured; brutal punishment is inflicted for the attempted escape; sickened but vowing freedom despite the dangers, the slave plots escape again. The reader, meanwhile, has seen 'life' on the plantation from several angles. In the O'Connor interview, Butler also acknowledges learning about, and subsequently reading, the narratives of Frederick Douglass and 'others who endured and escaped slavery.' In a note to me she has added: 'Very, very grim reading! It convinced me that (among other things) I was going to have to present a cleaned-up, somewhat gentler version of slavery. There's not much entertainment in the real thing.'

I AM AN OCTAVIA E. BUTLER SCHOLAR

Kathleen Kayembe

The Butler Effect

1: *I'm at a fashion show in my junior year of high school, a biracial Congolese-American geek surrounded not by Africans, but by African Americans. I don't look out of place, but I feel it. Even the book vendor's tables have nothing that represents my experience: second-generation halfrican raised in middle-class white suburbia.*

'What do you like to read?' the vendor asks as I turn to leave.

I pause and tell him, sure he has nothing for me – if there is spec fic with black anything, I'd have found it by now. To my surprise, he puts a book in my hands and says, 'You need to read this. This book will change your life.' I take it, sure he's wrong, but see a bald, beautiful, proud black woman on the cover. I read the back of the book.

The woman is African.

I read the first paragraph and surface pages later: yes, she is African, older than my grandmother's grandmother. Her journey will take her to America alongside the slave trade, and a race of black, mutant-superpower-wielding human beings will spin out from her and the man she meets in that first encounter. And the writing is good. Like, really good. I make myself stop reading and buy the book: Wild Seed. *It's the only Butler book he has.*

Some part of me must already have believed what the book vendor said, because those few minutes are fixed in my memory as a turning point, a revelation.

After *Wild Seed*, I devoured every Octavia E. Butler book our library had – perhaps why it didn't strongly register that so few of the books I read for school were about black people. After all, in Butler's worlds, I was represented: most protagonists were women and men who looked like me. I knew her characters, empathized with them, aspired to be them as they struggled through hardships and rolled and stumbled with the punches of living with other people and having superpowers. Butler taught me to write real people, to write flaws fearlessly, and to never pull punches on protagonists. She made me want to be a better writer.

I learned from *Bloodchild*'s essays that Butler was a hardworking black woman who wanted to be a writer all her life. Those glances into her process gave me hope and inspired me to write as much as I could. She wanted me to write, her essays said, and if she could persist in her writing and write black protagonists in science fiction while being a black woman and do it all to critical acclaim, then maybe – if I persisted and worked hard – I could too.

2: *I'm visiting Smith College, meeting women I don't realize will remain some of my best friends to this day, and see an Octavia E. Butler book on my host's bookshelf. It's been signed. 'She came to our Science Fiction class earlier this year,' Mel says. 'I think she's friends with one of the professors.'*

If that's true, I think, she might come again, and I can meet her, and she can sign my books, and I can thank her for everything she has been to me. The next year, I take that class.

Before Butler, I wasn't consciously aware that no one in the books I read – black or white – shared both my skin tone and cultural experience. I didn't realize some speculative fiction was shelved with African American Interests because bookstores assumed such interests were necessary to read books with black protagonists, no matter the genre. It didn't occur to me to question why my school assigned books with predominately white, male protagonists and authors; or why I, too, began in high school to write stories with predominately white, male protagonists.

3: I walk into Science Fiction with Bill Orem. We've just finished Imago. *Hope, already at her desk, says, 'Did you know Octavia Butler died last night?' And I realize: I will never meet her now, can never thank her now, can never read any more than what she's published. She was so young.*

After Butler, I returned to female protagonists, and even started writing black and multiracial protagonists, people who looked like me, shared my experience, but lived fantastic lives. They had interracial queer romances and mixed families, they solved mysteries and dealt with racism and sexism and people they didn't agree with, they rolled with or collapsed under the punches Butler taught me not to pull. Butler's books gave me permission to write what I knew while still writing what I loved. I'd been reading white female protagonists all through elementary school thanks to teachers' recommendations, and even written Japanese and Hispanic protagonists before the literary canon derailed me. But until Butler, it never occurred to me that a blind spot I had as a reader and writer was people who looked like me. My cultural experience was missing, and it belonged in speculative fiction.

4: I've been accepted into Clarion's class of 2016, but can't be happy about it yet; I'm still waiting to hear whether I'll get the Octavia E.

Butler Memorial Scholarship. Tuition is expensive – I can't afford it – and my mother is willing to pay my way, but I see how hard she works for how little she gets, and I know it'll cost her more than money. I slump into my car, tired from working closing shift at a local grocery chain for not much money myself, and check my email.

I've been awarded the scholarship.

I am an Octavia E. Butler Scholar.

Adrenalin and joy wash over me. My name is associated with hers. Nothing can erase this. This connection is mine. To top it off, some of my tuition will be paid. I read the rest of the email, wondering how much I'll still owe, and find out: nothing. It's a full scholarship. I can live this dream without the guilt of borrowing tuition from someone who can't afford it. I feel a sudden weightlessness with the threat of tuition gone. For the first time I am unequivocally happy about going to Clarion. Octavia E. Butler's memorial scholarship has saved me. Once again, she is changing my life.

Butler dreamed of sending writers of color to Clarion, of enabling us to enter the speculative fiction field successfully, of throwing down ladders for us to climb. I found out being a Butler scholar was like being a king or queen of Narnia: once was for always; we were her legacy. I am so proud to be in that number, so proud and admiring of her goal to nurture young writers who, like her, wanted to write science fiction and fantasy, and deserved to have their stories heard. I went to Clarion to become a better writer and editor, and gain a community of classmates. I didn't realize until my arrival that Clarion would connect me to a still larger community of previous graduates, spec fic writers and authors and editors, and a legacy of Butler scholars; it would open doors. Butler wanted that for writers of color. She dreamed of bringing us with her into the fold.

All writing is political – it cannot be divorced from the society it comes from. Butler's decision to write her experience as a black American into the dominant narrative of science fiction paved the way for others to do the same. Like the little black boy who rubbed Barack Obama's head, thrilled to discover the President of the United States had hair just like his, I read Octavia E. Butler and began to see myself in speculative fiction.

Nowadays, most of my protagonists – and, thankfully, more of the protagonists I'm reading in romance and spec fic – are black or multiracial. Part of me does it to write what I know, but part of me feels obligated to put more stories with black protagonists out there, to push demographics in speculative fiction closer to representing the American population. I've also realized that while my experience as a black person is different from what people expect when they look at me, it's no less valid in the social narrative – and if I don't write it, it may never be heard. I'd be erasing myself.

Writing, like the scholarship, doesn't happen in a vacuum. The push by We Need Diverse Books and others, the studies about representation and its effects on identity and aspirations in children, the statistics showing the disparity in demographics in TV and film versus the American population, the outpouring of joy when Obama became the first black president (he's biracial, but this is America) – all of it points to the danger of media displaying a single, dominant narrative, and the necessity of changing it to include many voices, stories, and narrative threads. Octavia E. Butler dreamed of science fiction that reflected her experience, and made it reality. In doing so, she sowed seeds in the minds of others: you belong here, this can be your reality, there is a place here for you. The Butler Effect continues in me, and in every writer she enabled to dream of adding their voice to the literary narrative of speculative fiction. Butler bid the silenced speak, and we spin out from her, a powerful legacy.

Kathleen Kayembe

Jeremy Sim

Dear Octavia,

Hi. My name is Jeremy, and I don't know you very well. I didn't grow up reading your books or stories. I never met you in person, and you passed away just two years after I had heard your name for the first time. So consider this a letter from an outsider.

I used to be an angry, stubborn, shy child. I say 'used to' – in many ways I still am. I came to writing like that: typing stories to myself in the dark, passively imitating writers I admired and stories I loved from afar. It felt good, like I was discovering a new world of my own. Maybe you felt that way too, typing away on your Remington typewriter as a child all those years ago. For me it was a kind of self-exile, I guess, taking myself out of the real world and losing myself in the pages and words of my own fiction. It was lonely, but at least it was satisfying. I didn't realize it at the time, but all the while I was writing a thicker and thicker wall around myself. A wall that no one could break through.

You want to know how all that changed? As a matter of fact, it was you. I had been writing on my own for almost a full decade with no success, when on a whim I applied for the Clarion West Writers Workshop: the same workshop you attended many years ago. To my surprise, I got accepted – but then the question rapidly evolved into: do I actually want to go? I had a strong sense of reservation about it, but I couldn't explain why: it just didn't seem like something that people like me *did*. There was a sense of imposter-hood in me, I guess, that had only been growing larger over the years. Surely, I thought, I wasn't the type of person they were looking for at a workshop like that.

I remember it was a scalding Los Angeles summer afternoon, and I still hear the voice of Neile Graham congratulating me over the phone. She said: 'Jeremy, it looks like you didn't check the box indicating you want to apply for the Octavia E. Butler Memorial Scholarship. May I ask why?'

I mumbled something along the lines of, 'Oh, that's not for me, is it?'

'It is,' she said. 'And you're welcome to apply for it, if you want. In fact, I'd encourage you to. I'm certain Octavia would want that too.'

I remember being distinctly surprised. Someone really wanted to support my writing? It baffled me a little at the time, like the world had been flipped upside down. So I did what anyone would do – I said okay. I applied, and I got the scholarship, and I went, and it changed everything. I'm sure you're sick of hearing how life-altering a workshop experience like Clarion West is, and how much a writer can change in six weeks – heck, you experienced it yourself in 1970, a full forty-one years before I did. So I won't go into that.

But the most important thing I learned at Clarion West wasn't how to write. It was this: that writing isn't meant to be a lonely thing. Art is community. For the first time, I had writing friends. For the first time, I understood that it was about more than just me, it was about friends and partners and mentors and students and rivals and struggling together, not alone. And when I finally read your novels, *Wild Seed* and *Clay's Ark* and the others, I realized you had known it all along. That community was everything. I saw the theme repeated over and over in your stories: the taking in of strangers and turning them into family. The importance of love and kinship. The acceptance of one's self as a node in an infinite framework.

Thanks to the community you worked your whole life to build, I'm now a node in your framework. I feel connected to people like Erik Owomoyela, Mimi Mondal, Lisa Bolekaja, S. Qiouyi Lu, Jaymee Goh, and Rochita Loenen-Ruiz, who have all benefitted from your legacy in the same way I did – even now, a full decade after your death. There's a community, all connected to you. And I don't even know how to begin thanking you for that.

Octavia, I don't know you very well, but that's what I remember you for. I think of a shy girl whose Aunt Hazel once told her, 'Honey, Negroes can't be writers,' but who grew into a fearless warrior who broke through the walled gardens and worked to pull together the disparate strands of the writing world into a cohesive, inclusive whole. Over the course of your career, you did so much to bring the marginalized into the spotlight, making yourself an example to the women and people of color who yearned to write great stories and stand together with the great sci-fi and fantasy writers of the past. You wove yourself into the tapestry, and pulled me in with you.

Just so you know, I'm still writing and slowly publishing stories about the things you care about: diversity, power dynamics, identity and culture. I'm working on a novel and a video game about the same things too, and I continue to work on them every day, drawing support from my community – which is stronger than ever. So that's what I've been up to. I'm taking shaky steps up from the platform you built for me, but I haven't forgotten what you stood for and what I have to keep standing for.

And one day, when I'm older, I'll extend the end of the string to someone else. Someone who's on the outside, looking for a way in, but only knows how to sit alone and wall themselves off. I'll tell them: 'This isn't my string. It's here for you, too.' And I'll tell them that I came as far as I did because a long long time ago, way back in the twentieth century, there was a girl named Octavia Butler who started out on the outside, all alone, but broke through.

Sincerely,
Jeremy Sim

Mary Elizabeth Burroughs

Dear Ms Butler,

I am writing you because you've helped me before, and I think – I hope – you can help me again.

Let me explain. You once said that you wrote speculative fiction in order to 'see yourself in the world.' You didn't see anyone like you in novels and short stories, so you simply wrote yourself in. The seeming ease with which you came to such a watershed decision to create is something I am still stunned by.

But I want to know more.

Was your choice that simple? Did the drive to create become a moral imperative for you early on in your career, willing you on during the pre-dawn mornings before enduring hours of tedious menial jobs? How did you commit day after day, for years, despite several critics, speakers on panels, even readers communicating to you that representing people of colour in SF was an insignificant aim? Was your yearning to offer something for everyone so strong that it reconsidered carrying the daily weight of getting by, making do and the cold disinterest of whole swathes of people? I ask because I am gobsmacked just as much by your efforts as I am by the imaginative, compassionate depth of your works.

I ask because amongst other things, I am a writer who is deep in the muck and sometimes I feel as if I should just stay right down there, as quiet as I can be.

You see, I'm an Other myself. My father was black and my mother white, so I am mixed. Actually, the word we use today is 'multiracial' – that's the proper vocabulary – but I did not grow up in this sort of a world. A world that has for better or for worse become rigorously self-aware, one in which liberal-minded adults gift youngsters with kindly-sounding, expansive labels that ambitiously aim to simultaneously honour and articulate the vast complexity of their cultural heritage.

No, the '80s were not like that, as I am sure you are well aware, Ms. Butler, and what this meant for me was that certain white boys and certain black girls in schools in Florida took issue with my existence. It meant I've tasted mouthfuls of dirt, felt the eraser-less ends of pencils dug into the meat of my back, those metallic bands leaving circular engravings rather akin to the phases of the moon. It meant that at twelve, I would get shoved up and held against walls with breathy whispers from older boys about how mixed girls did things other girls didn't ...

Don't misunderstand me – I am damn proud of my parents coming together to make my sister and me – but in my head, I'm just mixed, full stop. My formative years did not in any way suggest the world was appreciative of my existence or eager to hear anything I had to say. Consequentially, I developed a certain comfort with violence. Likewise, I've developed a persistent watchfulness, a disinclination towards speaking and an overwhelming inclination towards writing and drawing.

But here's where you come in, Ms. Butler. Though I had access to books that kept me from crumpling in on myself and wound up preserving the integrity of my interior self – glorious books with tesseracting and wardrobes and interplanetary 'buggers' and plants from outer space that ate dirty socks – I do not recall encountering many characters who dealt with a complexity of issues that I could relate to. There were no children who were transported to dark fantasy lands and had to be canny enough to code-switch; no children who used free or reduced school lunch, for example, only to discover they had a special destiny. To be fair, I did read about the concerns of Others but only in 'issue' books and some 'literary' works. I didn't get to encounter anyone like that going on exhilarating, transformative quests in a novel of speculative fiction, adventure or mystery until I was a young adult.

That's when I discovered you.

It was the summer I realized that I was creatively adrift and somewhat socially isolated in a masters writing program for literary fiction in Mississippi. My epiphany was prompted by three texts: *Mojo: Stories of Conjuring*, edited by Nalo Hopkinson, *Magic for Beginners* by Kelly Link, and *Kindred* by you.

Kindred made me holler in delight at having found it. While the plot is deceptively straightforward, one in which we follow a black woman who is repeatedly transported from the 20th century West coast to 19th century plantation South to save the life of her white, slave-owning ancestor, its characterisation and conceptual foundation are anything but. It dramatizes how a variety of compromises, humiliations, and acts of violence must be endured in order to remain alive when one is systematically dehumanised and oppressed. You composed art about the nobility in survival, and I'm amazed by it. By the notion that remaining alive and whole is a worthy act. It spoke to me as a human. Then as an artist, I wanted to know how you managed to imbue Dana with relentless empathy in spite of her increasingly distressing circumstances? How did you render the story to feel so breathless and believable? And how did you do all of that without a whiff of righteousness or holier-than-thou-ness?

In short, your novel ignited me.

It drove me to research your works and career. I learned about your time at Clarion, which in turn spurred me to apply myself. I even felt emboldened enough to ask for financial assistance. And what do you know; I got in and won a scholarship in your name.

Dear Ms. Butler ... did you know, all those years ago when you wrote that page of affirmations on the back of one of your journals – a series of promises you aimed to keep to yourself ('I shall be a bestselling writer ... I will send poor black youngsters to Clarion ... I will help poor black youngsters broaden their horizons ... So be it!') – that you actually would?

How did you maintain your faith in yourself? How? What other messages did you whisper to yourself in the morning before you began your day or use to soothe yourself after some disappointing human interaction? Was it just the therapeutic art of writing that buoyed you? Was that enough ... ?

I am desperate to know, so that when I'm entrenched in the muck of life, as still and as quiet as can be, I will persist. Amid writing at 3 a.m. while my son and partner sleep, well before I teach Australian high-school students English, I aim to continue, no matter the number of rejections.

In a way, this is an unabashed thank-you letter. Thank you for creating a legacy that inspired the Carl Brandon Society to send me to the Clarion Writers' Workshop. Thank you for writing stories about complex, wildly thoughtful introverts who explore the world and seek to understand others. Your work broadened my horizons. I thank you, truly and deeply, for helping me realise that I have a voice worth using.

With gratitude and absolute admiration,
Mary Elizabeth Burroughs

Indra Das

Dear Octavia E. Butler,

When you died, I hadn't read a single story by you.

I knew of you. I remember seeing your face in a sea of white ones amid the pages of the bulky hardcover *Encyclopedia of Science Fiction* that I had as a child. A black woman, proudly seated shoulder-to-shoulder alongside the white giants of the Canon, garlanded with the same awards, the same accolades, the same fame and selling power. There were no Indian faces in that encyclopedia, not even Indian-American or Indian-British or otherwise diasporic. (I should mention that I'm from Calcutta, India.)

I still didn't read your work. There were no books by you in Calcutta's dusty second-hand bookstores (there weren't any major chain bookstores in the city back then), or in the Calcutta Book Fair, or within the austere stacks of the Saturday Club library. There were sci-fi and fantasy books in those places, but by white men, mostly. At the time, I mostly just read the work of white authors. I don't regret reading them. I do regret that you – and others who weren't white, weren't straight, weren't men, yet struggled and succeeded in carving out their place in the marble-pale Mt. Rushmore of anglophone genre literature's Hall of Fame – weren't *also* there on my shelf.

But there you were, in my beloved SF encyclopedia (this edition was published around 1997). A prized possession – painted with book covers and posters and movie stills lurid and artful, tracing a history of science fiction from the seventeenth century to the twentieth. There were other non-white writers listed, but I don't remember any other non-white women writers in there. (That could be down to my memory, to be fair.) It was written, compiled and published by a white American man. At the time, I associated science fiction with the West, and the West in general, primarily with white people. Your face stuck out to me. I didn't stop to think about why it did, of course. I was just a kid. I grew up in a world long claimed by white supremacists, nativists and megalomaniacs in the garb of job creators and politicians, rightful heirs to the colonialists, imperialists and slavers my ancestors and yours fought so hard to kick out of their palaces and plantations. I'm still growing up in that world. I just question it more now.

But back then, I hadn't read Octavia E. Butler. Non-white people – black, brown, Asian, indigenous peoples around the world – we were all secondary to white people and cultures, because that's just the way history had arranged us. Someone had to lead, and if it was white people, so be it. Back then, I'd watched *Mississippi Burning* and read *Uncle Tom's Cabin* and thought – there was this horrible, unfair thing called racism in the past, and it got solved because good white folks helped kick the bad, racist white folks to the curb during the '60s, after Martin Luther King Jr. marched on the streets and convinced them to clean up their own house (the house that was America, Land of the Free). I thought racism was dead in America, and therefore the world, because America was the leader of the world. And all that talk about how visitors to America should avoid black neighborhoods because they're filled with criminals and muggers, and how Chinese people talked funny, and how 'Arabs' were terrorists and dictators, from my fellow brown-skinned Indians? Well, that was just people joking, I assured myself, because society – Society – had assured me so. No one was getting hurt. No one was enslaving anyone. No one was wearing white hoods and burning crosses.

Maybe if I'd read *Kindred*, I'd have started questioning earlier.

The first time I read one of your stories was in 2012, at the Clarion West Writers Workshop in Seattle. Apt, because your career kicked off at Clarion West's counterpart and antecedent, the Clarion Workshop. Apt, as I was able to attend because of the Octavia E. Butler Memorial Scholarship, established by the Carl Brandon Society to help people of color participate in those two writing workshops, which can help give emerging writers a running start in a challenging field. That scholarship was started to honor your legacy. It was started by people who read your work, and were inspired by it – and by your life. After all, you had been a young black woman growing up in a racially segregated nation, who decided she wanted to contribute to a literature dominated by white men. You wrote to yourself, as I now write to you: 'My books will be read by millions of people!' And they were, and still are. We're still at a place where writers like me need examples like you – to show them they can be famous, award-winning, bestselling, influential and beloved authors without being white. Because it doesn't come easy to *anyone*, black, white or brown.

When I was reading 'Bloodchild' at a rented sorority house in Seattle under the auspices of the Clarion West Workshop, I was finally communing with the person who had allowed me to be there. And make no mistake – being there made a difference to my career as a writer who is not American, and not white, in a world where international publishing is still mostly white and West-centric. I met people I would not have otherwise met, wrote stories that I would not have otherwise written, made lifelong friends and colleagues who support me to this day. I saw firsthand that even in an inequitable world, there are kind, supportive people who will help balance the scales, even if only for a brief moment in what is ultimately a historical context. After reading 'Bloodchild', I wrote non-stop for an entire night, producing a story that was sold on its first submission. Inspiration matters.

I might as well throw aside the shackles of modesty and confess to you, who so boldly outlined your aspirations without shame – I want to win a Hugo, and a Nebula, like you did. I want my books read by millions. I want more excellent writers who aren't cisgender, men, white, or straight to win awards and have millions of readers too. I want readers and writers who feel threatened or slighted by this to understand that this wish doesn't preclude them or their art. There is space for us all here on this tiny blue dot.

You also wrote to yourself: 'I will send poor black youngsters to Clarion or other writer's workshops.' It heartens me that you are still, in a sense, sending writers who can't afford writing workshops to Clarion and Clarion West. I can't call myself poor, having been born with the privilege of a middle-class boy in a nation scarred by endemic poverty. I'm not black. But I certainly couldn't afford Clarion West at the time I got in, if not for the scholarship that bears your name and my close proximity to Seattle. (I lived in Vancouver then, forever an immigrant drifting between continents.) I hope that it would make you happy that you played a part in helping me, a youngster from a country quite far from the United States of America, achieve my teenage dreams of becoming a writer read by thousands, if not millions.

My debut novel is now published in several countries. I'm

not sure if I'm the first Indian author that genre stalwart Del Rey Books has ever published in the United States and Canada, but I think I might just be. It's a start.

I'm writing this in 2017. An abusive, misogynistic, racist white supremacist demagogue and his allies are in one of the highest positions of political power in the world. You knew him as Donald Trump. We need you more than ever. We need the kind of incisive, socially aware art that you created with such confidence – books like the Xenogenesis trilogy (or Lilith's Brood), which cut straight to the heart of humanity's self-destructive urges and imagine the incandescent beauty in resisting the same. I read the first volume of Xenogenesis while revising my first published novel – I borrowed an old hardcover edition from the public library, with an inexplicable cover showing a white woman peeling back some sort of green tube to reveal another white woman. The protagonist of *Dawn* is Lilith Iyapo, a black woman. There is not a black woman in sight on that cover. I imagine you hated it.

Now, the collected trilogy has a black woman front and center on the cover. Now, there is a TV show of *Dawn* in the works. Now, a Neo-Nazi-endorsed billionaire supervillain is President of the United States. With progress comes backlash.

You wouldn't be surprised at the state of the world today. Dismayed, but not surprised. For some, geopolitical turmoil, global warming, a world choking on its own hatreds mean that art fades into the background, proving its impotence in the face of reality's callous brutality. But if we're where we are with art in the world, imagine where we'd be without it. Art will always remain vital, because it inspires people. Ultimately, only people can change where we are as a species.

In your absence, the people you've inspired will do their best to compensate for it. I hope to be one of them. I've read many of them – authors of varied sexuality, genders, race, ethnicity, nationality, background, who are taking their place at the table despite the furious chest-thumping of bigots. They mention your name, often, in interviews. They're winning awards, publishing books, fiercely resisting bigotry inside and outside the bloody, public arena of the Internet. You'd be proud of them.

Know that they, too, are proud of you.

Yours,
Indra Das

Lisa Bennett Bolekaja

Dear Octavia,

The first time I discovered your books, I was still a college student working at a bookstore that catered to books about Black people. It was called Pyramid Bookstore in San Diego, California. Everything was yellow – yellow shelves and special yellow book displays shaped like pyramids to highlight popular books. I remember it being a bright and vivacious place to work. Kwame Toure had visited us. Rosa Parks had a book signing there and posed for pictures with our staff. Chuck D from Public Enemy bought books from me. So many important figures from the arts, academics, and activists' communities visited us. I received a serious education of the Diaspora and Black American history in the years I spent working there.

I was stocking the shelves with a brand new series of books that highlighted the work of Black Women writers, and two of your books, *Kindred* and *Wild Seed*, were part of the collection I put on the shelf. I stopped. Looked at the cover of *Wild Seed*. A Black woman with my skin color was on the cover, and her head was shape-shifting into different animals. I looked at your name. I had no idea who you were. I picked up the book, read the description on the back.

Who are you?

That's what I thought. I glanced at the other book, and read the blurb on the back. A Black woman time travels back to slavery days? Several times? What?!

Needless to say, these two books did not remain on the shelf. I bought them and read them both during one weekend. I was transformed. Zora Neale Hurston, Toni Morrison and Alice Walker were my Womanist writing foremothers. They centered me in my historical Blackness. But finding you by pure chance, just placing books on a shelf, I discovered my future Blackness. (As the writer/blogger Renina Jarmon says, Black Girls Are from The Future.) I cannot begin to tell you how much you have transformed my life. How you have been the catalyst for me gaining some dear new friends and a new tight-knit SFF writing family. I am crying as I write this because my heart is so full. You once wrote in *Parable of the Sower*, 'All that you touch, you change.' If only you knew how prophetic those words were. Touching your books, reading them … my path as a writer was changed by your life.

A friend handed me a flyer at my bookstore and said you would be doing a book signing at Eso Won Books in Los Angeles. I begged another friend to drive me up to see you. I sat in the back of Eso Won just in awe of your voice and your presence. A few years later when I moved to Leimert Park in Los Angeles, I had a chance to see you in person again. I brought my copy of *Parable of the Sower* for you to sign. I timidly asked you how you got your start during the Q&A. You told me about the Clarion Science Fiction and Fantasy Writers Workshop. You praised it and told me to apply. I had never heard of it. But through library research I was able to find out about this magical thing called 'Clarion'. I didn't apply though. I didn't have the money, and because I was working full time and making so little, it would be difficult to go out of state for six weeks. But I kept the idea in the back of my mind. One day I would apply, because you spoke so highly of it, and how it transformed your life.

Fast forward a couple of years and I was once again at Eso Won Books. I was in line at another book signing to see you. I finally got in front of you and for some reason you remembered my face. You asked me, 'Did you ever apply to Clarion?' I told you I hadn't, but you gently convinced me to do it. Give it a shot. I didn't want to tell you that I couldn't afford it. Growing up within a low-income household and working paycheck to check was still embarrassing for me to confide in people about. And to tell a writing hero 'I can't' was too shameful. I smiled and said I would. One day.

When word came that you had passed away in 2006, it was like the world had cracked in two. The loss of you was so visceral. It was like a favorite relative had died. Your work was so important. I believed you had so many years ahead of you, so many books to give us. It wasn't until after your transition that I learned of your health issues. I learned more about the grinding poverty you endured to write the books and short stories that we cling to like verses from a holy book. Even today Octavia, it is difficult to speak your name in a room full of people without my throat tightening, or my eyes watering, because it isn't fair to not have you here with us.

In 2011 I applied for the next Clarion Class of 2012. I joked with people that since the Mayan calendar predicted 2012 was the end of the world, why the hell not apply? Also, Ted Chiang, one of my favorite contemporary SF writers, was teaching for a week. I took my shot. Sent in two short stories. I also applied for the Carl Brandon Society's Octavia E. Butler Memorial Scholarship that was created a year after your death. The job I was working was threatening to lay everyone off. I was finally in a position to have six weeks off in the summer of 2012. If I didn't get the scholarship, I wouldn't be able to go. I told myself, 'If you get in and can't go, that's okay, because you got in. You did what Octavia asked.'

I resigned myself to just seeing what the future brought.

I was over the moon when I received the news that I made it into Clarion. Thoughts of, 'But what about money?' were pushed to the side for a few days. I got in. I wanted to enjoy that sweet victory for as long as I could. However, when I got the phone call at work that I would be the recipient of the 2012 Octavia E. Butler Memorial Scholarship, I ran to my friend Kelley and we hugged. Then I went for a walk to hide behind a tree and cried my eyes out. The stress of not knowing if I would have a job in a few months, the stress of worrying about trying to find money to go to Clarion if I did get in, just melted away. Because of your life I became the writer I needed to be. But because of your death, I would be able to attend Clarion ... the workshop I first heard about because you told me about it all those years ago. Listen, God has cosmic jokes.

A few weeks after I sent in my Clarion application, I went to visit your gravesite. A dear friend of mine, Dr. Ayana Jamieson, had told me where you were buried in Altadena. We met online at the Black Science Fiction Society webpage when she posted a message about your burial site. When you passed away in Seattle, I thought you were buried there. I didn't know your final resting place was back where you grew up in California. Ayana and I often visit your gravesite together during your birthday month. I bring scissors with me just in case the grass hasn't been cut around your headstone. We had a birthday party for you there once. Some people may think that sounds morbid, but it was fun. We had a birthday cake, a giant balloon, and I played some Motown songs because I heard that you liked it. The moment I knew I could go to Clarion, I drove up to Altadena from San Diego a giddy mess. I sat near your headstone and read one of the stories I wrote to get into Clarion out loud. I poured some libations for you and prepared to dig in for an intense writing bootcamp.

My beloved Octavia. You were right. Clarion re-shaped me. Some of the fiercest writers and some of the smartest feminists I know were in my 2012 class. We called ourselves the Awkward Robots. We didn't pull any punches with our critiques or opinions. The introvert in me had to pull away to be alone at times, but to have the time to just write and think of nothing but creating worlds was bliss. I was also able to go into the archives and read what you wrote while you were in Clarion. I saw the crossed-out words, typos, and the glimmerings of brilliance that was to come. I also took the time to read Nalo Hopkinson and Ted Chiang's archived stories. When I looked up the names of the instructors that Ted Chiang had the year he went, I was snatched up in my feelings again. I had no idea that you were one of Ted's instructors. And now he was mine. Like I said before, God has circular jokes. (By the way, my favorite Ted short story 'The Story of Your Life' was turned into a movie. It's called *Arrival*. I think you would like it a lot.)

I can't say it enough. After leaving Clarion, everything took on a forward momentum that would never have happened if I didn't go.

Laurie Edison, the artist who made your one-of-a-kind owl pendant, donated her talents to make an owl necklace for every Octavia E. Butler Scholar that the Carl Brandon Society chooses. A year after being in Clarion, the Carl Brandon Society asked me to become part of their Steering Committee. (I get to work alongside your good friend Nisi Shawl, my writing Godmother!) I asked to facilitate your Memorial Scholarship. Every April the Carl Brandon Society reads the work and personal essays of the Clarion students who have applied for your scholarship for both Clarion and Clarion West. Much deliberation takes place to choose writers whose work we think embodies the multiple intersections that your visionary work contemplated. Each year for the past four years I have gone to the UCSD campus where Clarion is housed for the summer. I carry a new hand-crafted owl necklace for the newest Butler Scholar and I tell myself I won't cry when I place it around the neck of the writer we have chosen. But I do. I always do. Because I wish you could see that we are bringing one of your dreams to life.

Recently a page from one of your journals was shared with the public, and we saw that you wrote about wanting to send poor Black youngsters to Clarion. The scholarship in your honor does that and more. Many of our Butler Scholars come from around the world. We are Black American, Black/Native, Asian, Roma, Mexican, Southeast Asian; from countries as far away as Nigeria, Australia, India, and the Netherlands. Some of us are genderqueer, gay, bisexual, gender non-conforming, biracial and multi-racial. If you were to put all of the Octavia E. Butler Scholars into one room, we would look like the United Nations of SFF writers. You did this Octavia. Your Scholars have gone on to be published in numerous magazines and anthologies, written books, been nominated for major writing awards, started new SFF magazines, and one of them co-edited this book of letters to you. (Hi Mimi!)

I write all of this to you so that you understand the impact you have made on the world. You threw a pebble on to water and it is rippling beyond what you may have imagined. It is my hope that we make you proud. I hate to mention this but we are now living in a world that you predicted so long ago. Black Lives, Native Lives, Disabled Lives, Queer Lives, Trans Lives, and all the other marginalized lives here in our country are under attack. America elected a trash president straight out of your Parable books. He doesn't believe in science or climate change or anything that affects the environment. He also used a slogan you used nearly twenty-four years ago about 'Making America Great Again.' Black people have been dying from police shootings and protesting in the streets again for basic human rights, and the Native Americans have been fighting for their land and water yet again (and also being shot like dogs by the police). We are living in a real-life dystopia like you predicted in your books. In a way, all writers have to become like your creation Lauren Oya Olamina. We have to plant Earthseeds with our words to protect us all from the racism, sexism, classism, ableism, and all the other isms that are being openly unleashed with the stamp of approval from a man not worthy of the title of commander-in-chief. Especially after having our first Black president and extraordinary First Family who tried to bring us together as a Nation. Our work is cut out for us.

I want to try and end this very long letter with something more profound than just 'Thank you'. Those two words seem so small for all that you've done for me. You unknowingly guided me to other Black women whose work I admired, and whom I now can call my friends. You wrote a blurb for Nalo Hopkinson and I sought out her work, and now we hug and laugh each time we see each other. Nalo led me to Tananarive Due, who gives me joy with her eternal optimism and her reminders that we are amazing. Connecting with my brilliant friend Ayana linked me to Walidah Imarisha and Adrienne Maree Brown who created *Octavia's Brood: Science Fiction Stories From Social Justice Movements*. Ayana's sphere of influence led me to Ruha Benjamin and Moya Bailey. All three of them created the astounding symposium 'Ferguson is the Future' at Princeton where your influence was deeply felt and recognized. Last summer Ayana and Moya (along with my Clarion

Mentor/Guide Dr. Shelley Streeby) spearheaded 'Shaping Change' at UCSD, an entire three-day conference dedicated to your life and work. I'm telling you, Octavia, these women are beyond brilliant.

Nisi Shawl bought my first short story and was my first real editor. She edited the anthology *Bloodchildren: Stories by the Octavia E. Butler Scholars* that was used as a fundraiser for your scholarship. Nisi led me to K. Tempest Bradford, and from there came Sofia Samatar, N. K. Jemisin, Mikki Kendall, Chesya Burke, Andrea Hairston, Jennifer Marie Brissett, Ibi Zoboi, Kiini Ibura Salaam, Nnedi Okorafor, Alaya Dawn Johnson ... and the list can go on and on now. Links in the chain of Black women who are writing the future. Our numbers are growing day by day. You paved the way for us, by being the first and often only Black woman writing SF. My world is richer and more meaningful with them in it.

I will continue my work with the Carl Brandon Society. I will support the Clarion Foundation as you did. I will do my best to bring up as many new writers as I can, especially those from marginalized communities. I will still cry if I'm in a room with people who love your work as much as I do. And I will write the stories that only I can.

Thank you. Thank you. Thank you.

I hope I make you proud.

With love and much admiration,
Lisa Bennett Bolekaja

P.S. I still have not taken back the copy of *Survivor* to the Santa Monica Library like you asked me to years ago. I'm too ashamed to take it back after all these years of forgetting to return it after I moved. Can I just donate a bunch of brand new books instead?

FORGET TALENT.
THERE IS ONLY THE WORK

Christopher Caldwell

Dear Octavia E. Butler:

Tonight I write to you from Scotland, across an ocean from the place I was born. I am afraid. I am resolute. I have begun writing again after a slow three months of feeling unable to put words in any intelligible order. One of *your* words echoes over and over in my mind. *Persist.*

It is snowing in Scotland. The winds are high. People in Glasgow are bundled up in coats with their heads down, necks tucked against their chests. Everything is gray. Americans have elected someone terrible. The dull inevitability of a bleak future stretches before me. I am a descendent of slaves. Everyone I love is in danger. I am queer and black and afraid to return to my own country. But change, even terrifying change, does not always signify destruction. I must persist.

When I was a child, my grandfather told me about our forebear, Delia. She was a cook in a plantation house near Baton Rouge. She was fine-boned and pretty, and favoured by her master. He never sold off her children. Not even when a harvest wasn't profitable. When emancipation came, she stayed on the plantation and received a pittance of a wage. Sometimes, my grandfather told me, to make a little extra money, Delia'd go into town wearing fine clothes and use sweet talk to get poor, hungry ex-slaves to give up their new freedom to become sharecroppers. I used to hate Delia a little. I was old enough to have heard the phrase 'house nigger.' Old enough to know what a mammy was, and how a mammy was mocked for her body, her love for massa and his children, her loyalty to fine people in fine clothes in their fine houses with their fine cruelty.

When I was fifteen, I read *Kindred*. It changed the world for me. You turned the mammy on her head. Instead of a minstrel caricature, here was a person whose misfortunes were caused by those fine white folk and she was keenly aware of it. Sarah was a woman whose suffering and rage were rich and raw. She was bound by hatred and fear and love for the last person precious to her; she was bound to the service of people who only ever saw her as a thing. Sarah shifted my perspective into something new. Survival in a world of terror requires different sacrifices of us all. My grandfather said that the white folks bragged about loving Delia like a family member; he never said that she loved them back. I learned to forgive Delia. I learned to be ashamed that I was ashamed.

I had wanted to tell stories since I knew I could make up my own. But after *Kindred* I wanted to change the world for someone else the way you changed the world for me.

I read everything you published. I wrote my own stories. Most of them weren't any good. But I gave them to people to read, and listened to good advice about them. Then I wrote more of them. And I read. I read James Baldwin, Alexandre Dumas, Samuel R. Delany, Alice Walker, Toni Morrison, Ranier Maria Rilke, Haruki Murakami, and Tananarive Due. I learned more about your life. I read interviews with you. I cherished the fact that you were a Southern Californian who did not drive.

I never learned to drive. When you lived in Pasadena, my great-grandmother still lived in Altadena. I wondered if we took the same buses. I wondered if I would have been too shy to speak to you if I saw you on the bus. I saw that you sometimes taught at the

Clarion and Clarion West workshops. I was too shy and too unsure of myself to apply. Next time, I kept telling myself. Until that awful day in 2006 when I learned there would be no next time. My mother called to tell me. We had both devoured *Fledgling* days after its release and had spent the previous few months arguing about its narrative and speculating about a sequel. 'I'm so sorry. Did you hear the news?' she said to me. You were gone. You were my hero.

A year after your death, I applied to Clarion West. I learned from one of your instructors. I met people who loved you and whom you loved. I sat under the stars in the backyard of a grand Victorian house talking to someone who called you Estelle. I saw their sorrow, and felt my own was cheap and sickly. I still grieved for the tremendous loss of you. A friend of hers told me, 'You would have loved her, and she would have loved you.' It was a kindness that still brings me to tears.

Everything is gray. But the grayness cannot remain forever. A new quality of light will bring new perspectives. Life is stubborn. It continues in the strangest places, under the worst circumstances. The bleakness of the future does not stretch on towards eternity. But there is work to be done. As well as persisting, we must also resist. We must fight against the notion that people are things. We must each of us promote understanding, and kindness, and patience with each other. Hard changes will come. We must reach out to those who reach towards us.

I wonder if I have the talent to reach anyone the way you reached me. I aspire to so much. I know that the tools I have are imperfect, and the gifts I have are humble. I work. What else is there to do? Giving up is not an option. I pile up rejection slips and re-write and write something new and try to learn from my mistakes. I read and I envy writers with beautiful prose. I try to improve my own clumsy sentences. There is always the voice inside me that says I am just not good enough. Something else of yours echoes: *Forget talent.* There is only the work. I may never be good enough. And that's okay. I will do the work. I will persist.

Thank you for all that you shared,

Christopher Caldwell

Hunter Liguore

Facing Dyslexia

De ar Ms. uBtler:

I wnated to tkae a momeont out of ym day adn tahnk yuo fro bieng an isnpriation to tohse of us woh hvae dsyleixa. I hda been a fna of yuors snice cihldohod, but it wsa not utnil muhc latre, aftre my diagonosis, thta I begna oloking for othrse like me. Wehn I discovreed thta yuo – a belvoed author – also shraed this, and hda nt let thsi ostp you frm crfating novles, withtou it hindreing yuo, it offred me ohpe.

Like yuo – or so I'v e erad – omy taechres oloked at my oslw erading and sturggle to cpomlete assign emnts as being uninteersted in sch ool, or even a otruble-makre, ebcause I amde excsues abtou wyh I oucldn't fiinsh. I felt like osmething awsn't qutie rghti, but I dind't awnt to sya naything. Insteda, I absically ilved up to thier low expcteations for me. Whta savde me – and amybe yuo foun d this too – is thta I had a ivvid imgaination to crfta stroies. I mean, thta's wyh I love yuor oboks so much, espeically, *Paarble of teh Sowre*, whchi for me oshwed me eth knd of owrld tht aws opssible, if I wsa iwlling to owrk hrda to achnge it.

At smoe opint, I did ahve a te acher woh took an intreest, and noto nly owrked iwth me to gte the ehlp I need ed, but saw in me osme of the optential I had for ostrytelling. I carride aruond a noteobok, like yuo, to ercord all the idaes I'd ocme up with, btu I istll dind't eefl elik I ahd whta it atkes to be any kind of a iwrter, and so abnadoend it. But atht taecher, who'd encuoraged me siad – odn't igve up.

I've laerned over the yaers (now in ym ithrties) thta it is aesy to awlk awya frmo thnigs yuo love, even if noo ne is dircetly ushtting yuo down. It's likeo nce ethre is a group-mindste thta shuns yuo – like it did fro amny yaers, as a dsyleixc – then it osrt of amkes it aesy to let go.

Inm y twneties, thruogh yaers of wrok, then collgee, and wrok again, I mnaaged to ahng on to ym love of raeding. Becuase I'm a slwo raeder, I agrvitate more to listneing to aud io recrodings, whchi allwos me to oprcess the ostry, withuot the strgugle with the owrds. I also reraed, *Paarble of teh Sowre* and lla yuor wrok in gene ral. Oen of my favrotie things abuot yuo is that yuo dind't let yanthing keep yuo from yuor wrtiing. There is a quote I fuond, frmo yuo, thta sadi: 'I think thta there ocmes a time wehn yuo just ahve to do thta [techa uyorself], wehn ithngs ahve to astrt to ocme togteher for yuo or yuo dno't reaylly becmoe an eductaed eprson.'[1]

I evnetually staretd wrtiing agian. Btu this etim, I did it fro ymself, and noo ne else. I astrted to craete owrlds and ithnk abuot the future – my olve of sci-fi blos osmed, and I begna to 'edcuate myeslf' on thnigs I dind't know, like qunatum phyiscs, blcak ohles, and arcaeohlogy, whchi helpde me to feel empwoered – like the 'gruop-imndset' had been e rased, and bceause of yuo, I was abel to mvoe apst it, and bef ree.

I alos used whta was afmilira to me, incroportaing my dsylexia in iwth osme of ym characters – in my oboks it's part of whta maeks them magcial and able to svae the dya. Yuo o nce wrote, 'I thnik iwrters use absloutely eevrything thta happnes to us, and surley if I hda hda a differnet sort of childhdoo and still cmoe uot a writre, I'd b ea dffierent iknd of wrtier.[2] Fro me, thta's treu – if I awsn't dsylexic, I dno't ithnk I wuold've tried so ahrd to get it irght.

I wno't lie and sya it's nto a usper big strggle to blaance my dsylexai and still write and raed or exist in a word-infused world. But I've held on to yuor words – 'Do the thing thta yuo love and do it as well as yuo possibly can and be persistent abuot it.' Right? It's thta aesy.[3]

On abd days, I olok up all the ibrllaint poeple whoh ave shared uor dsylexai, like Albret Einstein, Whoopi Golbderg, Alexander Grahma eBll, Kiera Knightlye, Thomas Edisno, Bnejamni Frnaklin – he mdae the first Ameircan libarry in Phialdelphai, hwo cool is thta? It's been aruond snice 1874 wehn Dr. Pringle Morgan, in England, spent lnog enuogh with a yuorn gboy to discvoer he wsa having a ahrd time raeding – we etnd to olok at the apst as being elss 'owrldly' or techncail, or evne slowre, and yet I thnik somdeays, thnak ogodness osmenoe noticde itbeofre the Intrnet age.

Sme adys I rellay ahte the owrd, **dys lexai**. But to atke its pwoer away, I fonud uot thta in Grkee, it only maens 'poor' or 'inadequate' (dys) and 'lexis' or 'word.' So itis less ascry, less lik e a disaese.

I do ahte m yreglar 'ocming uot' evry etime I amke a hgue imstake. Soemtimes I dno't awnt to sya anything, becasue there are smoe epople who stlil thnik thta it me ans 'lwo intellignece.' Actaully – and yuo're proo fo fit – it's qutie teh ooppsite. In afct, we ecxel at upzzle sovling; we copmrehend stoires and ahve execllent thikning siklls – we gte the bgi pictrue, wehn othres can't. Soemtimes we're teh onse wit hthe big gest vocab. So whta if we need ujst a littl e xtra tim eto oprcess it – w eneed to oslw dwon tdoay!

Ms. Bulter, I hpoe thta yuo know whta an inspirtaion yuor owrk has been to me – rgeat novles, wiht graet inisghts and wsidom – I'm srue yuo aherd this a lot. For me th o ugh, yuo wer e oen of teh ifrst role omdels I had, woh also had dsylexai, and who ddin't let it stpo her.

In thee nd, I've been wrtiing and erading and elerning, and not let ting it slow me dwon. Yuo once said, 'Yuo dno't star tuot wrtiing good ustff. Yuo star tout wrtiing crap and thikning it's good ustff, and then grdaually yuo get ebtter at it. Thta's ywh I sya oen of the msot vaulabel traits is perisstence.'

Fro me, I do whta I ahve to doto get oni nthis owrld, and dno't owrry too umch baout whta othres are oding. Wehn I reocmmend yuor oboks, and epople ask why this authro, I say, beacuse this wrtier was perisstent. She dind't let nayone geti nthe awy of whta she awnted – and ewll, it's the best yuo'll find.

With grtaitude for inspriing me,
Hnutre Liugore

[1] Interview with Octavia Butler by Joshunda Sanders: www.inmotionmagazine.com/ac04/obutler.html.

[2] The Yale Center for Dyslexia & Creativity: dyslexia.yale.edu/butler.html

[3] Octavia Butler Interview Excerpts, *Locus Magazine.* http://www.locusmag.com/2.../Issues/06/Butler.html

Joyce Chng

*Missives Through The Multiverse: Ephemeral Letters to
Octavia Butler*

Dear Octavia,

I hope my words reach you through the ether, like fragile bare
bones becoming bird-shaped(?) and taking wing. My letters carry
my dreams, my aspirations, and my thoughts. They also carry the
joys, the determination, and the pain of Earthseed, sowing and
growing.

Baby writer picked up *Parable of the Sower* when her soil
thirsted for nourishment. Baby writer read the book, put it down a
couple of times, and picked it up again. It was not an easy book to
read. Many of the things hit home and hit hard. Like punches on
the solar plexus. It was a journey not only for Lauren, but for baby
writer who had thought the book was gentle, a kind encouragement
that would cradle the heart and give it love. Instead, it was bare,
hard, rich, deep, and conflicted just as Lauren Oya Olamina was.
Her world collapsed, safety (as she knew it) was gone; she learned
how to cope with her hyperempathy, and created a belief system
that centered on self and radiated out into the community.

Baby writer didn't like Lauren at first. She was not an easy
person to like. But then, must all girls in fiction (and non-fiction)
be likeable, like princesses who would instantly command love
(and turn instantly into pushovers or doormats)? Lauren reminded
baby writer so much of herself. Many levels, so many parts edged
like hard flint, so many parts soft and protected by the flint,
because the teenager was still growing. And as society crumbled

around her, Lauren grew stronger as her awareness of self crystallized. When her followers listened to her, Lauren became a prophet-leader and her belief system became a religion. Yet, did her religion define her, or did she define the religion? Her mistakes were not the sum of who she was. This is a vital lesson for many people, especially for girls and women, for boys and men. For everyone.

Octavia, baby writer was me.

Joyce

———

Dear Octavia,

I hope my words reach you once more through the ether. My last letter talked about how baby writer read *Parable of the Sower* and didn't really love it straightaway. Instead, it took a few readings, a lot of courage to finish it. Hard lessons are often difficult to swallow. We always want to listen to nice things, sweet things, things that have been tailored for us like bite-sized news. Nobody wants to listen to hard lessons that taste of bitter earth and bitterer tears. Most of us would rather listen to lies or sugar-coated half-truths because we bloody well want to feel good about ourselves.

Baby writer was struck by the words of Earthseed:

All that you touch
You Change.

All that you Change
Changes you.

The only lasting truth
is Change.

God

is Change.

(*Parable of the Sower*, Grand Central Publishing, updated edition, 2000, 3)

Those were powerful words. For baby writer who was still searching for the right (well, that felt right to her) path, these words were seeds that were planted, germinated, and grew roots. The words taught me a truth that resonates true even now. God (or Goddess) is not predestination. We have a part to play too. This truth teaches us that we have power too and that we too have to be sensitive of the impact we make on ourselves and on others. And that we have to learn how to change and cope with change. Things are not static. Stagnancy breeds toxicity and entropy. We have to change and change has to come, no matter what.

Joyce

———

Dear Octavia,

I hope my words have landed safely in your hands, wherever you may be in this vast multiverse. This (hopefully not the last) letter has my dreams, some realized, some still in seed form. I am telling you these dreams to give myself the hope that somebody in the multiverse also understands them.

Baby writer has, by now, written fiction. A few books, poetry, and some personal words. Baby writer stills feels like a baby writer, because learning doesn't necessarily stop at a single point in Life. I am still riding on a steep and jagged learning curve, a lot of ups and downs. At the moment, I have slid to one of the downs, odd because at the time of writing this letter, the old year has burned away in self-immolation and the new year is barely two days. Old things have followed me into the new year, old fears that have grown terrifying in size and shape. I wish I could have the strength of Lauren, who has taught me to be human, and to be vulnerable. I would like to hide in a corner and weep, because that's my only response at the moment. I have so many seeds planned and planted. I want them to come into fruition. I do not want them to fail.

The baby new year has brought with it a slew of uncertainties. The planet is falling apart at the seams. Megalomaniacs and tyrants dominate. Hatred, bigotry and division seem big and unmovable. The unreal has become real. Lies are indiscernible from truth. People are fearful, terrified and looking for hope. Your words are becoming too real:

Choose your leaders
with wisdom and forethought.
To be led by a coward
is to be controlled
by all that the coward fears.
To be led by a fool
is to be led
by the opportunists
who control the fool.
To be led by a thief
is to offer up
your most precious treasures
to be stolen.
To be led by a liar
is to ask
to be told lies.
To be led by a tyrant

is to sell yourself
and those you love
into slavery.
(*Parable of the Talents*, Warner Books, 2000, 201)

So, I turn to you for advice, for this hope, for inspiration. Because you have inspired me so much, even with *Parable of the Sower*. That we can all be sowers, in our own way. Yet we all have to learn the hard way, because resistance requires also self-belief, willpower and trusting in good people. These truths shine fierce light on the liars and tyrants. These truths also demand we hunker down and fight. Resistance is hard work, with blood and tears and physical labor. A belief system is strengthened by belief. People have to believe in themselves first, just as Lauren had to believe in herself. We have to depend on faith. We need to have faith. We need to have dreams. We need to dream. We dream. Dreaming is a powerful verb. Dreaming is action.

We really need to have Earthseed now. Perhaps we are Earthseed. Perhaps now we are the Change that Changes us.

Dear Octavia, your words are Change. May my words sow seeds in people, seeds that grow promise, hope, resistance, and kindness.

Dear Octavia, thank you.

Thank you.

Joyce

Stephen R. Gold

Ms. Butler:

You may remember me from the 2005 Clarion West Writers Workshop. I was one of eighteen students, and you were our First Week instructor.

What an exciting and disorienting week for me! I'd been writing seriously for four years, but remained unpublished. I lacked basic knowledge and skills, such as deconstruction and short-story structure. In spite of this, I'd applied to a workshop that involved intensive writing and critique of speculative fiction. And there I was, cocooned in Seattle for six weeks with a bunch of strangers who shared my passion for SF.

I got in largely (I assume) on the strength of a short story I sent in with my application. Lacking anything newer to offer, I submitted it for first-week critique.

Perhaps you recall it. The protagonist was a pious fisherman's daughter with the ability to lure fish by singing to them. My manuscript ended with her forcible abduction by foreign sailors, who easily separate her from her young son.

It evoked varied critiques. Going around the classroom that morning, my fellow students repeatedly astonished me with their reactions. Some thought my story was set in the Caribbean, and one labeled it 'magical realism.' (I had to look up what that meant!) I was also told that my first-person narration sounded too bookish for an illiterate fisherman's daughter.

The feedback enlightened and humbled me. Scribbling

notes and absorbing all I could, I said little.

As the instructor, you got to speak last. With visibly suppressed fury, you asked, 'Do you think people of color don't love their children?'

I've long wondered why you reacted that way. Were you or someone you loved ever pressured to give up a child for adoption? Or were you releasing pent up anger after being subjected to such prejudices all your life?

I was stunned. I'd never heard that prejudice before, and my story had no people of color in it. I said, 'No, ma'am!'

When a question is posed in the negative, it's easy to misconstrue the answer. I meant that I assumed people of color do love their children. I wish I'd clarified that.

Harsh though it felt at the time, your question helped me eventually revise my story. I removed the miscue which had led readers to infer a Caribbean setting. I laid better groundwork for the climax, disclosing the protagonist's love for her son and motivating her decision to go calmly with the sailors. Revision improved the story by boosting its emotional pitch. But that came weeks later.

Later that same day, I waited outside your office for our one-on-one. I was anxious. I knew my story had offended you, and I didn't expect you to be any gentler in private than you had been in class.

Our conference, though awkward, wasn't as bad as I'd feared.

The memorable moment came when you asked whether I loved my protagonist. I was puzzled. She was a fictitious character. Was it even possible to love a fiction? A moment's consideration convinced me it was. But while fond of her, I had invented dramatic events to advance the plot. Given the physical and emotional distress they caused her, I couldn't claim to want the best possible outcome for her. (Such, at the time, was my notion of 'love.') After pondering for most of a minute, I admitted I didn't love her.

You recommended writing about something I loved, and we proceeded to other matters.

Later, trying to put your advice into practice, I wondered if I'd understood you correctly. 'Love' is a verb with many senses. In what sense should authors *love* their protagonists?

I see literary characters as fragments of the author's psyche. From that perspective, I did love my protagonist – in the sense of emotional bonding, at least. Like her, I felt distant and alienated from the community where I grew up. Like her, I was separated from my son – by career and divorce, in my case. Much of her pain was familiar. That made her easy to write.

From that same perspective, failure to love my protagonist might reflect guilt over being an imperfect parent myself – the sort who leaves a young son to attend a six-week writing workshop, for instance. But I doubt you meant I should write characters without faults; literary consensus regards a 'fatal flaw' as the key to a good character.

And I'm sure you weren't suggesting I write about God, pets, close kin, or trusted comrades. If by 'love' you meant divine, familial, or fraternal love, you wouldn't have posed the question.

But perhaps you believed my life experience as an assimilated, light-skinned American male had left me ill-equipped to invent sympathetic characters with dissimilar backgrounds. Perhaps you were suggesting that if I didn't love (in the sense of 'relate to') the Other, I should write about other assimilated, light-skinned American males. In other words, 'Write what you know.'

If that's what you meant, then I disagree. Learning about others and their viewpoints was what attracted me to historical and speculative fiction in the first place. In preparation for the workshop, I'd read *Wild Seed* and spent a couple of happy hours in the mind of Anyanwu. Similarly, I've spent days in the head of that fisherman's daughter. Despite our dissimilar backgrounds, I believe I relate well to her.

And even if I'm deluded in that belief, I keep trying to see the world from her viewpoint. I can't seem to stop trying.

Viewpoint isn't just essential to fiction, it's essential to becoming human: learning to understand one another so we can treat each other decently. Based on what I know of you, I'm hopeful you'd agree.

Since the workshop, I've extended my story with some of the singer's adventures after her abduction. Like you, she endures terrible prejudice. Like you, she finds solace in books and develops a keen interest in historical research. Like you, she mentors others. And like you, her passing is sudden and tragic.

I didn't consciously insert these parallels into her story. In fact, I just noticed them today. They're coincidental. Well, probably coincidental. My mind refuses to let them go. It delights in finding such patterns in human experience, and that, I believe, is the root of storytelling.

Your mind, I imagine, must've had a similar bent. You were a master of patterns. You studied the patterns of power-hoarding in our society, and by translating them to other milieus, made them easier to recognize and understand. You had that ability, and you shared it with the world. Thank you! Thanks also for the help you offered aspiring storytellers like me.

I don't know where our humanity goes when our bodies die, but wherever you are and whatever you're up to, I hope you're surrounded by great stories.

Sincerely,
Stephen R. Gold

Michele Tracy Berger

'Positive obsession is about not being able to stop because you are afraid and full of doubts. Positive obsession is dangerous. It's about not being able to stop at all.'

Octavia Butler, 'Positive Obsession' in *Bloodchild and Other Stories* (page 133, 1st edition)

Dear Octavia,

You are an unacknowledged creativity guru. I have studied your struggles to become a speculative fiction writer during a time when that was almost unthinkable for an African American woman. I've been fascinated with your self-making in the face of adversity and your ability to stay creative despite the odds. Your work has influenced me as a speculative fiction writer, has shaped my understanding of the creative process and serves as a model for teaching about feminism and creativity. I feel as if you've been mentoring me all these years.

I discovered your fiction in graduate school in the early 1990s after consuming feminist science fiction authors of the 1970s and 1980s and dog-earing my copies of *Amazons!*, *Women of Wonder* and *Aurora: Beyond Equality*. It was, however, your nonfiction work that creatively baptized me and propelled me into action.

You came to Ann Arbor, Michigan in 1995 and read from your short fiction collection, *Bloodchild*. As a frustrated political science graduate student, I was just starting to acknowledge and make room for my deep desire to write speculative fiction. Hearing you read your two brief essays, 'Positive Obsession' and 'Furor Scribendi,' changed my life.

The word obsession can have a negative connotation. It can mean that we have an unhealthy fascination with an object or situation. In your essay, however, you use the term 'positive obsession' to indicate an approach that helped you realize your dreams:

> Obsession can be a useful tool if it's positive obsession. Using it is like aiming carefully in archery.
>
> I took archery in high school because it wasn't a team sport. I liked other team sports, but in archery you did well or badly according to your own efforts. No one else to blame. I wanted to see what I could do. I learned to aim high. Aim above the target. Aim just *there*! Relax. Let it go. If you aimed right, you hit the bull's-eye. I saw positive obsession as a way of aiming yourself, your life, at your chosen target. Decide what you want. Aim high. Go for it.
>
> I wanted to sell a story. Before I knew how to type, I wanted to sell a story.
>
> ('Positive Obsession', page 129)

You kept your focus on a publication goal through getting ripped off by an agent (who charged a 'reading fee'), through getting up at 2 a.m. and writing before you went to work, through numerous rejections and even a creative writing teacher who asked you,

'Can't you write anything normal?' You sold your first story at age twenty-three and then nothing for another five years.

Then you sold *Patternmaster*, your first novel. You persevered.

That day in Ann Arbor, I bought your book, and you signed it. Though I was too shy to say more than a sentence to you, I secretly vowed that nothing was going to stop me from becoming a writer. In a flurry of creative outpouring, I wrote several stories, including the first twenty pages of a novella that I loved. The next year, I applied to the Clarion Science Fiction and Fantasy Writers' Workshop. I was accepted and much to the chagrin of my dissertation adviser, took six weeks during the summer to eat, sleep and breathe speculative writing. I loved every minute of being in a community of writing faculty and students. That transformational workshop provided a crash course on how writing workshops operate, including how to be a good workshop participant (i.e. ways to give and receive critique). I workshopped my novella and received enthusiastic and helpful feedback. Clarion gave me my first taste of what being a disciplined writer meant.

At Clarion, I also learned about being an outsider within an already marginal group of 'nerds' who read and write science fiction. I was the only person of color in the group, the only person writing about nonwhite characters. I tried to imagine your experience there in 1969, more than twenty years before me. We don't know much about your time at Clarion except that you sold a story during it. Did you struggle with doubts about being good enough? Did people politely respond to your work?

In 'Positive Obsession,' you chronicled your almost crippling self-doubt and ruminated over the sexism and racism that you faced in the 1960s and 1970s. You gave words to the inner and outer demons that haunted me for decades. Was I getting rejected because my writing wasn't strong enough or because my work often centered on the lives of women of color and drew on tropes and themes common in African American literature? I lay awake many nights worrying that my characters and their struggles didn't seem 'relatable enough' to white editors and slush pile readers.

As a mentor, you continue to surprise me. Digging through the archives, historians recently found affirmations you wrote on the back of a notebook. Where and when did you find out about affirmations? Did you take a workshop? Or, more likely, read a book? Affirmations as a self-growth tool were popular in California long before they became mainstream. Affirmations as short, simple positive statements have lost the connection to mysticism they had when you used them. Now, psychologists, writers and coaches all advocate their use.

Did you practice saying them out loud in front of a mirror? Did you say them after you got another rejection letter, or people questioned your right to write science fiction?

I wonder if you used affirmations to combat the sorts of statements that I sometimes hear in my head:

It's never going to happen for me.

People will never understand my work.

It just sucks.

I savored reading your affirmation notebook from 1988, when you had had a taste of professional success after winning several awards for your novella 'Bloodchild'. Your greatest commercial successes still lay ahead of you and you could feel it. I admire that you were willing to try any method to keep focused. I think blogger Kiara Collins has it right when she notes that you 'literally wrote' yourself 'into existence' using affirmations (https://blavity.com/octavia-butler/).

When I look over your handwritten affirmations, I am struck by how you wanted your success to contribute to others. Several of your affirmations involved supporting African American young people. It's a reminder that creative success should ripple out and positively impact others.

I discovered your notebook halfway through my own experiment with affirmations. I had made a commitment to post one affirmation about writing and/or creative practice every day for the entire year on my blog, 'The Practice of Creativity'. I wanted to go beyond technique and discipline, and work on self-kindness and confidence. I discovered that this practice gave me a type of generous permission and freedom that I had not known before. Self-approval is the secret elixir of writing. And, if we have to fake it for a while, that's OK. You learned this lesson long ago.

I kept writing speculative fiction after graduate school and through the early half of an academic career. I've made more and more space for a creative life. In 2017, that novella I worked on at Clarion, twenty years ago, is being published with Book Smugglers Publishing – my biggest professional sale thus far. It is not lost on me that a small feminist-oriented press that has a commitment to selecting a diversity of voices fell in love with my work. The struggle for writers of color in speculative fiction continues to be well-documented.

Creativity is the millennial buzzword and books exploring the creative process and how to harness one's imagination are popular. Most of these books continue to draw their examples primarily from the lives of straight, white male artists. I teach a 'Women and Creativity' seminar and your work features prominently in it. Your essays provide a richly textured understanding of creative practice that evolves out of the experiences of African

American women's lives. It echoes Alice Walker's pivotal essay, 'In Search of Our Mother's Gardens,' in her groundbreaking collection of essays by the same name. You both remind us that creativity is simultaneously an approach to life and what one produces. *Creativity also trumps personal trauma.* In my class, your life is a beacon to students. We discuss how you faced and overcame classic external barriers (racism, sexism, classism, etc.) and internal barriers (self-doubt, lack of role models, etc.) that often define the trajectory of creative women. Reading your words emboldens them to dream big and persist.

In the afterword to the essay in *Bloodchild*, you say how difficult it was for you to write 'Positive Obsession'. Thank you for pushing yourself, persisting, and encouraging all of us.

Staying inspired,
Michele

References

Butler, Octavia, *Bloodchild and Other Stories*. New York: Four Walls Eight Windows, 1995. 123–136.

Collins, Kiara. 'Octavia Butler's personal journal shows the author literally wrote her life into existence,' Blavity Blog, January 28,2016. https://blavity.com/octavia-butler/

Walker, Alice. *In Search of Our Mothers' Gardens: Womanist Prose*. New York: Harcourt Brace Jovanovich, 1983.

Rachel Swirsky

Dear Octavia,

I don't know how to write this letter.

I don't believe in an afterlife, although it's lovely to imagine there is one for people like you. I hope it is as beautiful and transcendent as you deserve, though I can't put my faith in it.

This letter is necessarily a performance. It's written between me and an audience, framed by the echo of you. I don't know how to write as if it is anything else. So, I suppose I'll write what it is.

If you could read this, you wouldn't remember me. I was in your Clarion West 2005 workshop, the last one you taught before you died. It was one of the greatest honors of my life. I sat across the table from you, thinking, 'How can this be the woman who wrote *Parable of the Sower* and Lilith's Brood?' Simply because I could not imagine being so close to such genius. I was staring at you in the sunlight, your hands and profile limned by Seattle's summer gold, uncomprehending. I am not religious, but I saw in you the miracle of human brilliance, and it was dazzling.

You weren't much interested in the three stories I gave you. You wrote that one had spark; thank you for that. Still, listening to you talk about fiction, I began to realize how our aesthetics didn't match. Your work embodies mine. My work was orthogonal to yours. Fiction is like that sometimes. There's a strange alchemy between reader, writer, and text.

Of course, it would have been raw joy if you'd liked my stories, but your indifference in no way diminished the honor of hearing you speak, about my work and others'. I like to joke that the most valuable paper I own is your critique of 'Heartstrung': a half-page of penciled lines, ending mid-sentence when you (presumably) fell asleep over the paper. I call it a joke because it amuses me, but it's also true.

A few months after the workshop, I saw you during your tour for *Fledgling*. When I reintroduced myself, your stare was blank, and I collected your autograph and moved on. I had the immense privilege of being near you, but I didn't know you, not really.

So, how do I justify the ache I still feel, these eleven years later?

I ache for your work. I ache for your voice. I'm gutted for this world of ours you left so young. I ache for the words that should have been written that have been squandered on death instead.

I don't know whether or not to be grateful that you've been spared seeing the progression of the world. During one of our few conversations, you told me that you'd had to set aside your dystopic Parable series because it felt too close and painful during the turbulent Bush years. I'm grateful you've been spared the pain of seeing the increasing American embrace of fascist and neo-Nazi rhetoric, and its celebration in our halls of power.

But I wish you were here.

I've always been fascinated by your view on humanity: bleak, yet also tender in its way. You imagined us – revealed us? – as fundamentally, tragically bound by the limits of our bodies and minds, driven toward gratification and competition that so easily turn to greed and war. Simultaneously, you imagined slantways solutions, science fictional or fantastical. The love or indifference of aliens. Diseases affecting, transforming our minds. Psychic powers. Even divine intervention. The solutions were often –

perhaps always – fraught and impossible and conflicted, and yet they captured the allure of cooperation and solidarity. I do not believe your fictional worlds were ever meant as literal ways to navigate the murk of humanity. Instead, they illuminated and clarified the natures of our souls and societies, and taught us ways to imagine different possibilities, to see cracks of potential change in walls we'd thought impenetrable.

There are some things you would love about this world. I wish you could have seen the proliferation of astounding speculative fiction by powerful, smart Black women that has been awarded its due acclaim. N. K. Jemisin, Alaya Dawn Johnson, Nnedi Okorafor, and others who strive and succeed in the wake of your legacy, bringing Black women's imaginations into the future.

If you were here, could you help lead us out of this dark place?

Would it be too selfish to ask?

You were the most important science fiction writer of the twentieth century. You gave us a gift the world can never repay. Your words will bring light as long as there are people to read them.

In love, debt, and reverence,
Rachel Swirsky

Stephanie Burgis

Dear Octavia,

I'm trying to make a list of the specific things I owe to you ... and wow. This list may not be long, but to me, it is *important*. It starts with one of the biggest thanks of my life:

1. The fact that I attended the Clarion West Workshop

Of course I always wanted to go to a Clarion workshop ... *one day*. I'd worked as the assistant to the director at the Clarion East workshop when I was eighteen, and had felt wild with jealousy of the student writers there. I wanted *so badly* to be part of one of those workshops circles – and as a writer, this time, not just as the one who made the coffee. So I told myself I really would apply ... *one day*!

But somehow I never, ever had the nerve to apply *now* ... because let's face it, the Clarion workshops are for real writers, not just wannabe writers, riiiight? And the idea of calling myself a real writer – saying it out loud, in front of other people! – filled me with panic and a desperate fear of humiliation. So each year passed in exactly the same way, sighing wistfully over each Clarion notice in *Locus* and then letting it go. And it could have gone on that way forever ...

Except that one day, I found out that you would be giving a talk at a bookstore in a town only forty-five minutes away from me. Unfortunately, I didn't have a car that I could use to drive there. There were no direct bus routes, either. So I worked out a circuitous two-hour-long route to get out to hear you talk, because I *knew* I could not possibly pass up the chance to meet you in person.

. . . And oh, wow. Your talk was inspiring. Your frankness about what it took to become a published author was eye-opening. Your brilliance was not surprising (since I'd already devoured all of your fiercely intelligent books), but it was still stunning. Your presence was phenomenal.

. . . And you mentioned in the course of your talk that you would be teaching at Clarion West the next summer. So when I finally reached the head of the line to get my book signed by you, I said brightly – in the slightly pathetic hope of making a connection – 'Oh, I'm planning to apply to Clarion West this year!'

. . . And honestly, I thought I *might*. *Probably*. *Maybe*. At least if I could work up the nerve sometime over the next few months … which, okay, I probably wouldn't, but. . .

You could have smiled and nodded and let that moment go, moving on to the next person in the very long line. Instead, you frowned at me. You looked concerned. You said, very firmly, 'Then you'd better apply *quick*. They're already filling up fast!'

I gulped. I felt the full force of your attention focused on me. I said, 'I will!'

I went home in a daze.

And then that weekend – shaking and, at one point, crying with tension – *I actually finally did it*. I filled out the application form and wrote the personal essay and printed out multiple copies of the first chapter of my new book, which had always felt secret and private and far too vulnerable to show to anyone outside of my family.

I sent it all off, terrified and filled with the unshakeable belief that my rejection – no, my *humiliatingly dismissive* rejection –

would mark the final end of my lifelong delusions of being a writer.

But I got in!

. . . Which is how I finally became a person who *told* other people that she was a writer and began to treat her own writing seriously, rather than like a shameful secret – and how I finally learned to *do the work* to achieve my dreams, instead of just sitting back and fantasizing about them.

It's how I became a much, much *better* writer, one who would eventually become good enough to be published.

It's how I learned to be a *professional* writer (which is slightly different from just being a good one). It's how I found a community of supportive fellow writers to buoy me up. It's even how I met my husband, and how I moved to a different country!

In other words, going to Clarion was one of the most significant experiences in my life, and I would owe you *so much* just for inspiring that. But then something else that was equally important happened:

2. You were my Week 1 teacher, and you taught me one of the most important writing lessons of my life.

Every week, after the morning workshop session, each of the writers who'd been critiqued got to have one-on-one conferences with their teacher. You had chosen my chapter to be critiqued on the first morning, so on the very first day of Clarion West, I walked, feeling so nervous that I was literally trembling, up to your apartment to talk about my writing.

My chapter came from a historical science fiction novel set in Vienna in 1914, with aliens hidden in a family's basement. You said to me, as we discussed it that afternoon, 'I never could get a really clear visual of what the aliens actually looked like. Could you tell me how you see them?'

I laughed a little, embarrassed laugh, and I shrugged, and I said, 'Oh, I haven't really bothered to think that part through. I mean, the aliens are really just a metaphor, so that part doesn't matter so much. *Right?*'

Right?

You looked at me.

When I say look, I mean *a look*.

Your eyebrows shot up.

You didn't say anything. I think maybe you were too horrified to reply ... or else, you simply couldn't think of anything polite to say in response to that piece of inanity. After all, you were, as a teacher, invariably gracious, polite and kind.

But you were also always honest with us. And the message in your head came through very clearly in that look.

I said, very quietly, as you continued to look at me in silence, 'But... I'll think about that more carefully now?'

'Yes,' you said, with audible exasperation. 'You *do* that.'

And then, as you shook your head to yourself in lingering disbelief, you asked, 'Now do you have any questions for me?'

'Yes,' I said. I was still feeling small and honestly pretty stupid, but I somehow found the courage to ask what I'd been desperate to ask ever since our packages had first arrived, weeks ago, with copies of my chapter enclosed inside for everyone to read before we arrived. '*Why* did you choose my chapter for the first day's workshop?'

My secret fantasy, of course, was that you would reply immediately with something like: *Because yours was the best. Because I loved it. Because I saw your geeeeenius!*

But that wasn't you, and it wasn't what I needed, either.

Instead, you looked me in the eye and you said calmly, 'Because it was flawed enough to give people things to talk about, but good enough that you wouldn't be embarrassed by what they said.'

I looked back at you. I took a deep breath, as I absorbed it. I said, 'Okay.'

And I prepared myself to work harder than I'd ever worked before.

Because my work was *good enough* to start with ... but I was determined to get *much better*.

Because I wanted to live up to the standards that you'd set for me.

Ever since that day, every single time I've ever wanted to handwave a description or a worldbuilding point – and oh, do I struggle with that impulse all the time! – I remember that look that you gave me ...

And I try harder.

I do the work, just like you inspired me to do from the very first time I met you.

You set a standard that I will never match, but I am so grateful to have had it set for me.

Thank you, Octavia. Thank you so much.

Sincerely,
Stephanie Burgis

SECTION SIX

I LOVE YOU ACROSS OCEANS, ACROSS GENERATIONS, ACROSS LIVES

Bogi Takács

Dear Octavia,

You are my hero, my shining beacon. Words are inadequate. But I am writing you this letter because I owe you an apology.

To explain, I'll have to tell you something I have told very few people in the English-speaking SF community. I'll tell you something that makes me squirm and hide, that makes me feel ashamed of myself.

I'm not a native speaker of English. And a considerable amount of my English I have learned from pirated media – including your work.

When I'm starting to write this letter, I still don't know if I will dare to sign it, even though what I did was perfectly legal in my country of origin – Hungary – at that time, and to my knowledge it still is to this day. Now I live in the United States and I can get all your books from my public library. I live paycheck to paycheck, but I can sometimes even buy your books; one of my treasured possessions is a signed copy of your *Parable of the Talents*, purchased at a Midwestern antique mall and filled with newspaper clippings chronicling your career. Someone must have felt the same fierce gratitude that I feel toward you.

Without you I would not be writing today.

When I first began pirating your work, the word 'ebooks' did not exist yet. People said 'e-texts,' sometimes even 'e-textz' to express the risqué nature of warez, pirated data in a quintessentially late-nineties/early-aughts way.

I first came across your short stories: among them, *Speech Sounds*, in a .txt file. I still have it. It took away my breath – the way the science was woven in, in an understated but unambiguous way. At this point, Internet access was a preciously rationed commodity, in Hungary even more so than in the US; and people swapped books on IRC.

Early on I began to gravitate toward minority authors in English-language SFF, because I also belonged to a minority in my country of origin. On the few websites discussing the topic at that time, everyone advised: 'Read Butler, read Delany.' I only lurked in these spaces; I did not feel like I spoke enough English to participate in any discussion.

But while a few tattered, dog-chewed copies of old Delany paperbacks did turn up once in a while in the English-language bookshops in the capital (the only English-language bookshops in the country), I could not find your work. Delany probably benefited from his covers showing muscular Aryan barbarians – at this point I did not know of the term 'whitewashing.'

Amazon was a promising startup at this time; Jeff Bezos grinning on the cover of *Time*, surrounded by styrofoam pellets. Shipping books to my country was not only prohibitively expensive, shipments were also regularly stolen – a problem to this day.

I turned to warez.

I read *Parable of the Sower*. Of *Parable of the Talents* I could only find a corrupted copy, which I still read, only to be aggravated to tears when I found dozens of pages missing in the second half. Sure, I could understand someone wanted to mess with the pirates' heads. But I was a lonely and scared youngster in a not-so-developed country, and these books were a lifeline.

I could not finish reading *Kindred* at that time, only much later; it hit too close to home.

Years later, I found an only slightly mutilated copy of your Xenogenesis trilogy in one of the aforementioned bookshops. Its stamps said it had been a library discard from a Western country. We always got the discards – the clothes, the books. Something someone in the West had thrown away, I paid good money to get.

Even later, I made a friend from that Western country, also a minority person; they told me that the public libraries were downsizing, getting rid of everything, closing rural branches. They could not get a library copy of the very same Xenogenesis trilogy that someone had shipped to my country, and probably made a profit while doing so. I sat, stared at my computer screen, trying not to cry at the unfairness of it all. I wanted them to have my copy, but I had no money to send it to them. Would it be stolen en route? It was impossible to predict: when I started to apply to foreign universities, people even stole my application materials.

I made that book even more chewed-up than it had been before. I read it several times, halting, savoring, shuddering.

You spoke of power. Of exploitation. Of all the things most other writers shied away from. You wrote with an ease that seemed accidental, but upon reading you, had been illuminated to me as deliberate. You spoke – it seemed like you spoke to me. You understood. And I wanted to learn.

I felt I could write; that the shapeless tensions churning in me could be given form, allowed expression. That I could write about cruelty and hope. That I could write about all that had previously been off limits, when I tried my hand at short stories. That there was a *point* to science fiction beyond canny extrapolation. That my emotions could fit. That my life experience could fit.

Does my story have a happy ending? I moved to the United

States. I am in the process of immigration. I get heaps of books from my local public library, by all the writers of color, all the queer and trans people who were inspired by you – I struggle with carrying my hoard home. I have no need to pirate any of that. I stream movies from Amazon on the smart TV we bought on a Black Friday sale. For all intents and purposes, I live in a future of unimaginable riches, even while the IRS tells me I am officially low-income.

When I try to explain, few American writers listen. I like to imagine you'd listen, you who also thrived on public libraries, who spoke of 'grazing' the shelves, getting all the non-fiction that struck your interest, building it into your work in obvious and not-so-obvious ways. You who also spent countless hours on Greyhound buses, cramped up and cranky. Who tried to write while utterly exhausted from work, who saw the underside of the country and who understood all the warning signs.

I love you, across oceans, across generations, across lives. Please forgive me.

On the second try I did manage to sign this –

I remain, in eternal gratitude,

Bogi

Asata Radcliffe

Octavia,

It never occurred to me that a day of random browsing in an Albuquerque used bookstore would, six years later, lead me to having lunch with you on a college campus in northern California. The saying 'what a difference a day makes' came to life for me on that spring day in 2005, when I was pulled to the side by the director of the Women's Center library, Joy Fergoda. Joy pulled me close, and whispered, 'Would you be interested in having lunch with Octavia Butler?' My answer to her: 'How did you know?'

At the time, I was an undergraduate in my sophomore year at UC Davis. To be asked to meet you was a no-brainer, though I had never spoken to the librarian about you, or told her that I had a shrine of your books, that bordered on obsessive in my campus apartment. All of your books sat on what I had deemed the O.B. Shelf, in full view, to remind me daily that it was my calling to one day have my name among the next generation of science fiction writers. Whenever I mentioned your name to English teachers then (and sadly even today), none of them had ever heard of you, let alone read your work. I'll never know why Joy chose me, and I could only assume fate had played a hand.

The path to meeting you began in 1999, on a visit to a used bookstore in Albuquerque. I was having one of those *I'll let the book speak to me* days, not looking for anything in particular. The cover of your book *Dawn* struck me: a brown-skinned woman, lying with her eyes closed, her body wrapped in what looked like soft foliage, her hair braided back, a small bang on her forehead, wisps of hair on her neck, the same way I had worn my hair for much of my time in middle school. After seeing the word 'starship' on the back cover, I knew this was the book that had called to me.

Hours later, I had become engrossed in this science fiction world, an immersion I hadn't experienced since I first saw *Star Wars*. I swallowed up the entire Xenogenesis series, though finding the third book, *Imago*, proved to be almost impossible as your books weren't on the science fiction shelves in any of the retail bookstores. It was 1999. The Internet was barely up and running. Luckily, I found a Canadian website that carried the third book of the series. Waiting for that sequel to arrive in the mail mirrored the anxiousness I feel every year waiting for the next season of *Game of Thrones*.

Between the years of reading your books and meeting you, as the Internet began to expand its universe, I finally had the opportunity to read your own words in a few online interviews. You spoke of your discomfort with people wishing to classify your books under race, and how insignificant race truly was for you as it related to the epic mysteries of the universe. To learn this was how you felt mirrored my own views on character writing. Race was of no consequence to me though many applauded my efforts to contribute as a woman of color to a genre that had its doors closed to most not white and male. Your presence marked possibility, my open door. Race was simply the genetic coding that came with the package. And therein lies the paradox. It was the girl that looked like me on the cover of *Dawn* that pulled me to enter into your science fiction world. However, what kept me there was that race was not the driving theme of any of these stories.

And then there was *Parable of the Sower*, the first dystopian novel I had ever read. The Parable series is a trailblazer compared to what I feel are the snoozefest of the many redundant dystopian films now being produced, as you cast a female lead in a dystopia long before it became fashionable and profitable in Hollywood. You weren't casting your stories based upon meeting the need to fulfill a gender or race-based demographic. You were writing from your own purpose. The simplicity of your intentions are what made you stellar to me. You thrived on living in the outer rims, a place where you were quite content. Your books gave me permission to consider that I could actually write books like these myself. And then life offered the miraculous chance to meet you.

The day finally arrived. A discreet lunch with selected women had been organized, held in a small communal room in the campus Women's Center. There you sat with a welcoming smile. Wow. My shero, in flesh and blood. The magical world had become real for me in that moment. There were about seven of us once lunch began. You were nothing like you had been described in the few articles written about you, casting you as shy and soft-spoken. Quiet. A mysterious recluse. It amused me that you were quite the opposite. You asked us how we felt about current events, and said how much you obsessed over the news. We talked about sustainability. You laughed out loud. I thought, this woman knows how to have fun. You were the perfect host, breaking the ice of the initial quiet hesitancy among your guests. Once you began to talk, you didn't stop. I loved it!

After you signed my copy of *Parable of the Sower*, the librarian told me that I had been designated to walk you over to a second private gathering in another department across the campus. I was thrilled, and petrified, though it would give me the chance to finally be alone with you.

So there I was, on that warm spring day, guiding you across campus, your 6'0" regal stature towering over my 5'5". You asked me what I had written. I told you that being a full-time undergrad with a double major, I was frustrated that I might never have the time to write anything of significance. Instead of berating me for not waking up at 4 a.m. to write, your insight was spot on 'You're the type of writer who needs long blocks of time to write. Some can write everyday, but you're not one of them, and that's ok. So, make sure you make the time. Take a whole summer, or a few months. No matter what, do what you have to do to get that block of writing time. It is what you must do.' Once we arrived to the second meeting place, I was all giddy as I presented you to the faculty that awaited you. I handed you my only *Battlestar Galactica* DVD as a gift. You looked at me like I was such a geek. And I was. A geek that walked away with a huge grin on her face. After your thank you and a smile, you said, 'And when you finish something, feel free to send it to me.' It was an invitation I will always treasure.

Sadly, I never got the chance.

Barely a year later, one spring to the next, I received a phone call from an artist friend who lived in your hometown of Seattle. This friend had learned of your death before it hit the news. I spent the next several weeks devastated, trying to reconcile how you stumbled to your death in your own backyard. News reports cited that you had been ill, which was even more puzzling to me as you had so much life and energy months earlier when I saw you. The inexplicable suddenness of your passing felt like an undermining theft. I wondered if you knew, or had a feeling it was coming, the end. Or if it were just another day. I wondered if you were upset with yourself for not getting to complete the third book of the Parable series, one I had patiently waited for you to produce.

Laced within my grief, an idea came to me. Maybe I could finish *Parable of the Trickster* for myself, as a way for me to reconcile what your presence on this planet, and what your loss, meant to me.

There is no such thing as coincidence. Fate has a heartbeat. You came right to my doorstep, as a whisper in my ear, to a small college town that is a blip on the radar. For whatever reason, on that day, your presence was kept quiet. No fanfare. No lecture hall. I believe, with certainty, that forces from an invisible realm brought us together. Even though I missed the chance to hear your feedback on my writing, I hope that one day my work can resonate as yours did. I thank you for writing. You influenced my life forever.

'All that you touch
You Change.
All that you Change
Changes you.
The only lasting truth
Is Change.'
(*Parable of the Sower*, p. 1, 1st edition)

Asata

Nnedi Okorafor

Reprinted with permission from *Strange Matings*, 2013

butler8star@qwest.net

I still keep Octavia's email address in my Outlook address book. I used to send emails to it even after she passed. How poetic would it have been if I'd gotten a reply from Octavia from the spirit world via email? The mix of the mystical and the technological would seem very much like her. Or maybe not; Octavia once told me that she didn't like using email.

Nevertheless, for a minute, she did use email. I don't recall how I got her email address, as I was not personally close to her. I may have had it after I'd interviewed her or maybe I got it after the first time I spoke with her on the phone when I was at Clarion (East) in 2000. I had it, and *of course* I used it. Octavia's email address was butler8star@qwest.net.

I kept our online exchanges like little treasures, and not only because they were emails from one of my favorite writers. It was also because of the time period within which the emails were exchanged. And the subject matter. It was right after September 11th. About a month. When there was little else on most Americans' minds.

I happened to have just read *Parable of the Sower* for the first time. This novel did not help with the panic I was feeling. It scared the hell out of me, solidifying my reasons to feel panicky, paranoid, and untrusting of anything the American government said or did. All I could think about was just how fast society broke down in *Parable of the Sower*. How real it was. Things fall apart.

The 'war' in Afghanistan had just begun: the 'war' where the richest and most powerful country in the world proceeded to bomb one of the poorest, most troubled parts of the world. Octavia and I were speculating about what would come next.

Subject: Re: CNN Questions for bin Laden
Date: Thu, 18 Oct 2001
From: butler8star@qwest.net
To: nokora1@uic.edu

I think Bush will declare victory, pin medals on a few people and try to put war in the past just as soon as he begins to suffer politically – which may be this winter if what I've heard about Afghan winters is true and if Bush really does send in ground troops.

Meanwhile, the bombs and bin Laden will have brought forth a whole new generation of much-deceived young men eager to die for Islam – or just eager to get revenge against the people who bombed their relatives.

Octavia

————

Subject: Re: CNN Questions for bin Laden
Date: Thu, 18 Oct 2001
From: nokora1@uic.edu
To: butler8star@qwest.net

Yeah, you're right. They are both maniacs and they seem to understand each other as if they were identical twins. However, I think hearing Osama bin Laden speak will be a benefit for the 'people.' I don't see this war as a war between 'good' and 'evil.' I don't believe in that concept. I think it's a war of conditions, madness, and power.

This is off the subject but I hear that now the Taliban are teaching women how to fire guns. The same women that they wouldn't allow to move about without a male escort. Hypocrisy abounds.

Nnedi

———

Octavia was still seeing our president as smarter than he was. If President Bush had only done it the way she'd predicted. Nevertheless, Octavia was right about one thing, Osama bin Laden has received his legion of angry disgruntled maltreated followers.

In another email, we discussed some of the vibrations around the world caused by the September 11th attacks.

Subject: Re: CNN Questions for bin Laden
Date: Sun, 21 Oct 2001
From: nokora1@uic.edu
To: butler8star@qwest.net

Speaking of people who have been deceived, have you heard about what's happening in Nigeria? There has been tension between Christian and Muslims for decades there. But a few days ago the Hausas (who tend to be Muslim) went on a rampage and massacred Christians (mostly Igbos). They are saying all the killing was because of this jihad that's been called in the Middle East.

My family is still waiting to hear from some relatives we have in the city where all this took place. In a world where there has been such evolution in communication technology (at least in the 'second' and 'first' world), it's amazing how misinformed we still all are. I think the technology has only made it easier to manipulate and brainwash people.

Nnedi

———

Subject: Re: CNN Questions for bin Laden
Date: Sun, 21 Oct 2001
From: butler8star@qwest.net
To: nokora1@uic.edu

I'm so sorry to hear about this renewed trouble in Nigeria. I hadn't heard at all, and I pay attention to the news. I suppose a great deal is being ignored in favor of the 'war.' I hope your relatives are safe and well. One of my favorite quotes – so sadly true – is from Steve Biko: 'The most potent weapon in the hands of the oppressor is the mind of the oppressed.'

There is also the sad reality that it takes very little to set off young men who want to feel powerful and important, but who are either unwilling or unable to find constructive outlets for their energies. Testosterone poisoning. And men have the nerve to complain about women's hormonal mood swings.

Octavia

———

There are many things I loved about Octavia, but her unflinching political views remain my favorite. She had a way of maintaining them outside of politics. Many know the famous quote where Octavia describes herself as 'a pessimist, a feminist always, a Black, a quiet egoist, a former Baptist, and an oil-and-water combination of ambition, laziness, insecurity, certainty, and drive.' Each of these things is fundamental, not political. Like her writing, her statements were uncluttered, sparse, and always so so clear.

Years later, when I interviewed Octavia about her latest novel, *Fledgling*, for *Black Issues Book Reviews*, she said:

> I wanted to get away from the daily news, which was drearier and drearier and more and more awful each day. I'd read it and listen to it mainly on NPR. There isn't really much you can do about most of what's going on.

> You can support causes or shoot off your mouth but there really isn't a big difference you can make. With the most recent presidential elections, I was depressed for a long time; this was way before the hurricanes. I'd think about the war and watch as corruption became a more normal thing – so I wrote a vampire story.

I remember sputtering and stammering. I wanted so badly to assure Octavia that she had made an enormous difference in many lives. I recited to her all the ways in which her books and her existence had changed me. I told her that because of her I now knew that it was okay to write strange disturbing African characters. And that she changed the way I viewed gender and relationships. I stressed that she had shown me so many possibilities and variations in life. I wanted her to know that she had stretched my mind and it would never return to its former shape. Lastly, I told her that she had inspired, informed and energized legions of us. She just laughed and said that all this was encouraging.

On the night of September 11th, 2001, I wrote these paragraphs:

The black pigeon with white speckles was an overachiever. She had the blood of the archaeopteryx from millions of years ago coursing through her veins. She'd taken one look at the tall skyscrapers and known she would nest close to the top.

She sat on her eggs as she always did, gazing down at the world below. She cooed a sigh of contentment. Then something pricked her small mind. She knew she should fly but she did not. She had eggs. Babies. When she saw the giant metal bird careening toward her, she only stared, chanting a soothing mantra to her creator to do its will: Coo coo, coo, cooo cooo. Coo coo, coo, cooo cooo. It calmed her and she accepted her fate and became part of the blazing inferno of the World Trade Center.

That day, I had been thinking of that same powerlessness, the same futility that Octavia would later articulate during my interview with her. I sent the paragraphs above to Octavia September 11th, 2007, and asked her what she thought. I was curious. But I'll never know, because for the first time my email bounced back. Her address had been officially shut down for good.

Though she's gone, Octavia left us with so much to chew on. This is the beauty of the written word. It lives on when you are gone. It's as close to immortal as you can get. The written word continues to have the power to affect and change long after its creator has moved on.

To survive,

Know the past.

Let it touch you.
Then let
The past
Go.
From 'Earthseed: The Book of the Living,' by Lauren Oya Olamina, *Parable of the Talents*

K. Tempest Bradford

Dear Ms. Butler,

The first time we met was at Clarion West in 2003. You came to speak to our class in week three (before we all fell apart) and I saw you again a couple of weeks later at the party at Greg Bear's house. I know this was the last time I saw you because there's a picture of us standing on the balcony laughing. I don't know what I said or what you said to make this happen, I'm just glad I have evidence that it did. I don't remember much about that conversation except that I wanted to tell you a story and ended up not telling you the story because I thought: she must hear stories like this all the time and be sick of them. Later on I realized that this was a silly thought and decided that the next time I saw you, I'd tell you.

We never got a chance to talk again. So I'll tell the story now.

When I was in my sophomore year of high school I found an excerpt from *Kindred* in my English Lit textbook. I don't think we were assigned to read it – I don't remember having a discussion about it in class. All I remember is the effect it had on me.

Reading about Dana, a modern African-American woman yanked back in time to the 1800s where she witnesses and experiences the horror of slavery, upset me to a degree I was not aware I could be upset by fiction. For the first time I was able to directly identify with a character in fiction and question whether, if put into the same situation, I would be able to deal. The answer at the time was: No. Hell no. I had an anxiety attack just considering that question. All this because Dana is, like me, a Black woman.

I don't know how many Black characters were in the fiction I'd read up to that point, but I don't remember many. I don't remember imagining myself in the world or life of a character in a book before this, not even to fantasize. *Kindred* changed my entire relationship to books. I understood for the first time the power of narrative, and that both frightened and fascinated me.

I'll admit something to you now, something I know I didn't say back when we met because I would have been embarrassed to: I have never finished reading *Kindred*. I know, it's a tragedy! That book is so good. I know it is. But when I say I had an anxiety attack I'm not exaggerating for the sake of hyperbole. That happened to me while reading the excerpt. And I never went back.

It was many years before I encountered your work again and began to understand who you were and how you were important to the genre I'd come to love. The moment I connected the name Octavia Butler with That Book That Messed Me Up In Tenth Grade I knew I wanted to read the other books you'd written. Because you were a Black woman writing Black women in the future, traveling through time, creating new people and new religions. And even though I still couldn't think about Dana without tearing up a bit, I knew I wanted to read more by a writer who could do that to me. By then I understood that what you did was what all great writers are supposed to do. I wanted more of that.

It took me many years of reading science fiction and being part of the SF writing and fandom communities to understand how rare your specific genius was and still is. Instead of creating characters that anyone could relate to by creating characters that looked, acted, and sounded like most every other character in the genre, you created characters that reflected aspects of your existence and still made them relatable. Even though you did that over and over, each novel and short story more amazing than the last, each award you won more and more deserved, this is still something Black and other authors of color have to fight for in our fiction. I fear we're going to have to keep fighting for it for the next while. Sometimes I wonder what you'd have to say about that if you were still here.

Maybe you wouldn't say anything. You'd just hand me a copy of *Kindred* and expect me to finish reading it after all these years. To get to the end and see that Dana makes it through all the horrendous things she had to experience, things she did not spend her whole life learning how to cope with, and survives. Changed, damaged, but alive. If Dana could get through that, maybe I could, too. And if I could survive that, I'm strong enough to deal with whatever the real world throws at me.

Thank you,
K. Tempest Bradford

Kate Gordon

Dear Ms Butler,

My name is Kate. I live in Hobart, Tasmania, an entire world away from where you grew up and lived. When I was born, you were already famous; you were the age I am now, or thereabouts.

To the girl I was, when I fell for you, that idea would have seemed ridiculous. That you were grown up before I was born. That, by the time I 'met' you, your hair was turning grey.

That you might, not so very long after, die.

All of these facts seem strange to me even now because, when I was a kid sitting in my school library, reading your books, you were my friend.

I didn't know you were American. Didn't know what colour your skin was. I didn't even know, at first, that you were female – I'd never heard the name Octavia before. All I knew was that, when I read your books, I felt at home.

That's weird, too, though, isn't it? Because I was a kid growing up in rural Tasmania and your books are ...

Worlds away from there. Universes.

I was a kid in rural Tasmania who had been raised in a home that didn't love science fiction. I read Thomas Hardy, the Brontës, and Jane Austen. I loved those books but they didn't explode my heart.

Your books did. Your books twisted my soul.

I don't know how to tell you what they meant to me.

I was a kid who was different. I was shy, skinny, gawky,

painfully socially awkward. I never knew the right time to laugh. I barely ever said the right thing. The only time the world made sense to me was when I wrote things down. Or when I was reading. Everyone else seemed to get life. They could make sense of it. They were inside. I was outside.

You were outside, too.

And your books existed, for me, in that space that was outside.

Though your characters had names I couldn't pronounce, though most of the time I'm sure your themes and conceptions went completely over my teenage head, your books felt more real and true and logical than anything else that was going on in my world.

I was a kid who firmly believed I was born in the wrong time, in the wrong place, and yes, that sounds pompous but it wasn't arrogance. It was an ache. A hole within me. You filled that hole.

You, Tamora Pierce and Isobelle Carmody. You were the missing piece of me. As I sat in the corner of the school library, alone ...

I wasn't alone.

You were there.

You were my friends.

Four girls together, whispering secrets of other worlds. While the girls who made sense sat in the sun and tanned their legs and thought of new ways to make me feel freakish, I ran away with you into your worlds. I dreamed of being a shapeshifter like Anyanwu and like Daine in Pierce's Tortall books. I dreamed of being a telepath. Maybe then I could understand what was going on in the minds of those other girls.

You, Tamora, Isobelle and me. We would work it out. One day, we would create our own world.

The librarian at school – bucking the cliché of librarians being kind to misfits – didn't like me. Even she thought I was strange. It was the technician who worked only a couple of days a week who taught me how to organise the books – which order to stack them in, which chronology. She sourced some of your works that the library didn't already have. By the time I left high school, I'd read the Patternist series all the way through, and Xenogenesis. Some of the books I probably read twice.

I didn't read 'Bloodchild' until I was at university. College (what we call grades eleven and twelve) wasn't such a hard time for me. I found my tribe and they protected me. I needed you less. But university was a horror and I found comfort again in your words.

Even though, you know, humans playing surrogate to alien bugs shouldn't be comforting. It was. Because it felt feminist and brave and because it made me feel like, if Octavia could write a book like that, maybe I could write the dark things in my own head.

I knew, by now, that you were an American woman, that you were black.

I also knew your birthday and mine were only four days apart. Which I thought was extremely cool.

I knew – because the Internet existed now – that you had also been a child of libraries; you had also been bullied. That part of me that still believed in magic (the part that has never really died), wondered idly if we might both have really been telepaths. If you might, actually, have been sitting beside me in that library. Still a girl, the same age as I was – untethered by time or space. You were with me.

I thought, with a laugh, that if that were true you might

have taught me how to pronounce all those names.

In the years that followed I revisited your words, every so often. I remember hearing of your death not long after I married in 2006. It didn't feel right or real because you were still beside me, so how could you be dead?

You were still beside me, holding my hand. I was still the other. You still understood me in a way nearly nobody else could. By this time I wrote books, too, and they were all about girls who didn't quite fit in; girls who were often found in libraries, trying to make sense of the world.

In all those years – these, now, more than twenty years – between the kid in the library and now, I never read the book for which you are most famous.

Kindred.

Whenever people talk of you, they mention this book. It's your magnum opus. It's the book that saw you moved from the 'genre' shelves to the (apparently) more lauded 'literary' section. I should read *Kindred*, people said. I loved your other books. Why hadn't I read *Kindred*?

The answer was ...

I was saving it.

While there was still one book of yours that I hadn't read, you were still alive. You still had words to share.

Worlds to share.

Ms Butler, I just read *Kindred*. It broke me. It completed me.

And I'm glad I read it because you are still alive. Reading it didn't break the spell. You're still with me.

And you know what? That's the thing about books. They are never over. They never end. You can turn them over and begin again.

I love you across oceans, across generations, across lives

And I have a kid now myself. A girl. One day I'll read her your books.

I probably still won't be able to pronounce the names.

But I want her to know you too.

Love,
Kate

Cat Rambo

Dear Octavia:

I always think of you when I'm riding the bus, because I know that's one of the ways you wrote, riding and thinking about what you were working on. That seems so Octavia to me: a willingness to take a simple and very human experience and use it to make art. And a means of transportation taken by most people, rather than a privileged few.

I remember my first week at Clarion West, hearing you laugh when Leslie's dog Luke was tearing around the classroom as fast as he could, happy to see you. I remember getting a chance to talk to you about my stories, and the serious frown on your face as you said, 'Well it's very oddly shaped, but it's still a story.' And then we talked politics instead for an hour. I can hear your voice in my head, that deep resonant flute, but it's your laugh I remember more than anything else, because it was all laugh, coming up from the roots of your soul to make the world a brighter place just from hearing it.

To me, you represent what a writer should be: always working on craft, always engaged with the world. When you started writing, you said, you copied down an entire Phyllis Whitney novel in order to see how it worked. You knew that writing is more than a craft, though; that for some of us, like you, it is a calling, and the way we try to change the world.

I found out you had died while at a local convention, and I will confess that I have never liked that convention as a result, though it is utterly unfair to it. I just remember that gut punch of finding out such a monstrous unfairness: that you had slipped and died. That you were taken from us far, far, far too soon. You were my teacher, and we never got the time to move past that into friendship, and that's a sadness that will always linger with me.

I hadn't read your work before. When I got accepted to Clarion West and knew I'd be learning with you, I went and got as many of your books as I could, worked my way through *Kindred* and Lilith's Brood and *Patternmaster*. You were working on a vampire novel, what would appear after your death as *Fledgling*.

I pulled up your page on Wikipedia so I could check for the date on that last, and that picture still makes me cry, because it's you, thinking hard as always, gathering what you will say before you speak it, eloquently and truthfully. You gave us all a model to live by, and that's what great teachers do: teach by example as well as word. You made me more patient with my students, made me realize that there are many approaches to writing and all of them are valid, much like life itself.

I love you and I wish you were still here.
Cat

Amanda Emily Smith

Dear Octavia,

When I was fifteen, I discovered *Dawn* in Marigny Books, the local gay book store on Decatur Street. This was 1994, four years before we met. When I began reading, I knew you then through your words. I knew that you led me to question through the pages of *Dawn*. Your words made me uncomfortable, and in that discomfort, I grew into being. The idea of a creature that loved – no, needed – both men and women to survive scared and intrigued me. At that time, I struggled with romantically choosing women or men. I originally chose the former because the latter seemed too complicated. But, in your pages, I could examine this 'alien' sexuality, a sexuality existing outside the binds of choosing one option, the default – attraction to men. I could breathe and question through your pages. There, I was safe. There, I didn't have to choose.

By eighteen, I was sure I was a lesbian. My parents had just found out that summer. It wasn't the gay boyfriend or Indigo Girls' *1200 Curfews* blaring every night. It was pamphlets between my mattress on homosexuality and the church. In the end, it was the words that exposed me. My parents prayed daily for a change that would never come. They asked if I was practicing. If I had thought of men. At that time, I could not question my sexuality. I wore my lesbianism like a coat of arms, like an armor to save me from all the arrows shot at my chest, a fortress of gold-star commitment and lesbian culture to keep me safe from the proverbial angry village knocking at my gate. I had to. I was constantly being interrogated, criticized and challenged. Because of this, it was not safe to question myself and my heart. I could not examine my own desires. I could only resist. I saw no other way.

We met in 1998. You came to Tulane University via Newcomb College as the Zale Writer-in-Residence. I was only eighteen, a Wild Seed who months before had run away from home to love the way she felt. I was still struggling with the nature of this gift of queerness. I hadn't had my nervous breakdown yet. (That was still two years away.) As a Newcomb student, I was asked to tour you around campus. I felt honored just to be in your presence. I didn't realize how blessed I was to soak up your words. I would pry you to speak to hear your words. You answered with few but always just the right ones.

Words to remind me that you were not a god, you were a Black woman. You were a writer. You were mortal. I was not sad about this realization. Even mortals can be divine. You changed me. It was in those early days that your books planted a seed in my heart that took two more years to sprout. In this discomfort, I discovered that maybe I could love all the genders that call to me. And I was not this alien, I was a human. I did not have to force anyone to love me. It was then I came out as bisexual.

The words you wrote changed me, Octavia. Thank you for giving me space in your pages, in your words to be safe as well as uncomfortable with myself. Thank you for giving me characters that looked like me, who questioned their own reality. Thank you for writing my experience into your work.

It amazes me how you have touched so many lives. The man I will eventually call husband thinks of you as a mentor. You helped set the course of his life, and if you had not we might have never met. Though you are gone from this reality, your words are forever. Your Wild Seed will spread across the Earth writing, connecting, visioning and resisting. Your words will continue to shape us into being.

With Love Eternal,
Amanda Emily Smith

Vonda N. McIntyre, Sandra Y. Govan, Jeffrey Allen Tucker, Veronica Hollinger, Sweta Narayan, Marleen S. Barr and Joan Gordon:

(reprinted with permission from *Science Fiction Studies*, Volume 37, Number 3, November 2010)

Reflections on Octavia Butler

Remembering Octavia Butler – Vonda N. McIntyre

Everybody knew her as Estelle in 1970, at the Clarion Writers Workshop in Clarion, Pennsylvania. She was tall, quiet, dignified, and very shy. Harlan Ellison discovered her in a screenwriting workshop in Los Angeles, the city in which she lived for most of her life. Harlan has written that she wasn't a very good screenwriter, which doesn't surprise me much; her subjects and ideas and expressions were deep and complex. Screenplays have strengths, but 'deep' and 'complex' aren't high on their list.

At Clarion, Estelle and I roomed next to each other in a dormitory built out of cinderblocks. Cinderblocks are famously useless in soundproofing. The sound of typewriters echoed throughout the hallway on a more or less continuous basis.

I'm a night owl. I do my best work starting around midnight, or anyway I can't justify procrastinating any longer when midnight arrives. Estelle, on the other hand, was the archetypal morning person. After Clarion, she told me that at the workshop she started working about the time I packed it in for the night, and she hoped she hadn't kept me awake. I sleep like the dead; I hadn't even ever noticed her typewriter. I suspect the truth is that I kept her awake, but she never complained about it.

Estelle was tall and dark; I'm short and rather pale. I have a picture of the class from a convention we all attended, PhgLange, in Pittsburgh, where we're standing next to each other: a pair of opposites, for certain. She wore her hair in an Afro, and mine, when I was young, was rather curly, even more so in the miserable humidity of western Pennsylvania in the summertime.

I would occasionally bound through her doorway and ask what she thought of *my* Afro.

She would smile and shake her head.

When she turned in her first story, everybody in the class read it and gave a collective gasp of amazement. It was clear from the first page that she was an extraordinary writer as well as being an extraordinary person. Over the course of the six weeks of the workshop, her talent and range impressed her fellow workshop members as well as the instructors – a stellar list that included Robin Scott Wilson, Joanna Russ, Harlan Ellison, James Sallis, Samuel R. Delany, Fritz Leiber, Kate Wilhelm, and Damon Knight.

It was neat to watch her career flourish. She overcame her shyness and accepted speaking engagements. She was a terrific speaker, and the events made a big difference in the economy of her household.

In early years, when she had to get a day job to keep her head above water, she would take jobs that required no intellectual exercise, such as working in a laundry. Then she would get up early in the morning – two or three o'clock – and write before going to work.

That changed when her books grew more and more successful, and especially after the MacArthur Foundation awarded her one of its Genius Grants. They couldn't have picked a better recipient.

We kept in touch for more than thirty years. I would always visit her when I went to LA, and she taught several times at the second incarnation of the Clarion West Writers Workshop in Seattle, my home town. She liked Seattle; after her mom died and family responsibilities no longer kept her in the LA area, she moved here. In an amusing coincidence, she bought a house across the street from where I used to live. If Third Place Books had been there when I lived in the area, I might never have moved.

Octavia enjoyed Seattle; she liked the cooler climate and she loved the mountains. Seattle is smaller and more compact than LA, which gave her more access to concerts and plays, since she didn't drive. She would accept a ride, but she wouldn't often ask for one.

Her health, and some of the medication she took for it, affected her ability to write. Distressed, she started one novel after another; dissatisfied, she threw them away. She decided to read some lighter fiction instead of beating herself up all day every day about writing; she particularly enjoyed Charlayne Harris's Sookie Stackhouse vampire novels.

And she decided to write a vampire novel of her own: *Fledgling*.

Being Octavia, she wrote a vampire novel unlike any vampire novel you've ever seen, one that explores responsibility, love, obligation. She was thinking of writing a sequel.

We'll never see it.

I miss her.

Vonda N. McIntyre

Looking Back, Then Forward:
Reflections on the Vision of Octavia E. Butler.
Sandra Y. Govan

The immediate grief felt keenly when Octavia passed so unexpectedly lessened some with the passage of time – she died 24 February 2006 – but a sharp sense of loss remains. It is not simply personal loss; the feeling is more one of ironic absence, for Octavia departed too soon. She had more to do, more work planned. Furthermore, she died before seeing the idea of change, an idea explicitly championed in the Parable books, in the Patternist saga, and in the Xenogenisis trilogy, take hold and make a difference in this country. She left before she could witness the idea of hope, the 'audacity of hope,' to borrow a phrase, become operational and infuse the American body politic with hope, much like the clayark mutation spread in her novel, *Clay's Ark*.

Despite the claims positing that Butler articulated a dystopian vision, in 'A Few Rules for Predicting the Future,' an essay written for a special Collector's Edition of *Essence* magazine (Mar. 2000, 165-66), Octavia staunchly maintained that 'the one thing that I and my main characters never do when contemplating the future is give up on hope. The very act of trying to look ahead to discern possibilities and offer warnings is in itself an act of hope.' Sadly, she passed before witnessing the American electorate, despite our country's legacy of slavery and segregation, elevate an African American man to the Presidency of the United States. Talk about concepts making a real imprint!

I suspect Octavia would have enjoyed watching, or perhaps working in, what became the historic election of 2008, for she was an excellent student of history. Indeed, speculations about varying historic events are skillfully crafted into her fiction. The fascism so evident in *Parable of the Sower* and *Parable of the Talents* draws, in part, from the history of Nazi Germany. *Wild Seed* draws from nineteenth-century colonialism in West Africa. Butler reminds us in these books, as she does in *Kindred*, that 'we forget history at our peril.'

Just as Michael Jackson's fans will replay his music, dance to 'Thriller' in nightclubs, and watch his videos repeatedly, Octavia Butler's fans will continue to mourn her loss. We will miss her carefully realized characters with their gutsy determination, their insights, their strength and integrity. We will miss peering into Butler's windows to the past, miss her perceptions about imagined possible futures set in intriguing locales that gave us pause. We will also miss her rich and warm magnificent voice – whether we listened to her speak from a stage or heard her speak from the printed page. We will read and re-read her novels, stories, and essays – but, and here is the rub, we will also selfishly grieve that no additional work will be forthcoming. What is carved in our memories is as true for us as it was for Lauren Olamina, of Parable fame. 'Change,' Butler's mantra, is what we who remain now face. Change. She is gone. Change. We cannot bring her back. Our lives, as readers and writers, as fans or scholars and students, have indeed changed. We now live in a period where we can only be reminded of her vision. Or, as Lauren puts it more poetically, 'The only lasting truth / Is Change.'

Let me briefly reflect upon the truth of change in light of current events. When Barack Obama repeated the oath of office as President of the United States, we witnessed change.

On 8 August 2009, Judge Sonya Sotomayor, a Puerto Rican woman, was confirmed as the 111th Justice to the United States

Supreme Court. She is the first Hispanic, and only the third woman, appointed to the nation's highest Court. Her appointment demonstrates another astounding change.

The bankruptcy of American automobile manufacturers, the implosion and reorganization of the American banking system, water rationing in sections of this country due to prolonged drought, the recognition of a global economy with devastating global effects when things go awry are possibilities Butler's fiction contemplated long before these changes actually occurred.

Whether she speculated about the past or posited a possible alternate future, Octavia E. Butler was a woman and a writer of great vision whose prose left us a gift and a legacy. Our inheritance is the value of hope, the knowledge that change is certain.

Sandra Y. Govan

A *Tribute to Octavia E. Butler* – Jeffrey Allen Tucker

The only book that I literally could not put down until I had finished reading it was Mary Shelley's *Frankenstein*. However, I made it through two-thirds – about 200 pages – of Octavia E. Butler's *The Parable of the Sower* before I decided that I needed to take a break; it was that compelling. For a graduate student who was formulating an ethos about studying and teaching literature around empathy, Lauren's hyperempathy – a cornerstone for her Earthseed philosophy, but also a liability in a setting where violence and the physical pain it produces can erupt at any time – prompted a rethink, if not a renunciation. Moreover, Butler's representation of a near-future urban dystopia in Southern California resonated with recent memories of the 1992 uprising in Los Angeles.

There was a lot of pain and anger in this book about a woman's quest to understand God, herself, and others. When I did complete my reading of the novel, I recalled another text on humanity's alienation from the divine, *Paradise Lost*. A gripping tale, full of horror and wonder, with considerable intellectual heft to it, *Sower* was hard to beat. This novel also grabbed me, in part, because of its unflinchingly high-resolution representations of violence. The very notion, for example, that people could and would set anything, or anyone, on fire because they were addicted to a drug that transformed the sight of flames into orgasmic pleasure was deeply disturbing, but also fascinating. Perhaps part of my own pleasure in reading Butler has often been to see just how far she was willing to go with such images, which has often been further than I initially expected.

Cut to 2003, when a local literary organization, Writers & Books, chose Butler's *Kindred* for its annual 'If All of Rochester Read the Same Book ... ' program. It was an inspired selection; not only did it appeal to readers interested in various specific literary topics – African American literature, nineteenth-century American history, science fiction – it brought readers from each of these camps together, literally, into the same spaces to share their enthusiasms and ideas about this text and others. I participated in a panel on *Kindred* at a local bookstore and heard audience members ask questions such as 'Where can I find more science fiction like this?' and 'What else should I read to learn more about the history of slavery?' I suppose most great works of art successfully appeal across demographics, affinities, and subcultures; however, to actually witness a diverse audience make connections amongst themselves across difference by way of Butler's novel affirmed for me the value of art and literature.

So in contrast to the violence that represents the ultimate form of alienation between people (and peoples), Butler's work has produced a powerful effect on different readers, bringing together disparate parts to form a community. Similarly, many of Butler's stories are about constructing families of some sort: Acorn, the joining of Terran and Tlic, the Pattern, the Ina's group marriages. Alongside and against the antagonisms that energize these stories' plots, Butler asserts the value of symbiosis: relationships that are discomfiting, hard-won, and require all parties to make negotiations if not sacrifices. These symbiotic relationships are often necessary for survival and growth, however. I am not suggesting that Butler's many and diverse writings can be summed up by some slogan such as 'Can't we all just get along?'; rather, I want to convey how Butler wrote with a scientist's eye for the very small and the very large – for colorful specificities and for vast, powerful, but intelligible systems – as well as with a philosopher's or alchemist's appreciation for the synthetic, combining disparate, even oppositional elements to create something new, a process emblematized by the formulation 'science fiction,' which named the oeuvre of which she was a master.

Along these lines, the two personal characteristics for which I have the most respect are hard work and a vivid imagination. The former is a necessity for success in publishing (or any endeavor), and Butler has commented on her own, indeed, religious devotion to her work and the necessity, for writers, of doing the work of writing every day in the short essays 'Positive Obsession' and 'Furor Scribendi.' Butler also must have conducted a considerable amount of research on antebellum Maryland in order to fully render the Weylin plantation, on molecular biology to represent Oankali methods of genetic trade, and epidemiology to convincingly describe Duryea-Gode disease. As for her imagination, which evidently works in tandem with such research, I remain in awe of the images, concepts, and characters that Butler created: Doro's ruthlessness, 'the human contradiction,' God as the Second Law of Thermodynamics.

And now we live in a world without Octavia E. Butler. What do you do when the source of so much that you value is gone? For literary scholars, perhaps the answer lies in emulating Butler as well as possible, using our imaginations and working hard to produce new readings of her stories. A subject search in the MLA International Bibliography yielded 170 hits – literary criticism on Butler produced from 1982 to 2009, in over 45 different scholarly journals and over 35 volumes. But there is more work to do. I would like to see even more scholarship on the West African cultural antecedents of Butler's stories, queer approaches, inter-textual readings of Butler that compare and contrast her works inside and outside of the traditions of science fiction and African American literature, by both men and women, as well as analyses of the formal characteristics that contribute to her distinctive narrative style. Simply put, advancing further teaching of and research on the writing of Octavia E. Butler is the best tribute we can give her.

Jeffrey Allen Tucker

Realism for the Times – Veronica Hollinger

Octavia E. Butler's science fiction has attracted an uncommon amount of critical controversy. A lot of people have noticed that her stories crisscross a variety of conceptual and political positions and a lot of people have argued about what these crossings mean. Is she or is she not a feminist – perhaps even a queer-feminist? Are her stories really always 'about' slavery? What exactly are they trying to tell us about utopian community? How are we to evaluate her very complicated responses to the competitive and hierarchical nature of human nature?

It is gratifying to see how Butler's fiction has come to be read more and more in its own terms, has become less weighed down by its 'failures' to meet any number of critical, political, and aesthetic standards and expectations. Gradually we have learned (are still learning?) to appreciate Butler's unique brand of contemporary sf existentialism. Her fiction is the ongoing answer to questions she herself raised in a 1994 interview:

> What good is science fiction's thinking about the present, the future, and the past? What good is its tendency to warn or consider alternative ways of thinking and doing? What good is its examination of possible effects of science and technology, or social organization and political direction? At its best, science fiction stimulates imagination and creativity. It gets reader and writer off the beaten track, off the narrow, narrow footpath of what 'everyone' is saying, doing, thinking – whoever 'everyone' happens to be this year.

The quality of Butler's writing is suggested in part by the fact that it has attracted not only a lot of commentary from the academic community, but also a lot of very good commentary. Her writing makes us more responsible readers, and it encourages us to do some hard work of our own when we undertake to think about it as scholars. Sometime in the early 1990s, Sue-Ellen Case visited from

UCLA and we fell into a conversation about teaching sf texts. I remember how struck I was when she told me that many of her students insisted that *Parable of the Sower* was realist fiction, and not science fiction at all. That was a moment that gave me a new understanding of Butler's stories. She was one of the genre's most honest storytellers, and not only because of her commitment to bioscientific verisimilitude. Much more important, it seems to me, was her commitment to the unremitting physical and emotional experiences that provide so much of the texture of her fictional worlds: Lauren Olamina's hyperempathy, Lilith Iyapo's conflicted pregnancy, human/alien birth in 'Bloodchild,' vampire sexuality in *Fledgling*.

Butler was one of the great realists of science fiction. Her prose is so transparent, so efficient, and it pierces to the bone. Her stories refuse to simplify moral choices, which are treated with the complexity of authentically grown-up fiction. Her writing can be very quiet and sometimes the affect in her texts seems almost flat – perhaps because of the distanced/disciplined self-consciousness of her very hard-working protagonists, from *Kindred*'s Dana to *Xenogenesis*'s Lilith to *Fledgling*'s Shori. It is worth considering that Butler's prose represents – at the very level of the words on the page – the kind of iron control necessary to survive under impossible circumstances. The unvarnished and unromanticized face of human necessity takes on a resolute beauty in her stories.

I read the Xenogenesi trilogy and *Parable of the Sower* and 'Bloodchild' with my students, and they recognize that beauty. The Carl Brandon Society is building a scholarship fund in Octavia Butler's name. This will all continue. Once I sat with Octavia Butler at a dinner. That will not happen again.

Veronica Hollinger

Un-teaching Lessons: Butler's Bloodchild Collection
– Sweta Narayan

Octavia E. Butler's stories are many things, but perhaps their best single descriptor is *courageous*. They address topics where the hurt and fear is close to the surface, not without fear, but without flinching.

It's possible to miss this in her long science fiction, at least on a first read (though not at all in *Kindred*, which rips away one comfortable lie after another). Butler's sf novels open up intricate and vivid worlds, her characters are rich and complex, and their decisions bring cascading effects – such gorgeous flesh to mask that sharp subversive starkness of bone underneath. The underlying inequities and the lack of social privilege of the point-of-view characters are not the sole focus of the reader's attention.

Not so in her short fiction: it is all bone. The reader cannot ignore the underlying injustices, the characters' helplessness, the deeply personal and heartbreaking power dynamics and the pain that motivates their bad decisions.

Butler never settled for easy answers and, with every story in *Bloodchild and Other Stories* (1995), she challenges bad habits and easy ways out. She's not easy on the reader; her images are sometimes so raw one can feel the last held breath still in them. Her breath. Butler's short stories are as culturally different from most science fiction as she was from most writers and readers of the genre.

Science fiction (like fantasy) often claims to be about different worlds and new perspectives, but in most stories it's still boys who get to be heroes and white characters who get to save the day. Disabled characters will be magically healed and anyone hurt by the 'good' magic or technology privileging a point-of-view character stays off-screen. The implicit lesson in all of this is that only some types of difference are acceptable; only some points of view matter. Butler un-teaches that. She destroys the idea that the majority culture has the only valid point of view in science fiction.

In her title story, 'Bloodchild,' the main human character, Gan, is counted fortunate in some ways, but he is not a privileged character. He is faced with what it means to become the host for an alien's eggs, yes, and his helplessness is painful for him. But the worst part is that he has known this alien all his life and he loves her. The betrayal inherent in their relationship isn't abstract; it doesn't come from a distant Other or a hated enemy, it comes from his friend, his lover, whose needs conflict with his. He has a choice, but it's not a good one – no matter how he chooses, she *will* fulfill her needs in some way. His position is horrifically and organically dependent, and his decision is motivated more by jealousy and fear of loss than by care.

The dynamic is familiar to any non-privileged member of a culture. That love, that fear of loss, is why so many people hesitate to make waves, why it's easiest to be the invisible other, to put up with constant hurt from intimates. It is difficult to speak or write truth – not because of the abstract and unknown people who might react badly, but because of loved ones who do not want to hear that truth.

Butler's fiction doesn't flinch from the difficult and painful dynamics she experienced. She described herself as a hard worker; perhaps her work was hard because it wasn't comfortable. Because she walked new and personal paths; because she was thinking about and tackling hard problems and telling her own truth. Because courage is always hard; but perhaps teachers like Octavia Butler make it somewhat more possible.

Sweta Narayan

'The Book of Martha'/The Books of Octavia: An Appreciation
– Marleen S. Barr

When Octavia E. Butler granted me permission to publish 'The Book of Martha' in *Afro-Future Females: Black Writers Chart Science Fiction's Newest New-Wave Trajectory* (Ohio State UP, 2008, 135-50), she was quite explicit about the compensation she required. 'I would just like to receive a copy of the book. Having a copy is very important to me,' she said.

'Of course. No problem. I will be more than happy to send you a copy.'

'You won't forget?'

'No. I won't forget. I promise.'

But my anthology was published after Butler left us. I was never able to keep the promise. This appreciation, then, is my attempt to acknowledge and honor the promise in the best way available to me.

'The Book of Martha' is about a conversation carried on between a recently deceased black woman and god. Butler shared much in common with her protagonist Martha Bes. Like Martha, Butler was a tall black science-fiction writer who lived in Seattle. The story is replete with resemblances. Butler, Martha, and god look like each other. Because Martha dies young and talks to god, Butler's story has become especially poignant.

Martha can be understood as the word-made self-portrait Butler bequeathed to us: she is a spokesperson for Butler who comments upon the author's gifts and responsibilities. She functions as a guide to understanding Butler's own evaluation of herself in that she reflects the fact that Butler had so correctly assessed her own significance. The point is that this protagonist reflects Butler's extraordinary self-reflexivity and deliberateness about how she saw herself. My purpose is to honor Butler's memory by engaging in a discussion of 'The Book of Martha' that goes through the looking glass to explore the Martha/god/Butler mirror image. I wish to show that Butler, through Martha, indicates that the writer is given great responsibility: a bit of god-like power in the ability to create.

God assigns a specific task to Martha. She receives a directive which stipulates that humankind must stop acting like a murderous and wasteful adolescent and grow up to embrace peaceful and sustainable lifestyles. Butler's melding of science fiction and ecological awareness results in a god who sounds like Al Gore engaged in the process of authoring her/his (this god appears both as a female and a male) own version of Arthur C. Clarke's *Childhood's End*. God mentions treating the environment sensibly while informing Martha about how to accomplish saving humanity by borrowing divine power. God's statement combines Butler's interest in ecological concerns with an sf power-fantasy trope. Butler imagines empowering herself when she presents Martha as a science-fiction writer granted the god-given ability to rewrite humanity as she sees fit.

When Martha thinks about her oeuvre and decides to change people in a single positive way, she uses her new power in terms of textuality. (Butler, via Martha, announces that we can do things with words, that the illocutionary force is with us.) Martha, who shares Butler's concern about overpopulation, decides to author a new reality in which all people are limited to having two children. This protagonist's ability to make her choice real actualizes Butler's power fantasy about being able to improve and save the world by making a science fiction come true.

God moves from Gore-speak to the language of Star Fleet Command when s/he empowers Martha to break the Prime Directive. The protagonist can interfere with human existence by altering human reality; humans will have no choice about facing the consequences of her actions. Butler imagines science fiction to be a gift from god to a black woman as a way of saving the world. God provides this helpful hint about garnering the confidence to change the world: let there be science-fiction writing.

Martha's final decision about how to save humanity involves a dream merger between the real and the unreal. Butler most certainly derived satisfaction from dreaming about a better world. She was concerned with addressing ecological and social inequality throughout her life. She dreamed of improving the world and accepted the fact that the dreams which reflect her world-view would not become real.

Martha and god ultimately inhabit a dream vision of the mundane Seattle reality Martha and Butler share. Martha's small house, a mirror image of Butler's home, becomes a Borgesian juxtaposition of sameness and difference. The house is recast as a performance space in which Martha progresses in stages toward ultimately being able to see god in her own image. At first, god changes from the stereotypical white bearded man to a tall black man wearing contemporary street clothes. Martha responds to god depicted as a person of color in a feminine and humble way. Reflecting Butler's signature style which encompasses the mundanely basic, she offers god 'a tuna-salad sandwich' (147).

In the human creative imagination's entire history, no protagonist has ever offered god a tuna-salad sandwich. Charlton Heston cast as Moses, for example, did not give god part of a tuna-salad sandwich in exchange for parting the Red Sea. Martha's gesture rewrites the patriarchal narrative about how people properly interact with god; her action is domestically necessary (god has to eat too) – i.e., it is Butleresque in terms of simplicity, necessity, and directness. Butler further emphasizes that she creates god in her own image: the tuna-salad ingesting god Butler imagines also happens to be a fantasy novel reader.

This insistence upon using mirroring to personify god is also apparent when Martha is finally able to imagine god as someone who looks like her – a black woman: 'I see you as female now ... We look like sisters' (148). God becomes a 'sistah.' I would like to imagine that god is a wise woman of color, that she echoes someone who, like Butler and Martha, was economically disadvant-aged: when god changes from a white man to a woman of color, god speaks in the voice of Sonia Sotomayor rather than Al Gore. God alludes to the issue of how a female minority group member's particular life experiences would cause her perspectives to differ from those of white men. 'You see what your life has prepared you to see' (148), says god. These words, uttered by god presented as a wise black woman, can be read as a precursor to these words famously uttered by the wise Latina woman who now sits on the Supreme Court: 'I would hope that a wise Latina woman with the richness of her experience would more often than not reach a better conclusion than a white male who hasn't lived that life.' Although Butler did not live to see Sotomayor's achievement, she, I think, would believe that empathy should be a part of judicial decisions and that society needs the difference generated when women of color replace white men in positions of power.

Martha turns to the fantastic when she finally becomes confident about using her power: 'Make the dreams happen' (149) she tells god while echoing Captain Jean Luc Picard's commanding 'make it so.' Ironically, if Martha's dreams become real, the fictitious visions she authors will no longer be useful; her writing career will end.

We who care so much about Octavia E. Butler's writing must accept the fact that there will be no more new Butler texts. Her words have stopped. Our interpretations of those words, though, are part of the Borgesian infinite. The future will be replete with our interpretations/dreams of Octavia and her science fictions.

We no longer have Octavia E. Butler. We will forever have the books of Octavia.

Marleen S. Barr

Echoes and Hauntings – Joan Gordon

Octavia Butler's fiction arrived on the scene just after I discovered that science fiction was a field of study and a social network. Before 1975, I had been a lone reader of sf, accompanied only by my father who had introduced me to Asimov and Clarke when I was in, of course, eighth grade. But in 1975 I began graduate school and took a course (from Joe Haldeman and the late Larry Martin) in science fiction where I learned that this could be a life's work for readers as well as writers. Then came Butler's first five books, which I read as they came out – I have the old, tattered paperbacks to prove it – and they showed me how rich and powerful sf could be. They stood up magnificently against the other exciting novels I was reading by Toni Morrison and Paule Marshall and Alice Walker, also women of color and depth. And I read Butler's novels only for the delight and enrichment they provided, escape of a high order from the anxieties of graduate school since they offered a glimpse of much more important worries and much greater strength than was required of my life.

Later, as I slowly developed my scholarship in sf, came her novels and short stories of the 1980s – those were important to me in a different way. Now I thought of their rich ideas and how they might be analyzed. Again, they provided me with what I needed – now it was intellectual stimulation and inspiration, especially while I was teaching at an obscure and isolated college in Montana. But it took me until the 1990s to actually be able to teach her work and to write about her, and these acts of greater understanding made me appreciate her even more. Students always loved her work and we were always able to go more deeply into important ideas when discussing it. During this time, I had the opportunity to shake her hand at a couple of conferences, and felt, as everyone reports from such opportunities, her dignity, her kindness, her intelligence. When she won the MacArthur Award in 1995, it seemed only just.

Now, in 2010, it is hard to believe that it has been four years since her death, that we will not be reading the next installment of her Parable books or the sequel to *Fledgling*. Just as all her previous work left echoes and resonances that haunted me after the fact, these unfinished series leave ghosts of what was to come. She was an artist who provided every satisfaction of reading, from the delight of the pure experience to every level of analysis and exploration. She was an exemplar of what science fiction can offer. Like all great writers, she was not only supremely skillful but great of heart.

Joan Gordon

Alex Jennings

To Octavia Butler, Elsewhere

Dear Octavia,

It's been a while now, but I still feel your absence keenly. You were the first real author I met, and our interactions changed my life.

In the summer before eighth grade, my family moved from our home in Maryland to Paramaribo, Surinam. The dominant language there was Dutch, as it was a former colony of the Netherlands. It was hard to find books to read outside the library of the small Southern Baptist missionary school I attended there. The American Embassy where my father worked had a library in the Community Liaison Office; it was full of donated books and magazines. I first encountered your work in the pages of *Asimov's Magazine* and in paperback editions of your Xenogenesis trilogy.

Reading about characters who looked like me grappling with questions of sexual and species identity was powerful enough to fold new grooves into my brain. Almost all the characters I'd read about to that point were either white or written by white people. While I had no idea of your own racial identity in those pre-Internet days, something about your work and the experiences of your characters rang truer for me than anything else I'd read. I imprinted on your work, but in those days, I was still so young that I didn't think to seek out any more of it.

The next time I read you was in 2003, when I was attending The Evergreen State College. By then, I knew I wanted to be a writer, but I still wasn't sure what that meant. I had had the good fortune to encounter brilliant, caring teachers who believed in me, but when the leader of my writing workshop course told us you'd be visiting the school to speak to us, I knew exactly who you were, and that it was important to meet you.

You were tall and regal in your flower-print dress. Your voice was like none I'd ever heard. It was deep, authoritative, and smooth, without straining toward any of those qualities. This was before I discovered the music of Nina Simone, but hearing her sing in recordings is the closest thing I can think of to hearing you speak. You had a glow about you, a realness and a grace that I hope you were aware of. More than that, I recognized you in some essential way. In some way I couldn't put into words. You felt like family to me. What struck me most, though, is that when you finished speaking, instead of leaving right away, you sat at a table in the Writing Center and chatted with a few of us students for at least an hour. During that conversation, you asked me whether I wrote every day, whether I was committed to the craft. When I answered yes, you told me to apply to Clarion West, and that if I did, I'd get in.

Your statement was hard to bear. I wanted nothing more from life than to be a working author. I wanted so desperately to believe you, but I couldn't. You'd never seen my work. You would likely forget my name as soon as you left the room. In the end, I did as you told – you didn't suggest – me to do. You were right.

I've battled depression for a long time, but receiving the call from Clarion West showed me that life wasn't as small or as dim as I feared, that I could do at least some of the things I'd dreamed of. It didn't even occur to me that I would see you at Clarion, or that when I did you would remember me. But I did, and you did. And attending Clarion West exposed me to other heroes of mine – not just the instructors, but Ursula Le Guin, Greg Bear, luminaries in the field whose work I'd read and treasured after grabbing their publications from that cramped little Embassy library. I remember arguing with you about why the black characters in the *Matrix* movies had 'the dumbest lines'. I remember doing my best to make you laugh on the deck outside Greg Bear's house.

In the end, we spent precious little time together, but you, your work, and the guidance you gave me before you left had an enormous effect on me. It took me many years to begin to understand your influence on me. At first, I thought it was just that you were a real writer, one I had read and whose work was dear to me, who paid me attention and was kind to me. Still, your instruction to apply to Clarion West, and your statement that I would be admitted, bothered me until I read an article revealing how you wrote your own career into being. You wrote those statements about your own career with the same sort of authority and belief with which you spoke to me that day in 2003. You spoke my career into being just as you wrote yours, and I never even realized it until you'd already gone.

These days, I live, work and write in New Orleans. I've been here for ten years. I run a monthly readings series called Dogfish with some of my literary-minded friends, and it is the darling of my heart. There's a collective here called Wildseeds, inspired by your work. I've felt your spirit at their events, and at each one I attend, I think how proud you would be to have inspired them so. I'm still in touch with Nisi Shawl, whom I met at Clarion West. I look to her as not just a friend and a colleague, but as a mentor. I told her once that she had filled the void your passing left in my life, and she told me that hearing so made her terribly sad, because it made her feel your absence more keenly than ever. I often wonder whether you'd be proud of me, of my work, and I miss you every day.

I hope there is an alternate universe where you still live, and we are great friends. I hope I spend time with you whenever I make it to Seattle. I hope I had a chance to introduce you to the woman I intend to marry. I hope that that other version of me listens to Nina Simone and thinks of you, not because you are gone, but because you are there. I don't know how many times I've cried over losing you, but thank you.

Thank you for those tears, and for everything.

Love,
Alex Jennings

Cassandra Brennan

Dear Ms. Butler,

Ten years later and I'm still struck by the loss of your presence. Twelve books you left us as reminders and inspiration for us dreamers. An even dozen, full of prose and insight; characters with depth and grace in circumstances unforetold. Eighteen years ago, I remember telling you that your lecture at the Smithsonian was a birthday present from one of my oldest friends. You complimented me on my choice of friends and introduced me to one of yours, the irascible Mr. Walter Mosely. Not only did I have the pleasure of your lecture and an insight into how you did the damn thing, you talked with me about what it meant for you to write. To write, to create, to dream, to share, to be a maker of worlds requires discipline, deep breaths and a commitment to stay the course. Sacrifices must be made: sometimes financial, sometimes personal.

Instead of running a company, you chose to influence the unconscious collective that is the human animal. You risked the real American Dream of a safe retirement to give us *Kindred* and *Parable of the Sower*. Fifteen years later, I'm still letting Plan B suck me dry. I come home, beat down from the day, and I drag out space to create. Sometimes all I can do is find visual references to remind me of the next chapter or plot point I want to pull out of my head. I wonder if you would be disappointed in me. I wonder if you would be disappointed at the continuing low levels of representation of women and black people in science fiction and fantasy. There are ten thousands of us in my Black Science Fiction Writers social media group. I know you would like that.

The internet did not impress you when we spoke of its growing presence. I think you recognized its unlimited potential as a time thief. Given the frequency of my Facebook posts in direct comparison with my writing output, I hang my head in shame at the undeniable evidence of my procrastination. *One word at a time*, you told me, *that's how you tell a story*. It sounds easy and so does Bach's Cello Concerto #3 but I dare you to lay a hand on that bitch and call it a walk in the park. You were right – about non-fiction being a great source of inspiration. The ideas knit together when fact and fiction dance. The little sparks fly and ignite, leading into dark pathways that create themselves as you follow step by step.

Still no cure for cancer but there is a smart drug in trials now Ms. Butler. I don't know if it will lead to the genetic undoing that will be our downfall as a species but I'm hopeful. Not just to prove the point you're making in the Xenogenesis series but because you knew that we are only at our best when we have to fight for what we need to survive. The battle between our intellect and drive to self-destruct both propels us forward and drags us back with every step we take toward evolution into a higher state of being. I haven't lost my faith in humanity yet but as a Black woman in America, it has worn thin. In *Kindred*, you show us how we modern people might react to the burden our ancestors endured. Thank you for making it plain how deep those wounds still lie in our society. We have so much further to go but your voice is one that will guide us. *Kindred* is in college curriculums across the United States now, so the young ones will hear you.

I never liked you just because you were a Black Woman Science Fiction Writer. I liked you because you told great stories with a unique perspective and a voice I recognized. I remember asking you what you preferred to be called and if it mattered: African American, Person of Color, or Black. You told me Octavia or Ms. Butler were your first choices. After we all laughed, you said it didn't matter to you as long as it was done with respect. We agreed that the new term POC was more inclusive, which we both appreciated. I remember someone saying that Sunday dinner in most people's homes should look like the UN so we know we are all in this together. My favorite thing to remember is that you said you had been Black all your life and it fit you as you saw yourself. You said the term is comfortable and worn in the right spots like your good winter coat. This is where I got a glimpse of that zing of perspective you bring to your work.

One of my favorite examples of your unique eye is in a pivotal scene in the short story 'The Evening and the Morning and the Night'. An aspect of the Duryea-Gode Disease you created in that story has a fascinating twist. The women with two DGD parents and dominant personalities are able to lead the distracted poorly-socialized groups of DGD sufferers into a semblance of normalized functioning. These same women are repelled by each other like opposing magnets: a queen bee syndrome. I think there is an element of truth in proposing a biological factor in the complex relationships women as leaders face. Through exploring the possibility that our biology impacts our relationships with power, we may find a better understanding of how we connect and disconnect as social animals. Many of your stories lead us back to the idea of humanity as an animal, a basic truth we seem blind to in the course of our development as a species. Your work makes me wonder what we are missing by not actively examining this basic truth about who we are.

You told me you kept life simple in order to stay focused and do your real work. I feel like I failed you and myself. I did take risks: I walked away from the DC contracting corridor, moved to New York City to make a life with space for creativity. I came here with a little cash and a couch, resolved to create a life that worked for me. Fifteen years later, I'm in a hole I dug for myself with a career that sucks me dry every day. This path has given me a husband, a home, a circle of loving friends, one of whom is my personal editor and an artist who makes my stories a visual glory. Sadly, I am back to writing on the train, under the dryer at the hairdresser, and under the covers at one a.m. Somehow Plan B has taken over again. I told you then I didn't know how to stop this from happening. At least I'm writing. I'm still writing, which means I'm not done yet. The business card you gave me is in a place of honor on my desk. A simple white card with tasteful black letters, it says more than just your name to me. It says as long as I keep working, I'm not done. I'm not done Ms. Butler, I'm not done.

With Love and Hope,
Cassandra

L. Timmel Duchamp

A Letter to Octavia Butler

Dear Octavia Butler,

We met several times while you were living in Seattle, but probably because you and I shared the characteristic of being what people call 'deeply private persons,' our conversation was never personal. (My sense of this ran so strong that my dentist's observation to me that she had acquired a patient who, like me, was an SF writer and then named you, embarrassed me, as though it were an indiscretion.) Our first meeting was one of those polite exchanges with a handshake usual when formal introductions are made. On another occasion, we shared a two-day, emotionally intense workshop for mid- and advanced-career writers, moderated by Pat Murphy, in the basement of the house hosting that year's Clarion West Writers' Workshop. A number of the writers attending were, like you, authors I'd been reading voraciously even before I started writing SF myself (which is probably another way of saying, authors who'd formed my deepest sense of SF's forms, tropes, and narratives).

After the first day's session, Vonda McIntyre, another participant, drove you and me to her house, to pass the time before the workshop participants were all to meet at a nearby restaurant for dinner and then go on to a Clarion West party. I sat in the backseat while you and Vonda made the briefest of small talk. I remained silent, thinking about all that my reading self would have liked to say to you, would have liked to converse with you about. At Vonda's you took a nap, which fit what I knew about your health problems. Vonda gave me tea and knitted as we chatted the hour away.

I've often thought about that so-minor an encounter, which was not of course the last time we met. I'd managed to convey my admiration of her work to Vonda by then (however clumsily), but I couldn't imagine finding a way of telling you to your face how important your work was to me. (It's easy to understand why James Tiptree had the habit of writing fan letters to her colleagues.)

To be frank, the intersection between the individual human being who has written words I encountered on the page and the imaginary author conjured up by that encounter has always been difficult for me when the textual encounter precedes in-the-flesh acquaintance or friendship. The strongest textual encounters always create a distinctive voice in my mind that I 'know' in ways I can never 'know' an actual human being. In a few rare cases, the imaginary author comes with a face (as people I've listened to on the radio always seem to do). Imagined faces and voice never match those of the real author, of course.

In your case, for the first several novels of yours I read in the late 1970s and early 1980s, you figured, in my visual imagination, as a young Latina (I've no idea why). When I learned you were black, it did not really surprise me. And because I'd seen photos of you long before I met you, the only thing about you that surprised me was your solid, looming, yet subdued presence (which reminded me physically of Joanna Russ, whom after our first meeting I likened to a great bear). My overall impression of you was one of focused seriousness – an impression corroborated by all that you revealed of yourself in the many interviews of you I've read. I felt a special kinship with you when I learned that like me, you'd always been a serious person; even as a young girl you pursued your creative desires and ambitions with unfailing seriousness.

I know from my own experience that serious girls face a constant barrage of ridicule for daring to be serious (which I imagine goes double for girls of color). I'm sure you must often have been told to stop taking yourself so seriously. (Being serious, for girls and young women, seems to be equivalent to taking oneself seriously.) Somehow, despite being female and black, you managed to disregard such pressures. Your mother, I believe, supported your seriousness and ambition, perhaps because she was deprived of even the most basic education growing up as the child of Louisiana sharecroppers. I can't tell you how much I love that you were so serious.

I'd also attended readings by you before we first met, so I'd long since replaced an imagined voice with the real one. (Once I hear an author read, I hear that voice in my mind whenever I read her work. But then my memory retains the memory of a person's voice long after I've forgotten the expressions their faces take or the texture of their hair.) When you read from *Parable of the Sower* and participated in the Q&A that followed, your physical presence and general attitude (and the occasional trace of impatience revealed in your body language) radiated confidence and persistence. A friend attending the reading with me later expressed disappointment that you hadn't laid out your wisdom for all of us, thirsting for it, to gulp down at one go. But you'd been and were still giving us your books, weren't you? You gave a lot of interviews in an amazing variety of venues. Preaching, even to the choir, wasn't your way.

After you died, not yet sixty, Seattle's SF community held a heavily attended, almost unbearably emotional memorial for you. I was asked, like several other writers, to choose a passage from a favorite book of yours to read at the memorial. The idea of choosing a single work as my favorite flummoxed me. Finally, I chose *Wild Seed*, which is probably the book of yours that most influenced me as a writer; certainly it is the one I've reread the most. But most of your novels have worked powerfully on me. After the recent US general election, when many of us were shocked and dazed, unable, after a month of 24/7 media hysteria, to concentrate enough even to read, I decided that what I needed to do to reclaim my ability to think was to choose a book I valued and set myself to read it. (Though it mostly isn't, sometimes reading can be medicine for mind, the heart, the soul.) I decided, of all the books I loved, that it must be *Dawn*, the first novel of your Xenogenesis trilogy. *Dawn* is not the book of yours closest to our current moment of reality— that would, of course, be *Parable of the Sower*, which to my mind is too damned close for comfort – but it is a book about the need to combine resistance with survival, and a book that raises the question of whether humans might be wired for self-destruction.

The need to combine resistance with survival is an old theme of yours, of course; it was there from the beginning and can arguably be found in every novel you published. The power imbalance that Lilith faces is extreme, yet she finds ways to negotiate and influence the outcome of the situation. The moral ambiguities and uncertainties are painful, and yet she doesn't lose her soul. White USians tend to think of struggle as all-or-nothing, where the winner takes all and the loser gets nothing. You knew that history doesn't work like that. Rereading *Dawn* effectively rebooted my brain. I ceased being numb. I recalled past struggles and knew that what we faced was nothing particularly new, even if it now confronts us with one of our worst collective nightmares. After re-reading *Dawn*, I thought about the work ahead, and though that made me sad and tired, I was no longer dazed and hopeless. And today, one week after the infamous inauguration marked by a week of rising resistance, I'm energized and good to go. I need to be, since in the face of such threat only massive, collective resistance will save us.

Thank you, Octavia. I can't tell you how grateful I am that you worked so hard, through so many attempts at your novels (now revealed in your archived papers and manuscripts), through so many years of persisting to create the stories that have meant so much to me through the forty years I've been reading and remembering them. Your imagination has enabled me and kindled many of our souls with the bright fire of resistance.

With admiration and respect,
L. Timmel Duchamp

Rasha Adbulhadi

Dear Kindred Teacher,

I'm sorry this letter, written more than ten years too late, won't reach you. I'm sorry I wasn't fast enough; I'm sorry I didn't mail that package I promised in time to catch you in 2005. Would it have caught you at your doorstep and given you reason to pause, to sit down curious and delighted for a moment, and would we then still have you? I don't think I could have been that important, but dear God of Change, if I could have done anything to keep the tree of your life rooted here just a little longer, I would have spent the money I didn't have to get it to you. I wish I had known, I wish we had the work you were still making, and I am still so glad I met you.

Tonight I cast a blessing out to the roommate who asked me: *Isn't Octavia Butler that author you like so much? She's going to be at the library downtown tonight.* I remember sitting in a red velvet chair in the auditorium of Chicago's Harold Washington library, one of maybe a dozen people in the audience, and being tuned electric to your voice reading. I think I may have embarrassed you, or maybe you were embarrassed for me, or perhaps just confused by this ambiguously ethnic kid who stood up and said: *I feel like I'm going to turn into a tree listening to your voice, this is just amazing.* I loved your work too much to have any self-consciousness.

I didn't have extra money to buy *Fledgling*, the book you were traveling to promote, the book you wrote when you weren't writing *Parable of the Trickster*. I bought it with grocery money. I didn't think I'd love it, and I still don't know if it wants me to love it. Some books don't exist to be loved – they have other business to do. I feel that from a lot of your writing, and still I find myself caught on its tangles. I wish you'd had more time to elaborate the new trains of thought you were so obviously on. Hybrid families, chosen families, polyamory, older women who long for other women, and the very troubling and troublesome sexual aspects of very young women. All of this is present in *Fledgling*, through which you extended your neat trick of offering us disability as talent to show us a character whose blackness makes her more powerful at the same time as she is young and new and vulnerable and discovering her way in the world. There are books to be written about what you did in *Fledgling*.

Your business card has hung above every desk I've ever used since that day – the business card you gave me when I promised that I didn't want or expect a reply, that I wouldn't send you my own writing, that I just wanted to send you gratitude and a care package. I hadn't asked for your card, just any address – your publisher's even. That day, a rectangle of heavy paper seemed like a shining assurance of the power of literature. Today, it reminds me that no sequels are promised and that putting things off has a cost.

At a bookstore in Oakland in 2012, I asked for your writing (I was looking for *Survivor*, the one you said you'd prefer people didn't go looking for), and in a turn of magic, the proprietress of this fine establishment revealed that she had known you. Sometimes loss makes a bridge. She told me stories that are hers alone to tell, and I will not repeat them here, but I was grateful to know about your sparkle and silliness and freedom from her.

At a cafe that afternoon in California, the friend I was meeting wondered what rooms of women you were in and what ideas were cooked up in their company. My friend has doubts about the myth of the solitary author genius. I have sympathy for those doubts, and I know that anything good I've written has come from documenting the best (and maybe sometimes the worst, and even occasionally the uncomfortably in-between) of what I have been witness to. For that reason, I am grateful to you as both solitary adventurer and witness.

Reading your interviews has given me as much as your fiction, which still reveals new cellular architectures with each reading. I thrill at the thought of your archives. I long to have a project that would give me worthy reasons to beg time with your unpublished papers. I eagerly await the writings of scholars who have been to your archives, scholars like Dr. Alexis Pauline Gumbs and Dr. T. Pickens. I cannot wait to think the new thoughts that are being spawned from the meetings of these brilliant minds with your pollinating paths of thought. These women and others are already shaping future generations; they are writing the thoughts that haven't been thought all the way yet, thoughts that feel ticklish now and may, like yours, seem prescient – visionary – in twenty years, in forty. I am honored and really just so excited to be on the planet at the same time as the cohort of people who have read your work, been fed by and been shaped by your words and worlds. I am grateful to come in a generation after yours. I wish we had had a little more time to offer you our gratitude and our elaborations.

Your short stories really aren't praised often enough. The ending of 'Amnesty' wrecks me and strangely reassures me – they've already lost the war, and like us, they are living in the aftermath. I think often about 'The Evening and the Morning and the Night' – how it polishes the themes of *Mind of My Mind*: the wounded young woman helping people to live together through the discovery of her necessary power, how her power is rooted in damage done to her intergenerationally, and how even this healing power can make her dangerous. Again and again, you take us through the twists of discovering our power at the same source as our wounds, and finding in our power – in our greatest offerings to others – the greatest dangers we pose to them. Always in your writing, danger cuts both ways. Even in asymmetrical power relationships there are things that the less powerful have that the powerful need – their bodies, their reproduction, their talents.

When I met you, I brought my copy of *Wild Seed* and thanked you for how delicious it was. You told me you'd written it as a reward to yourself for finishing *Kindred*, which had been much harder. I told you that in my honest opinion I thought *Parable of the Talents* was the most brilliant sequel I'd ever read because it both continued the story and completely changed the way we read the first book, forcing us to contend with the way mothers and daughters wrestle for the truth of their shared stories. Even now, your seeds are planted in my work as I wonder what a pre-apocalyptic literature looks like: how do we know when we're in the apocalypse? How do we know, short of full blown catastrophe, what a societal emergency looks like, and where do we apply a tourniquet and just what kind of hospital can we get to?

I think about you and Philip Levine, working manual labor jobs early (and even midway) into your writing careers. Because of you I am reassured in my natural declination away from investing in a professional arts degree. Because of you I read Theodore Sturgeon and took delight in his confirmation that stories are everywhere just lying around waiting for us to see them and follow them down their holes. Because of you, I found Delany and Due and Jemisin.

Dear teacher, you are one of my guiding lights, my hard heroines. I know your path is not mine, not in origin, and not in destination, but you are one of the shining sights by which I can set my bearings. Your work and your life help me know where I am in this landscape. You gave me tools before I knew I needed them. Now it's my job to leave some more for the folks who come after me.

yours and mine and ours,
Rasha

Steven Barnes

Dear Octavia –

When I learned that I had a chance to send you one last letter, I leaped at the opportunity. It isn't that there were things unsaid between us, but more that it was important for you to understand how very much you meant to those who only discovered you after your transition.

You would be so proud! Allow me to list some of the things that they appreciate the most:

1. **The clarity of your thought.** You never wasted a word, or an image. Unlike most of us, you always seemed to understand your core themes, and your view of humanity and the world. Everything fit together, and that gave you the freedom to create a kind of poetry in the interweaving of plot and theme and character.

2. **You did your homework.** It is so obvious that you understood the 'game' of science fiction, the combination of 'what if?' 'if only?' and 'if this goes on ...' that creates the greatest works in our field. YOU RESEARCHED. Exhaustively, intensively, obsessively. And that allowed you to create with clarity ... you knew your world, so we could believe in it and come along for the ride, wherever you chose to take us.

3. **You had a clear view of humanity, and never blinked.** I remember you saying that the things that most worried you about our species were 1) our hierarchical nature and 2)

our tendency to place our own tribe higher on that hierarchy. While this led you to feeling pessimistic at times, you were willing to go wherever your truth led you. That level of courage and commitment is rare.

4 **Despite your concerns about humanity's destructive capacity, you never lost hope.** You always held onto an iota of faith, in even your darkest moments. Like a single star in the darkest night, you never ceased to shine, and in shining, showed those of us wandering in the darkness that there could, indeed, be order and purpose in the world. You loved us, you really did. And do. And that warmth of heart pierces the coldest night.

5 **You went to the edge.** I've never known an artist who invested more of herself in her work, and yet clung to sanity. Not one. Although of prodigious gifts, you also cut off all lines of retreat, invested everything you had in being the best writer you could be, even if that turned you, at times, into an almost nun-like figure, solitary in her prayer cell, obsessing over every sentence of the sermon you prepared for the nurturance of our minds and hearts.

6 **You never fell over.** And this is where the rubber meets the road. Genius can consume us, and many were destroyed in its obsessive flame. This was never you. Every time I saw you, you were an avatar of warmth and welcome. If you felt loneliness, you balanced it with a hearty sense of humor. If you felt depression, you balanced it with a joy in life's absurdity. If you saw darkness, you balanced it with a belief in logic and light. You were one of those human beings who make me proud to be human.

7 **And on a more personal level ...** you always wanted me to be a

better writer, and believed in me, even when I didn't always believe in myself. Oh, I was always cocky, but you saw through that, and encouraged me to think more deeply, write more honestly, care more about readers in fifty years than sales tomorrow. Thank you, and bless you.

I'll always love you, and consider it one of the joys of my life that we could be friends. And family.

Looking forward to seeing you again ...
Steve

SECTION SEVEN

SCIENCE FICTION STUDIES
MEMORIAL

A Memorial to Octavia E. Butler

De Witt Douglas Kilgore and Ranu Samantrai

This article is reprinted with permission from *Science Fiction Studies*, Volume 37, Number 3 (November 2010). It appeared in an issue of *Science Fiction Studies* focused on Butler; hence the occasional reference to 'essays' throughout the piece.

Since Octavia E. Butler's untimely death at the too-young age of 59, friends, colleagues, and readers have honored her life and work. The Carl Brandon Society established a scholarship fund in her name. The national media informed the general public that an important science fiction writer and past winner of the MacArthur 'genius award' had died. Notable contributions to Butler scholarship since 2006 have ranged from Ritch Calvin's invaluable research in 'An Octavia E. Butler Bibliography (1976-2008)' to Ingrid Thaler's recently published *Black Atlantic Speculative Fictions: Octavia E. Butler, Jewelle Gomez, and Nalo Hopkinson* (2010). Recent conference programs for the Science Fiction Research Association (SFRA), the International Conference for the Fantastic in the Arts (ICFA), and the Modern Language Association (MLA) show continued interest in evaluating the content and influence of her work. This activity indicates that she has become an essential part of what we mean when we speak of science fiction. That is a measure of immortality. The present commemoration is a part, then, of a larger attempt by writers and scholars to honor Butler in print. It is our hope that this tribute in *SFS* will call attention to that ongoing scholarly activity, and will invite further critical engagement with her work.

Much has been said about Butler's contributions to cultural/ literary debates regarding the neo-slave narrative, utopianism, and cyborg feminism.[1] The common thread in all her work is her persistent demonstration that the genre's fantastic investment in science enables critiques of the meaning of biological difference in the organization of human life and destiny. Within the science fiction community, we tend to congratulate ourselves about the genre's relative openness in matters of race and sex. But we also know that, while for some authors the genre's conventions prompt the imagination of alternatives to our social arrangements, for others they provide justification for extending into imaginative perpetuity the segregations and discriminations that have naturalized phenotypic hierarchies.[2] Perhaps Butler's interest in the genre was sparked by this contradiction. Certainly its stark juxtaposition of these conflicting tendencies made science fiction the proper vehicle for her literary engagements with our raced and gendered world.

Butler approached sf askance, choosing to write self-consciously as an African American woman marked by a particular history. Her example clarifies the stakes for any particular minority breaking into forms seen as ethnically exclusive: the necessity or simply the desire to see oneself complexly represented in one's culture. Butler entered the field at a time when science fiction did not serve that function for white women or for people of color. In 1983 Thulani Davis criticized a genre that lacked the richness and possibilities she sought in her own life: futures in which living black cultural communities survive, grow, and influence the world around them, and in which black women are recognized as actors to be reckoned with. In her pithily titled essay, 'The Future May be Bleak, But It's not Black' (1983), Davis argued that sf commonly creates futures in which white men thrive and dominate (17). Such is the strength of the genre's conventions that even black authors such as Samuel R. Delany and Ishmael Reed defer non-ironic representation of black futures (19). Writing around the same time, Ursula K. Le Guin also criticized the genre's habit of casting the future as the 1880s British Empire: 'All those planet ... conceived of ... as colonies to be exploited ... the White Man's Burden all over again' (88).[3] And Butler, an ardent champion of the genre, nonetheless recognized its limitations when she noted that 'In earlier science fiction there tended to be a lot of conquest: you land on another planet and you set up a colony and the natives have their quarters some place and they come in and work for you' (Kenan 31). Butler's career is a partial answer to such concerns.[4]

Butler is one of the few writers who reached a significant non-genre audience during her lifetime. As Robertson notes in this issue, she is placed as readily in the category of American literature as in science fiction. Butler herself said that she was responsible to three audiences: 'the science-fiction audience, the black audience and the feminist audience' (Potts 72). To each group, she offers a mirror, but the reflection therein can be strange and unsettling. For instance, she holds the distinction of being the first prominent exponent of sf to have published a story in *Essence*, the lifestyle magazine for African American women.[5] It is safe to say that most *Essence* subscribers would have been more familiar with the realist canon of American literature than with sf. The Black and Afro-American Studies programs that flowered in the 1970s would have influenced how the young college-educated women targeted by the magazine read the story.

How might they have responded to Butler's vision of a future in which they certainly matter, but not because the promise of equality pursued by Black Studies has been accomplished?

As the essays in this issue make clear, the tales Butler tells are not simple future-history scenarios extrapolating utopian solutions to contemporary troubles. Her narratives can be grim and are often tragic. Her characters are never uncomplicated paragons of good, messiahs determined to lead their people from fear and oppression into the light. Dominance and submission, masters and slaves characterize the future as well as the past; rape is a constant danger in even sympathetic social relations. Her view of the human prospect may ultimately be hopeful but it is never sentimental. Resolution, if and when it comes, is hard. If it is fair to say, as some scholars have, that science fiction tends to create technical fixes for racism and racial politics (erasing race as a part of the future), that charge cannot be leveled at Butler.[6] Her futures are populated with recognizably raced subjects and textured by histories that cannot be left behind.

Readers of *Kindred* (1979) will recognize that Butler looks to history and culture to explain the significance of race. Indeed, her treatment of race as a social phenomenon is the most widely discussed aspect of her work. But her most trenchant investigations result from the inclusion of science in the mélange of cultural material that she brings into focus. Informed by evolutionary biology and the potential of genetic engineering, Butler developed a fantastic sociobiology grounded in the materiality of bodies. In her work, race is not only a function of human variety but also a species marker that informs behavior and potential. Crucially, because she does not assume that biology determines destiny (McCaffery and McMenamin 62; Potts 67), she finds hope in recasting humanity as a species. The trope of a radically, sometimes violently, remade *homo sapiens*, altered either due to its own mutations or as a consequence of its encounters with other kinds of beings, runs from her Patternist books (1976-84) through Lilith's Brood (1987-89) to her Easrthseed novels (1993-98) and to the naturalized vampires of *Fledgling* (2004).

The result is never the scenario made familiar by *Star Trek* and its variations, in which sentient species/races remain distinct. Butler's theme is contact – appropriately figured as miscegenation and contamination – that shatters any illusion of the inviolable individual or species. She does not envision a liberal-pluralist federation in which heterogeneity of the whole shields homogeneity of the parts. Nor is the result the mixed-race blessed community, as in Marge Piercy's *Woman on the Edge of Time* (1976). Instead, in Butler's oeuvre political hope is presaged by the catastrophe of sex, often non-consensual, between races – encounters that decimate unmodified humanity before any new condition can be established. Her point-of-view characters – the human beings who invite readerly identification – are stalked, emasculated, disenfranchised, and enslaved before they are altered from the inside out.

Readers for whom science fiction is an adventure in which the white, male hero saves humanity (most often in the form of a scantily clad woman) will find in Butler a challenge to generic conventions. But her work pushes the genre to speak to our deepest, culturally burdened horrors as well as to our transcendent hopes. For Butler, the most intimate fear is located at the meeting point of race and sex, the former the license for and the latter the tool by which a historically enfranchised class has controlled the bodies and destinies of peoples considered inferior. If humanity as a whole is subject to the fear of bodily violation and exploitation, in Butler's futures it is black women who have the longest familiarity with it. Such unfortunate experts know the best strategies for survival. Lilith of *Dawn* (1987) and Alanna of *Survivor* (1978), for example, are intensely xenophobic before their forced mating with their respective extra-species mates. In contrast with the more familiar narrative of imperiled white masculinity, their encounters lead not to war – the scenario in which a heroic resistance can be mounted, exclusions can be made and enforced – but resignation, accommodation, and assimilation. Butler's investments highlight the difference that a writer's unique social and historic embodiment can make in her work.

But if the reader of conservative sf might be disappointed, so might those who share the expectations articulated by Thulani Davis. For Butler does not write fiction that faithfully and joyfully represents familiar black communities as a condition of the future. With the single exception of *Kindred*, she did not write condition-of-the-people stories in the manner of a Toni Morrison or an August Wilson. Even when they do not include extra-terrestrials, the communities she creates are always hybrid, composed of individuals and families who share oddities across the range of more conventional phenotypic differences: African, European, Asian. Butler's fantasies posit racial hybridity as the potential root of good family and blessed community life, a prefer-ence she attributed to her experience growing up in places not strictly segregated by race:

> When I put together my characters, it doesn't occur to me to make them all black or all white or whatever. I never went to a segregated school or lived in a segregated neighborhood, so I never had the notion that black people, or any other

ethnic or cultural type, made up the world. (McCaffery and McMenamin, 13)

Butlerian hybridity differs from the futurist pluralism popularly projected by the *Star Trek* franchise or James Cameron's *Avatar* (2009) in that her alternative communities are directed by the historical experiences and desires of Africans and African Americans. The new peoples that develop from inter-species miscegenation are not postracial (as in Arthur C. Clarke's *Childhood's End* [1953]), even though they confound familiar racial arrangements. The result is not the revelation of some anodyne golden age, either in the distant past or the far future. Doro, for example, one of the most powerful directors of her fictive universe, is also one of its great monsters (*Wild Seed* [1980]). His tragedy lies in his failure to achieve his own dream of racial perfection despite a multiple-millennia effort. Nevertheless, Butler's hybrid communities, created as they are by African protagonists, do provide glimpses of a social order that resolves some of the terror of our own. In *Wild Seed* the motherly shapeshifter Anyanwu serves as counterweight to the demonic Doro, offering a utopian alternative that tames his patriarchal tyranny. The families they create challenge the ubiquitous real-world assumption that communities are an expression of homogeneity. Butler uses the trope of racial hybridity to propose affiliations that proceed, however bumpily, from the fact of difference. And repeatedly in her novels, from the relatively mainstream *Kindred* to the vampire/courtroom procedural *Fledgling*, she questions the convention that enfranchised leaders and majorities always shape the nature and fate of communities. Instead, her focus is on 'minority' characters whose distance from centers of power increases their potential for reconfiguring their social and political worlds.

For some scholars the concept of afrofuturism has become a useful way to situate imagined futures in which active black communities are central to human destiny (Lavender 189-92, Bould 180). Mark Dery initially proposed this term for black popular writing that is influenced by but tangential to science fiction. Dery argued that such writing indicates the existence of a realm of black expressive activity relatively free from white intervention (182-87). That he did not see afrofuturism as completely removed from science fiction is indicated by his inclusion of Samuel R. Delany as a respondent to his first article about the concept. Examples of strong subsequent afrofuturist texts include Nalo Hopkinson's *Midnight Robber* (2000) and Nnedi Okorafor-Mbachu's *The Shadow Speaker* (2007), extrapolating as they do futures directed by distinct Africanist epistemes. In contrast, Butler's tendency to separate her black protagonists from their birth families, forcing them to make new homes among strangers, strains the communalist intent of afrofuturism. Although she comes closest to depicting working African and/or African American communities in *Kindred* and in parts of *Wild Seed*, the black families in those narratives are fractured or in the past, and always superseded by a more racially heterogeneous present and future.

Perhaps Butler can be read as offering a weak version of afrofuturism: she places an afro-centric sensibility at the core of her narratives but does not project the social or political survival of traditionally racialized communities. Rather, the segregations she imagines most powerfully are the fantastic substitutes of Patternists and mutes, Oankali and humans, Ina (vampires) and humans, insect-like aliens and humans. And even in these cases her project is to find porosity in apparently commonsensical and unbridgeable biological barriers. This insistence on hybridity beyond the point of discomfort makes Butler's work neither an outrider of black cultural nationalism nor an accommodation to a white-dominated liberal pluralism. She exceeds our common ways of defining and resolving racial politics.

Octavia E. Butler entered science fiction at a time of profound change in the United States. She found in the genre the tools for imagining a radically different world, and dramatically changed the field. The sf community recognized the impact of her voice with both of its most prestigious prizes, the Nebula and Hugo awards. Without writers such as Butler, it is possible that sf would have ossified and remained too closely wedded to an invalidated hegemony. In her life, as in her work, Butler showed us that change comes from unexpected places: from the minority actors who challenge the certainties of the majority and from the violation of the settled boundaries that organize our understanding of the world.

NOTES

We wish to thank the many scholars, writers, and artists who have contributed to this commemoration over the past several years. Your efforts remain a part of this project. We dedicate it to your diligence, patience, and passion for Octavia Butler's work. Special thanks are also due to Carl Phillips for encouraging us to undertake this project and to the editors of SFS for nurturing it to completion.

[1]   See, for example, Stewart-Shaheed, Warfield, and Yu.

[2]   For the former see Kilgore, and for the latter see Rieder.

[3]   Davis cites Le Guin as an innovator in science fiction's handling of race

(Davis 19).

[4]   Davis devotes a single line to Butler's position as a 'black sci-fi writer' but does not explain why Butler does not satisfy her call for a black future (Davis 19).

[5]   It is a version of the first chapter of *Wild Seed*. Calvin shows that the magazine reviewed her work several times in the decades following the 1981 publication of the *Wild Seed* excerpt (Calvin 486).

[6]   Elisabeth Anne Leonard and Isiah Lavender III have highlighted the generic tendency to create 'color-blind' futures that 'avoid wrestling with the difficult questions of how a non-racist society comes into being and how members of minority cultures or ethnic groups preserve their culture' (Leonard 254) or project 'racial anxieties onto the body of the alien without seeming to notice that the humanity united against this external threat is suspiciously monochrome' (Lavender 185). See also Bould (177–78).

WORKS CITED

Bould, Mark. 'The Ships Landed Long Ago: Afrofuturism and Black SF.' *SFS* 34.3 (July 2007): 177–86.

Butler, Octavia E. *Bloodchild and Other Stories*. New York: Four Walls, 1995.

—. *Dawn*. 1987. New York: Popular, 1988.

—. *Fledgling*. New York: Seven Stories, 2005.

—. *Kindred*. 1979. Boston: Beacon, 1988.

—. *Parable of the Sower*. New York: Four Walls Eight Windows, 1993.

—. *Survivor*. 1978. New York: Signet, 1979.

— *Wild Seed*. 1980. New York: Popular Library, 1988.

Calvin, Ritch. 'An Octavia E. Butler Bibliography, 1976-2008.' *Utopian Studies* 19.3 (2008): 485–516.

Clarke, Arthur C. *Childhood's End*. 1953. New York: Del Rey, 2001.

Davis, Thulani. 'The Future May Be Bleak, But It's not Black.' *The Village Voice* (1 Feb. 1983): 17-19.

Dery, Mark, 'Black to the Future: Interviews with Samuel R. Delany, Greg Tate, and Tricia Rose.' *Flame Wars: The Discourse of Cyberculture*. Ed. Mark Dery. Durham: Duke UP, 1994. 179–222.

Hopkinson, Nalo. *Midnight Robber*. New York: Warner, 2000.

Kenan, Randall. 'An Interview with Octavia E. Butler.' 1991. *Conversations with Octavia Butler*. Ed. Conseula Francis. Jackson: UP of Mississippi, 2010. 27–37.

Kilgore, De Witt Douglas. *Astrofuturism: Science, Race, and Visions of Utopia in Space*. Philadelphia: U of Pennsylvania P, 2003.

Lavender, Isaiah, III. 'Critical Race Theory.' *The Routledge Companion to Science Fiction*. Ed. Mark Bould et al. London: Routledge, 2009. 185–93.

Le Guin, Ursula K. 'American SF and the Other.' *The Language of the Night: Essays on Fantasy and Science Fiction*. 1979. New York: Berkley, 1982. 87–90.

Leonard, Elisabeth Anne. 'Race and Ethnicity in Science Fiction.' *The Cambridge Companion to Science Fiction*. Ed. Edward James and Farah Mendlesohn. Cambridge, UK: Cambridge UP, 2003. 253–63.

McCaffery, Larry and Jim McMenamin. 'An Interview with Octavia E. Butler.' *Across the Wounded Galaxies: Interviews with Contemporary American Science Fiction Writers*. Ed. Larry McCaffery. Urbana: U of Illinois P, 1990. 54–70.

Mehaffy, Marilyn and AnaLouise Keating, '"Radio Imagination." Octavia Butler on the Poetics of Narrative Embodiment.' 2001. *Conversations with Octavia Butler*. Ed. Conseula Francis. Jackson: UP of Mississippi, 2010. 98–122.

Okorafor-Mbachu, Nnedi. *The Shadow Speaker*. New York: Jump at the Sun, 2007.

Piercy, Marge. *Woman on the Edge of Time.* 1976. New York: Fawcett, 1991.

Potts, Stephen W. '"We Keep Playing the Same Record": A Conversation with Octavia Butler.' 1996. *Conversations with Octavia Butler.* Ed. Conseula Francis. Jackson: UP of Mississippi, 2010. 65–73.

Rieder, John. *Colonialism and the Emergence of Science Fiction.* Middletown, CT: Wesleyan UP, 2008.

Stewart-Shaheed, K. Denea. 'Re-Membering Blackness in the Neo-Slave Writings of Octavia Butler and Zora Neale Hurston.' *Reclaiming Home, Remembering Motherhood, Rewriting History: African American and Afro-Caribbean Women's Literature in the Twentieth Century.* Ed. Verena Theile and Marie Drews. Newcastle upon Tyne, UK: Cambridge Scholars, 2009. 233–51.

Thaler, Ingrid. *Black Atlantic Speculative Fictions: Octavia E. Butler, Jewelle Gomez, and Nalo Hopkinson.* New York: Routledge, 2010.

Warfield, Angela. 'Reassessing the Utopian Novel: Octavia Butler, Jacques Derrida, and the Impossible Future of Utopia.' *Obsidian III: Literature in the African Diaspora* 6.2–7.1 (Fall 2005-Summer 2006): 61–71.

Yu, Jeboon. 'The Representation of Inappropriate/d Others: The Epistemology of Donna Haraway's Cyborg Feminism and Octavia Butler's XENOGENESIS Series.' *Journal of English Language and Literature* 50.3 (2004): 759–77.

SECTION EIGHT

AN INTERVIEW WITH
OCTAVIA E. BUTLER:
'WE KEEP PLAYING
THE SAME RECORD'

Stephen W. Potts and Octavia E. Butler

This interview originally appeared in *Science Fiction Studies*,
Volume 23, Number 3 (November, 1996).

'We Keep Playing the Same Record':
A Conversation with Octavia E. Butler

For readers of this journal, Octavia E. Butler literally needs no
introduction. Her exquisite, insightful works – especially the three
XENOGENESIS novels, (*Dawn, Adulthood Rites, Imago*) and her
award-winning story 'Bloodchild' – have been discussed and
analysed more than once in these pages.

One usually has to get up early in the morning to reach Ms.
Butler. A private person, she prefers writing in the predawn hours
and eight AM is frequently out of the house on the day's business.
She has other claims to uniqueness: she is a native of Los Angeles
who does not drive; she is a woman of color working in a genre that
has almost none, and she is a science-fiction author who has
received a prestigious literary award, to wit, a 1995 grant from the
MacArthur Foundation.

The following conversation took place by telephone early
one morning in February 1996. It has been edited only to eliminate
digressions, redundancies, and irrelevancies and to bridge some
technical difficulties; Ms. Butler was given the opportunity to
review and amend the finished version.

Stephen W. Potts: Your name has been turning up with increasing
    frequency in journals (such as SCIENCE-FICTION
    STUDIES) devoted to the serious study of science fiction.

Do you read reviews or literary criticism of your work?

Octavia E Butler: I do, but I tend to get angry. Not when I disagree with someone's interpretations, but when people clearly have not read the whole book. I'm not too upset when they are factually wrong about some incident, which can happen to anybody, but I am when they are inaccurate about something sweeping. For example, somebody writing a review of *Parable of the Sower* said, 'Oh, the Earthseed religion is just warmed over Christianity,' and I thought this person could not have been troubled to read the Earthseed verses and just drew that conclusion from the title.

SWP: I ask because a substantial part of modern literary theory dwells on relationships of power and on the human body as a site of conflict: between men and women, among classes and races, between imperial and colonial peoples. These issues intersect nicely with the subject matter of your fiction. I was wondering if you were at all familiar with cultural theory.

OEB: Ah. No, I avoid all critical theory because I worry about it feeding into my work. I mean, I don't worry about nonfiction in general feeding in – in fact, I hope it will – but I worry about criticism influencing me because it can create a vicious circle or something worse. It's just an impression of mine, but in some cases critics and authors seem to be massaging each other. It's not very good for storytelling.

SWP: The first work of yours I read was the story 'Bloodchild' in its original printing in *Asimov's*. I remember being particularly impressed that you had taken the invading bug-eyed monster of classic science fiction and turned it into a seductively nurturing, maternal figure.

OEB: It is basically a love story. There are many different kids of love in it: family love, physical love ... The alien needs the boy for procreation, and she makes it easier on him by showing him affection and earning his in return. After all, she is going to have her children with him.

SWP: In fact, she will impregnate him.

OEB: Right. But so many critics have read this as a story about slavery, probably just because I am black.

SWP: I was going to ask you later about the extent to which your work addresses slavery.

OEB: The only places I am writing about slavery is where I actually say so.

SWP: As in *Kindred*.

OEB: And in *Mind of My Mind* and *Wild Seed*. What I was trying to do in 'Bloodchild' was something different with the invasion story. So often you read novels about humans colonizing other planets and you see the story taking one of two courses. Either the aliens resist and we have to conquer them violently, or they submit and become good servants. In the latter case, I am thinking of a specific novel, but I don't want to mention it by name. I don't like either of those alternatives, and I wanted to create a new one. I mean, science fiction is supposed to be about exploring new ideas and possibilities. In the case of 'Bloodchild', I was creating an alien that was different from us, though still recognizable – a centipede-like creature. But you're not supposed to regard it as evil.

SWP: Something similar is going on in the XENOGENESIS trilogy, isn't it? while teaching the books in my university classes, I have encountered disagreement over which species comes off worse, the humans or the Oankali. Humanity has this hierarchical flaw, particularly in the male, but the Oankali are the ultimate users, adapting not only the entire human genome for its own purposes but ultimately destroying the planet for all other life as well. Are we supposed to see a balance of vices here?

OEB: Both species have their strengths and weaknesses. You have small groups of violent humans, but we don't see all humans rampaging as a result of their Contradiction. For the most part, the Oankali do not force or rush humans into mating but try to bring them in gradually. In fact, in *Adulthood Rites*, the construct Akin convinces the Oankali that they cannot destroy the human beings who refuse to participate. The Oankali decide that humans do deserve an untouched world of their own, even if it's Mars.

SWP: In the case of both humans and Oankali, you offer sociobiological arguments for behavior: humans are bent toward destroying themselves and others; the Oankali are biologically driven to co-opt the genome of other species and to literally rip off their biospheres. Do you largely accept sociobiological principles?

OEB: Some readers see as me as totally sociobiological, but that is not true. I do think we need to accept that our behavior is controlled to some extent by biological forces. Sometimes a small change in the brain, for instance – just a few cells – can completely alter the way a person or animal behaves.

SWP: Are you thinking of Oliver Sacks's books, such as *The Man Who Mistook His Wife For a Hat*?

OEB: Exactly. Or the fungus that causes tropical ants to climb trees to spread its spores, or the disease that makes a wildebeest spend its last days spinning in circles. But I don't accept what I would class classical sociobiology. Sometimes we can work around our programming if we understand it.

SWP: The exploitation of reproduction and, by extension, of family arises in a number of your works. Doro in the Patternist novels is breeding a master race and uses family ties with heroines like Anyanwu in *Wild Seed* and Mary in *Mind of My Mind* to help keep them under control. Family ties control the problematic bond between Dana and Rufus in *Kindred*. Reproduction and family lie at the crux of the relationship in 'Bloodchild' and between the humans and Oankali in XENOGENESIS. Do you intentionally focus on reproduction and family issues as a central issue, or did it just happen?

OEB: Perhaps as a woman, I can't help dwelling on the importance of family and reproduction, I don't know how men feel about it. Even though I don't have a husband and children, I have other family, and it seems to me our most important set of relationships. It is so much of what we are. Family does not have to mean purely biological relationships either. I know families that have adopted outside individuals; I don't mean legally adopted children but other adults, friends, people who simply came into the household and stayed. Family bonds can even survive really terrible abuse.

SWP: Of course, you show the power of such bonds operating in either direction; for instance, Anyanwu in *Wild Seed* and Dana in *Kindred* both ultimately take advantage of the fact that their respective 'masters' need them.

OEB: They don't recognize those men as their masters.

SWP: I was putting the word in quotation marks. Are you

suggesting that people in subordinate positions should recognize and exploit what power they do have?

OEB: You do what you have to do. You make the best use of whatever power you have.

SWP: We even see that humans have more power than they realize over the Oankali. Especially with the construct ooloi in *Imago*: they have no identity without human mates. Aaor devolves into a slug.

OEB: The constructs are an experiment. They do not know what they are going to be, or when it is going to happen. And they do not need humans specifically, even though they prefer them; they can bond with anything. But they have to bond.

SWP: I would like to go back a bit in your literary history. Who were your authorial influences as an apprentice writer?

OEB: I read a lot of science fiction with absolutely no discrimination when I was growing up – I mean, good, bad, or awful [laughs]. It didn't matter. I remember latching onto people and reading everything I could find by them, people like John Brunner, who wrote a lot. I could pick up Ace Doubles at the used book store for a nickel or a dime, so I was always reading John Brunner. And Theodore Sturgeon – by the time I was reading adult science fiction, he had a considerable body of work. Of course, Robert A. Heinlein. I can remember my very first adult science fiction, a story called 'Lorelei of the Red Mist.' If I am not mistaken, it was Ray Bradbury's first published story. Leigh Bracket began it and he finished it.

SWP: Can you think of anybody outside of science fiction?

OEB: I tended to read whatever was in the house, which meant that I read a lot of odd stuff. Who was that guy who used to write about men's clubs all the time? John O'Hara. It was

Mars for me. I like British between-the-wars mysteries for the same reason. They take place on mars; they're different worlds.

SWP: Might we suggest that since John O'Hara writes about upper-class white culture, his world would be almost as alien to you as the world of science fiction?

OEB: Absolutely. There was a book of his stories in the house, as well as books by James Thurber and James Baldwin. I did not read any Langston Hughes until I was an adult, but I remember being carried away by him and Gwendolyn Brooks. When I was growing up, the only blacks you came across in school were slaves – who were always well treated – and later, when we got to individuals, Booker T. Washington and George Washington Carver. Booker T. Washington started a college, and Carver did something with peanuts; we never knew what. We did not read anything by a black writer except [James Weldon] Johnson's *The Creation*, and that was in high school. We managed to get through adolescence without being introduced to any black culture.

SWP: I was in that same generation, and I remember that it wasn't really until the seventies that we started opening up the canon. Actually, the issue is still controversial, judging from the so-called 'culture war' over how inclusive the canon should be or whether we should even have one.

OEB: Yes, it's too bad when ... well, there was one person I had a lot of respect for, but he could not find a single black person to put into the canon, so I lost my respect for him rather badly.

SWP: On its surface, *Parable of the Sower* looks like a change in direction from your earlier work.

OEB: Not really. It is still fundamentally about social power.

SWP: But it is much more a close extrapolation from current trends: the increasing class gap, the fear of crime, the chaos of the cities spreading to the suburbs, the centrifugal forces tearing our society apart.

OEB: Yes. It really distresses me that we see these things happening now in American society when they don't have to. Some people insist that all civilizations have to rise and fall – like the British before us – but we have brought this on ourselves. What you see today has happened before: a few powerful people take over with the approval of a class below them who has nothing to gain and even much to lose as a result. It's like the Civil War: most of the men who fought to preserve slavery were actually being hurt by it. As farmers they could not compete with the plantations, and they could not even hire themselves out as labor in competition with the slaves who could be hired out more cheaply by their owners. But they supported the slave system anyway.

SWP: They probably opposed affirmative action.

OEB: [laughs] Right. I guess many people just need someone to feel superior to to make themselves feel better. You see Americans doing it now, unfortunately, while voting against their own interests. It is that kind of shortsighted behavior that is destroying us.

SWP: Are these problems somehow unique to American society?

OEB: Oh no, of course not.

SWP: I was sure you'd say that.

OEB: We are seeing a particular American form here, but look at the Soviet Union. When capitalism took over, it is amazing how quickly they developed a crime problem. Unfortunately, the most successful capitalists over there now seem to be the criminals.

SWP: Which is ironic because in classic Soviet Marxist theory the capitalist class was associated with the criminal class.

OEB: That may be the problem. We are getting into murky territory here: I heard about an old man in Russia who tried to turn his farm into a successful private enterprise, but his neighbors came over and destroyed his efforts. He was not a criminal, but to them that kinds of individualistic profit-making was criminal behavior. I guess to succeed in Russia you have to be someone who (a) doesn't care what the neighbors think and (b) has a bodyguard. And if you're in that position, you probably are a criminal.

SWP: To get back to *Parable of the Sower*, Lauren Olamina is empathic –

OEB: She is not empathic. She feels herself to be. Usually in science fiction 'empathic' means that you really are suffering, that you are actively interacting telepathically with another person, and she is not. She has this delusion that she cannot shake. It's kind of biologically programmed into her.

SWP: Interesting. So what is happening, say, when she feels the pain of the wounded dog she ends up killing?

OEB: Oh, even if it is not there, she feels it. In the first chapter of the book, she talks about her brother playing tricks on her – pretending to be hurt, pretending to bleed, and causing her to suffer. I have been really annoyed with people who claim Lauren is a telepath, who insist that she has this power. What she has is a rather crippling delusion.

SWP: So we should maintain some ironic distance from her?

OEB: No.

SWP: We should still identify with her.

OEB: I hope readers will identify with all my characters, at least while they're reading.

SWP: Through Earthseed, Lauren hopes to bring back a sense of communal purpose and meaning by turning people's eyes back to the stars. It made me think: the space program of the sixties really was part of the general hopefulness of the decade, part of our sense that anything was possible if we strove together as a people.

OEB: And that was the decade of my adolescence. We keep playing the same record. Earlier I was talking about it: we begin something and then we grow it to a certain point and then it destroys itself or else it is destroyed from the outside – whether it is Egypt or Rome or Greece, this country or Great Britain, you name it. I do feel that we are either going to continue to play the same record until it shatters – and I said it in the book, though not in those words – or we are going to do something else. And I think the best way to do something else is to go someplace else where the demands on us will be different. Not because we are going to go someplace else and change ourselves, but because we will go someplace else and be forced to change.

SWP: Do you think we will be better for that change?

OEB: It's possible. We could be better; we could be worse. There's no insurance policy.

SWP: I gather that we can expect another book to pick up where *Parable of the Sower* left off.

OEB: *Parable of the Talents* is the book I am working on now.

SWP: It will be interesting to see where you go with the story.

OEB: Well, in *Parable of the Sower* I focused on the problems – the things we have done wrong, that we appear to be doing wrong, and where those things can lead us. I made a real effort to talk about what could actually happen or is in the process of happening: the walled communities and the illiteracy and the global warming and lots of other things. In *Parable of the Talents* I want to give my characters the chance to work on the solutions, to say, 'Here is the solution!'

SWP: *Parable of the Sower* was published by a small press (Four Walls Eight Windows), as was your collection *Bloodchild and Other Stories. Kindred* was republished by a small press (Beacon). As a successful science-fiction author, what made you turn to less commercial publishers?

OEB: I had probably reached some kind of plateau in science fiction, and I couldn't seem to get off it. I knew I had three audiences at least, but I couldn't get my science-fiction publisher to pay any attention. I could tell them all day and all night, but they would answer, 'Yes, that's right,' and then go off and do something else. You know, the best way to defeat an argument is to agree with it and then forget about it. I had wanted to try one of the big publishers not normally associated with science fiction, and then my agent came up with this small publisher. I thought I would take the chance.

SWP: Would you like to break down some of the walls between generic marketing categories?

OEB: Oh, that's not possible. You know how we are; if we kill off some, we will invent others.

SWP: I ask in part because I noticed that Beacon Press published *Kindred* as a book in its 'Black Women Writers' series.

OEB: Yes, I mentioned having three audiences: the science-fiction audience, the black audience, and the feminist audience.

SWP: And being marketed through such categories doesn't trouble you.

OEB: Well, they're there, as I was just saying, and there's nothing you can do about it.

SWP: I remember that during the New Wave of the Sixties –

OEB: Oh, where is it now?

SWP: – I was among those who believed that science fiction was moving to the forefront of literature.

OEB: Well, parts of it did move into the mainstream. In other cases, people simply did not call what they were doing 'science fiction.' I mean, Robin Cook did not announce that he was doing medical science fiction, and Dean Koontz does not publish his work as science fiction. And there are a lot of people who write science fiction although the word does not appear anywhere on the cover or inside. It doesn't mean they don't like science fiction; it means that they want to make a good living.

SWP: As I pointed out initially, your treatments of power, gender, and race coincide with many of the interests of current literary theory, and your own race and gender inevitably come into literary critiques of your work. Has being an African-American woman influenced your choice of theme and approach?

OEB: I don't think it could do otherwise. All writers are influenced by who they are. If you are white, you could write about being Chinese, but you would bring in a lot of what you are as well.

SWP: I can't help noticing – as you yourself observe in your essay 'Positive Obsession' – that you are unique in the science-fiction community. While there are more women working in the field than there were thirty years ago, there are few African-Americans, and I still cannot think of another African-American woman.

OEB: I have heard of some who have published stories. The ones who are actually writing books are not calling themselves science-fiction authors, which is right because they are actually writing horror or fantasy. For instance, the woman who wrote the lesbian vampire stories, the Gilda stories, Jewells Gomez – she's not science fiction but she is fantasy, and that's in the family. But I don't think she even presented her work as that.

SWP: Do you think many people are still under the impression that science fiction is primarily a white male genre?

OEB: Yes. In fact, sometimes when I speak to general audiences they are surprised there are a lot of women in science fiction. Because people do have a rather fixed notion of what science fiction is; it either comes from television or they pick it up somehow from the air, ambiance.

SWP: Any last words to the science-fiction critical community about how to approach your work?

OEB: Oh, good heaves, no!

SWP: [laughs]

OEB: As far as criticism goes, what a reader brings to the work is as important as what I put into it, so I don't get upset when I am misinterpreted. Except when I say what I really was so-and-so, and I am told, 'Oh, but subconsciously you must have meant this.' I mean – leave me alone! [laughs] I don't mind attempts to interpret my fiction, but I am not willing to have critics interpret my subconscious. I doubt they re qualified.

WORKS CITED

Butler, Octavia E. *Adulthood Rites*. NY: Warner Books, 1988.

– 'Bloodchild.' *Isaac Asimov's Science Fiction Magazine* (June 1984). 34–54

– *Bloodchild and Other Stories*. NY: Four Walls Eight Windows, 1995.

– *Dawn*. NY: Warner Books, 1987.

– *Kindred*. 1979. Boston: Beacon Press, 1988.

– *Imago*. NY: Warner Books, 1989.

– *Mind of My Mind*. NY: Warner Books, 1994.

– *Parable of the Sower*. NY: Four Walls Eight Windows, 1993.

– 'Positive Obsession,' *Bloodchild and Other Stories*, 125–135.

– *Wild Seed*. NY: Warner Books, 1988.

Sacks, Oliver. *The Man Who Mistook His Wife for a Hat*. NY: Summit Books, 1985.

AUTHOR BIOGRAPHIES

Rasha Abdulhadi grew up between Damascus and rural south Georgia and cut her teeth organizing on the southsides of Chicago and Atlanta. She is a cultural worker, educator, community technologist, and once and future farmer and beekeeper, as well as a member of Alternate ROOTS. Her work appears or is forthcoming at sinnerscreek.com, *Mizna Journal of Arab American Art, Tiny Tim Review*, and an anthology on Arab American Aesthetics, ed. by Therí Pickens Ph.D. She manages one of the oldest used/rare bookstores in Washington D.C.

Raffaella Baccolini teaches Gender Studies and American Literature at the University of Bologna, Forlì. She has published several articles on dystopia and science fiction, trauma literature, women's writing, memory, and modernist literature. She is the author of *Tradition, Identity, Desire: Revisionist Strategies in H.D.'s Late Poetry* (Patron, 1995) and has edited several volumes, among which are *Dark Horizons: Science Fiction and the Dystopian Imagination* (with T. Moylan, Routledge, 2003), *Le prospettive di genere: discipline, soglie, confini (BUP, 2005), Utopia, Method, Vision: The Use Value of Social Dreaming* (also with T. Moylan, Peter Lang, 2007), *Humor and Gender: Interdisciplinary and International Perspectives* (with D. Chiaro, Routledge, 2014), and Tom Moylan's new edition of *Demand the Impossible* (Peter Lang,

2014). She is currently working on the representation of 9/11 in American popular culture.

Dr. Moya Bailey's work focuses on marginalized groups' use of digital media to promote social justice as acts of self-affirmation and health promotion. She is interested in how race, gender, and sexuality are represented in media and medicine. She currently curates the #transformDH Tumblr initiative in Digital Humanities. She is also the digital alchemist for the Octavia E. Butler Legacy Network. She is an assistant professor in the department of Cultures, Societies, and Global Studies and the program in Women's, Gender, and Sexuality Studies at Northeastern University.

NY Times Bestselling author **Steven Barnes** has written over thirty novels of SF, fantasy, mystery and adventure. He lives in Southern California with his wife and collaborator, American Book Award winning horror novelist Tananarive Due with whom he won the NAACP Image award for *In the Night of the Heat*. He can be reached at www.stevenbarneslife.com.

Michele Tracy Berger is a professor, a creative writer, a creativity coach and a pug-lover. Her short fiction, poetry and creative nonfiction has appeared, or is forthcoming in *Glint, Thing, Flying South, Oracle: Fine Arts Review, Carolina Woman, Trivia: Voices of Feminism, Ms., The Feminist Wire, Western North Carolina Woman*, various zines and anthologies. Michele was a 'My View' monthly columnist for *The Chapel Hill News* from 2012-2014. Her award winning blog, 'The Practice of Creativity' was featured in *Southern Writers Magazine*. In 2017, her science fiction novella,

'Reenu-You' will be published by Book Smugglers Publishing. She currently sits on the board of the North Carolina Writers' Network.

Tara Betts is the author of two poetry collections, *Break the Habit* and *Arc & Hue*. Her writing has also appeared in *Near Kin: A Collection of Words and Art Inspired by Octavia Estelle Butler and Octavia's Brood: Science Fiction Stories from Social Justice Movements*. She teaches at University of Illinois-Chicago.

Lisa Bennett Bolekaja is a writer, screenwriter, and film critic. She co-hosts the screenwriting podcast 'Hilliard Guess' Screenwriters Rant Room' (available on Itunes and Stitcher). Her work has appeared in *Long Hidden: Speculative Fiction from the Margins of History, The WisCon Chronicles: Volume 8, How to Live on Other Planets: A Handbook for Aspiring Aliens* and *Uncanny Magazine*. She's an Apex Magazine slush reader, a former Film Independent Fellow, and a staff writer for *Bitch Flicks*, an online intersectional feminist film review site. She's also a member of the Carl Brandon Society. She divides her time between L.A., San Diego, Italy, and shit talking on Twitter. Come holla at her @WhatFreshHellIsThis.

K. Tempest Bradford is a speculative fiction writer, a journalist, a podcaster, a teacher, and a professional harsher of squee. Her short fiction has appeared in *Strange Horizons, Electric Velocipede*, and other science fiction and fantasy magazines as well as *Interfictions, Federations*, and *In The Shadow Of The Towers*, among other anthologies. She teaches writing classes at WritingTheOther.com on creating inclusive fiction alongside author Nisi Shawl. She also volunteers her time as a board member of the Carl Brandon Society, an organization dedicated to increasing racial and ethnic diversity in the production of and audience for speculative fiction. When not writing fantastical fiction, she produces a podcast about technology called The Write Gear, talks about literature on NPR Books, and reads every short story she can find. You can find her fiction, criticism, and list of projects at KTempestBradford.com.

Recovering musician **Cassandra Brennan** struggles to find coffee and solace in Brooklyn NY with the emotional support of her Thor-lookalike husband and apartment full of strangely needy plants. She has been a regular contributor to *Full Throttle NY/NE Motorcycle* magazine and looks forward to releasing her graphic novel series *M-Theory* this year.

Jennifer Marie Brissett is the author of *Elysium, Or The World After* (Aqueduct Press), winner of the Philip K. Dick Special Citation Award, and shortlisted for the Locus and Tiptree Awards.

Stephanie Burgis grew up in America and now lives in Wales, surrounded by castles and coffee shops. She is the author of two historical fantasy novels for adults (*Masks and Shadows* and *Congress of Secrets*), a series of MG Regency fantasy novels (beginning with *Kat, Incorrigible*), and a new MG fantasy series that begins with *The Dragon with a Chocolate Heart*. She has also published over thirty short stories in various magazines and anthologies. To find out more and read excerpts from her novels, please visit: www.stephanieburgis.com.

Mary Elizabeth Burroughs is a graduate of Clarion Writers Workshop at UC San Diego and University of Mississippi's MFA program. A native of Florida, she now lives in Sydney, Australia where she teaches English to high school students. Her published fiction has appeared in *Black Static*, *Phantom Drift: A Journal of New Fabulism*, and *Bloodchildren: Stories by the Octavia E. Butler Scholars* (Aqueduct Press).

Christopher Caldwell is a queer Black American living in Glasgow, Scotland with his partner Alice. He was the 2007 recipient of the Octavia E. Butler Memorial Scholarship to Clarion West. His work has appeared in *Fiyah*, *Bloodchildren: Stories by the Octavia E. Butler Scholars*, and *Obsidian: Literature & Arts in the African Diaspora*.

Gerry Canavan is an assistant professor of twentieth- and twenty-first-century literature at Marquette University, specializing in science fiction. He is the co-editor of *Green Planets: Ecology and Science Fiction* and *The Cambridge Companion to American Science Fiction*, as well as co-editor of the academic journals *Extrapolation and Science Fiction Film and Television*. His first book, *Octavia E. Butler*, is available now from the Modern Masters of Science Fiction series at University of Illinois Press.

Born in Singapore, but a global citizen, **Joyce Chng** writes mainly science fiction and YA. She likes steampunk and tales of transfiguration/ transformation. Her fiction has appeared in *The Apex Book of World SF II*, *We See A Different Frontier*, *Cranky Ladies of History*, and *Accessing The Future*. Her YA includes a trilogy about a desert planet and a fantasy duology in Qing China. Joyce also co-edited a Southeast Asian steampunk anthology titled *The Sea Is Ours: Tales of Steampunk Southeast Asia* with Jaymee

Goh. Her Jan Xu Adventures series, an urban/contemporary fantasy set in Singapore, is written under the pseud. J. Damask which she will tell you is a play on her Chinese name. She can be found at http://awolfstale.wordpress.com and Twitter (@jolantru).

Indrapramit Das (aka Indra Das) is the author of debut novel *The Devourers* (Del Rey / Penguin India), which was shortlisted for the 2016 Crawford Award. His fiction has appeared in several publications including *Clarkesworld Magazine, Lightspeed Magazine, Asimov's Science Fiction, Strange Horizons,* and *Tor.com,* and has also been widely anthologized in collections such as *The Year's Best Science Fiction* (St. Martin's Press). He is an Octavia E. Butler scholar and a grateful graduate of the 2012 Clarion West Writers Workshop. He grew up in Kolkata, India, and has worn many hats, including dog hotel night shift attendant, TV background performer, minor film critic, occasional illustrator, environmental news writer, pretend-patient for med school students, and video game tester. He is currently working as a consulting editor for Indian publisher Juggernaut Books while writing a second novel. He divides his time between India and North America, whenever possible.

L. Timmel Duchamp is the author of the five-novel Marq'ssan Cycle, which was awarded a Special Honor by the 2009 James Tiptree Award jury; *The Waterdancer's World* (2016); two collections of short fiction, *Love's Body, Dancing in Time* and *Never At Home;* the short novel *The Red Rose Rages* (Bleeding); and numerous uncollected stories, for which she has been a Nebula and Sturgeon Award finalist and short-listed numerous times for the Tiptree Award. She lives in Seattle.

Sophia M. Echavarria is a 2013 recipient of the Octavia E. Butler Memorial Scholarship. She studied English Literature, African American Studies and Creative Writing at Princeton University and spent time in the Creative Writing MFA Program at UC San Diego. Sophia lives in Long Beach, CA with her cat Pimienta and is trying to write from the in between.

Tuere T. S. Ganges, a South Jersey native, writes and teaches in Baltimore, Maryland. She was a June 2009 recipient of the Archie D. and Bertha H. Walker Foundation Scholarship to the Fine Arts Work Center in Provincetown. 'The Death of an Astronaut', flash fiction first published in *Referential Magazine*, was nominated for a Pushcart Prize in 2010. Her fiction has won prizes at the Philadelphia Writers Conference; and has appeared in *Mythium Literary Magazine*, *Wigleaf*, and *Fiction Circus*. Her monologue, 'Black. Belly. Box.' was performed in the 2016 production of *In Full Color* and another was selected to be performed in the 2017 production. *Wilted and Other Stories*, her collection of short fiction, is available digitally on Amazon.com. She is currently a contributor for BlackSciFi.com and the consulting editor of the anthology, *The Scribes of Nyota*.

Stephen R. Gold passes for an assimilated American male. He enjoys the privileges thereof and wishes them extended to all people. Raised in Pennsylvania, he lived a year abroad when he was eight. At ten, he self-published a story about anthropomorphic ducks. Stephen moved to California in 1986, where he married a Piers Anthony fan and fathered a son. After a great-uncle mocked his novel-writing ambitions, he applied for (and was accepted into) the 2005 Clarion West workshop, where he met Octavia Butler.

In his spare time, he shelves books at a public library.

Jewelle Gomez is the author of eight books including the cult classic, Black, lesbian, vampire novel, *The Gilda Stories*, whose twenty-fifth anniversary edition was recently published by City Lights Books. Her adaptation of the novel for the stage, *Bones and Ash*, was performed by Urban Bush Women Company in thirteen US cities. She is also the author of *Waiting For Giovanni*, a play about James Baldwin. Her new play about singer/songwriter Alberta Hunter, called *Leaving The Blues*, premiers at New Conservatory Theatre Center in spring 2017. Follow her @VampyreVamp; www.jewellegomez.com.

Kate Gordon grew up in a small town by the sea in North West Tasmania and now lives at the other end of the island, with her husband and daughter. Kate's YA books include *Writing Clementine* (2014), *Thyla* (2011), *Vulpi* (2012), and *Three Things About Daisy Blue* (2010). Kate frequently conducts author talks, school visits and conference presentations around Tasmania. She writes teacher notes for several major Australian publishers and has been an ambassador for the National Year of Reading and was the recipient of 2011 and 2012 Arts Tasmania Assistance to Individuals grants. Kate is now an assessor for these grants, and has also served as a judge on the 2015 Premier's Literary Prizes. Kate was a guest speaker at the 2015 Tasmanian Writers and Readers Festival. In 2016, Kate was the recipient of the Ena Noel Award from the International Board on Books for Young People and her novel, *Writing Clementine*, was published by Random House Germany. Kate blogs at www.kategordon.com.au/blog and you can find more about her and her books at www.kategordon.com.au.

Rebecca J. Holden is a fan and scholar of feminist science fiction. She earned her Ph.D. in English from the University of Wisconsin-Madison and has been teaching in the Professional Writing Program at the University of Maryland, College Park since 2008. She has published essays on various science fiction writers and reviews in *Foundation, Science Fiction Studies*, and *Women of Other Worlds: Excursions through Science Fiction and Feminism.* With Nisi Shawl, Holden co-edited and contributed to *Strange Matings: Science Fiction, Feminism, African American Voices, and Octavia E. Butler* (2013). She also edited a collection of pieces on WisCon, a feminist science fiction convention, titled *Regenerating WisCon* (2014). In 2014, Holden co-chaired the annual SFRA (Science Fiction Research Association) conference.

Tiara Janté is a writer hailing from north-east Pennsylvania. She has a passion for speculative fiction – especially science fiction. In addition to writing, she is Co-Founder of Oak PR, a boutique public relations firm specializing in literary public relation. She is also Co-Editor of *Black Girl Magic Literary Magazine*, a quarterly magazine featuring speculative fiction by and about black women, and she is a regular contributor to Black Sci-Fi.com. Her debut sci-fi novel *Exo* will be released Spring 2017. Connect with her via her website at: www.tiarajante.net.

Valjeanne Jeffers is a graduate of Spelman College, a member of the Carolina African American Writer's Collective (CAAWC) and the author of ten books: including her Immortal series, and her most recent Mona Livelong: Paranormal Dectective Series. Her first novel, *Immortal*, is featured on the Invisible Universe Documentary time-line, and her novella, *The Switch II: Clockwork* was nominated as best eBook novella of 2013, by the eFestival of words. Her writing has been published in numerous anthologies including: *60 Black Women in Horror Fiction; Steamfunk!; Genesis Science Fiction Magazine; The Ringing Ear: Black Poets Lean South* (as Valjeanne Jeffers-Thompson); *Griots: A Sword and Soul Anthology; Liberated Muse I: How I Freed My Soul; PurpleMag; Drumvoices Revue; 31 Days of Steamy Mocha; Griots II: Sisters of the Spear; Possibilities; Black Gold*, and most recently, *Fitting In: Historical Accounts of Paranormal Subcultures, Sycorax's Daughters* (in press), and *The City: A Cyberfunk.* Valjeanne is also one of the screenwriters for the horror anthology film, 7Magpies (in production). Preview or purchase her novels at: www. vjeffersandqveal.com.

Alex Jennings is a writer, actor, teacher. Born in Germany, he was raised in Gaborone, Botswana, Paramaribo, Surinam, Tunis, Tunisia, and the United States. He spends too much time on social media and considers himself an 'Afternoon Person'. He lives and works in New Orleans.

Alaya Dawn Johnson is the author of six novels for adults and young adults. Her novel *The Summer Prince* was longlisted for the National Book Award for Young People's Literature. Her most recent, *Love Is the Drug*, won the Andre Norton Award. Her short stories have appeared in many magazines and anthologies, including *Best American Science Fiction and Fantasy 2015, Zombies vs. Unicorns* and *Welcome to Bordertown*. In addition to the Norton, she has won the Nebula and Cybils Awards and been nominated for the Indies Choice Award and Locus Award. She lives in Mexico City where she is getting her master's in mesoamerican studies.

Kathleen Kayembe is the Octavia E. Butler Scholar from Clarion's class of 2016, with short stories forthcoming from *Lightspeed* and *Nightmare*. She writes paranormal romance as Kaseka Nvita, co-hosts the Write Pack Radio weekly writing podcast as herself, and lives on Twitter as @mkkayembe. A longtime member of the St. Louis Writers Guild, she organizes write-ins instead of movie outings, and falls in love with the world every time she uses a fountain pen.

Hunter Liguore is an Associate Professor of writing at Western CT State University. A three-time Pushcart-Prize nominee (including 2017), her work has appeared in various publications, internationally, including: *Bellevue Literary Review, Irish Times, New Plains Review, Writer's Chronicle, The Writer Magazine, Amazing Stories, James Gunn Ad Astra, Strange Horizons, Perihelion SF, Tincture Journal, SCI-PHI Journal, Black Denim Lit, The Rattling Wall: Pen American USA*, and an upcoming wildlife anthology from Ashland Creek Press, among many others. She is the first place recipient of the 2015 Ethnographic Fiction competition sponsored by the American Anthropological Association. Her forthcoming eco-fiction novel is due out in 2017 with Harvard Editions; she has literary representation with Regal Literary Agency.

Barbadian author, editor and research consultant **Karen Lord** is known for her debut novel *Redemption in Indigo*, which won the 2008 Frank Collymore Literary Award, the 2010 Carl Brandon Parallax Award, the 2011 William L. Crawford Award, the 2011 Mythopoeic Fantasy Award for Adult Literature and the 2012 Kitschies Golden Tentacle (Best Debut), and was longlisted for the 2011 Bocas Prize for Caribbean Literature and nominated for the 2011 World Fantasy Award for Best Novel. Her second novel *The Best of All Possible Worlds* won the 2009 Frank Collymore Literary Award, the 2013 RT Book Reviews Reviewers' Choice Awards for Best Science Fiction Novel, and was a finalist for the 2014 Locus Awards. Its sequel, *The Galaxy Game*, was published in January 2015. She is the editor of the 2016 anthology *New Worlds, Old Ways: Speculative Tales from the Caribbean*.

Zora Mai Quýnh is a literary poet and writer whose short stories have appeared in the anthologies: *The Sea is Ours* ('The Chamber of Souls') and *Genius Loci: The Spirit of Place* ('The South China Sea'). Her short story 'The Chamber of Souls' was translated and featured in the Czech version of *The Sea is Ours*. Her short story, 'The Seashell' was nominated for a Sundress Best of the Net Award for fiction, given honorary mention by the literary magazine, *Glimmer Train*, and will be featured in this year's 2016 APAture. Her essay 'On the Topic of Erasure' was published in the anthology, *People of Color Destroy Science Fiction*. Her creative non-fiction essay, 'Meta Eulogy: Nguyễn Ngoc Loan By A Vietnamese American', published at DiaCRITICS, was nominated for a Sundress Best of the Net Award for creative non-fiction. She was a finalist for the 2014 Barbara Deming Writing Grant. She is currently working on her first novel.

Asata Radcliffe is a writer and filmmaker. She received her MFA in Creative Writing (Fiction) from Antioch University. Her writing includes fiction, sci-fi/speculative, essays, and she is a reviewer for Kirkus Reviews. She is the Creative Director for Little Thunder Films. Asata's documentary and independent film work investigates culture, the interstitial in society, and the abstract in art. She is currently creating a collection of speculative film and writing, including a series of speculative novellas. Her most recent work, *Creative Sovereignty*, (2016) appears as the first essay to be published in the debut issue of Lady/Liberty/Lit. Her writing also appears in the anthology *Dawnland Voices 2.0: Indigenous Writing from New England & the Northeast*. She can be found at https://asataradcliffe.wordpress.com/.

Aurelius Raines II writes and lives in Chicago with his wife, Pam, and his two sons. He likes to write about the human condition and is obsessed with entropy. He is the author of two books of poetry, *I've Got A Hole In My Lip …* and *Love Songs To The Revolution*. His short stories and essays have been included in the upcoming anthologies *Dead Inside, Black Power* and the online journal *Timbooktu*. When he is not writing, he teaches science to middle-schoolers by showing them how to use biology, chemistry and physics to survive the end of civilization.

Cat Rambo lives, writes, and teaches atop a hill in the Pacific Northwest. Her 200+ fiction publications include stories in *Asimov's, Clarkesworld Magazine*, and *The Magazine of Fantasy and Science Fiction*. She is an Endeavour, Nebula, and World Fantasy Award nominee. Among her nonfiction books are *Creating an Online Presence for Writers and Ad Astra: The SFWA 50th Anniversary Cookbook*, coedited with Fran Wilde and which contains Octavia Butler's pineapple fried rice recipe. Since 2010, she has run The Rambo Academy for Wayward Writers, an online writing school. She is the current President of the Science Fiction and Fantasy Writers of America. For more about Cat, as well as links to her fiction and classes, see http://www.kittywumpus.net

Connie Samaras is a Los Angeles artist and sometimes writer. Her most recent photography project, *The Past is Another Planet*, is based on Butler's papers housed at the Huntington Library, Pasadena. The first part of this series premiered in the exhibition *Radio Imagination: Artists in the Archive of Octavia E. Butler*, the Armory, Pasadena (Oct 2016-Jan 2017) curated by Clockshop, Los Angeles. A part of this series was also recently shown in the group exhibition, *The Stand*, P! Gallery, New York (Jan-Feb 2017). An extensive monograph published in conjunction with a 2013 survey show of her work, *Tales of Tomorrow*, is available through D.A.P. art books. Among her upcoming projects is a multimedia installation based on the correspondence between Joanna Russ and James Tiptree Jr./ Alice Sheldon.

Nisi Shawl's acclaimed alternate history/steampunk novel *Everfair* was a 2016 Tor publication. Her collection *Filter House* co-won the James Tiptree, Jr. Award and she has been a Guest of Honor for WisCon, the Science Fiction Research Association's convention, and Austin's Armadillocon. Shawl co-edited *Strange Matings: Science Fiction, Feminism, African American Voices*, and *Octavia E. Butler;* and *Stories for Chip: A Tribute to Samuel R. Delany*. Since its inception she has been Reviews Editor for feminist literary quarterly *Cascadia Subduction Zone*. She's the coauthor of *Writing the Other: A Practical Approach*; and teaches the workshop it's based on. Shawl is a founder of and board member for the Carl Brandon Society, a nonprofit supporting the presence of people of color in the fantastic genres; she also serves on Clarion West's board of directors. She lives in Seattle, taking daily walks with her mother June and her cat Minnie at a feline pace.

Jeremy Sim is a Singaporean-American writer and the author of over a dozen short stories, including appearances in *Cicada*, *Crossed Genres*, and *Beneath Ceaseless Skies*. He is a graduate of Clarion West Writers Workshop, where he was awarded the Octavia E. Butler Memorial Scholarship in 2011. He has called many cities home, but currently lives in Seattle, where he works as a video game writer.

Amanda Emily Smith is a Dillard student, a poet, reiki practitioner, sex-positive activist, yoga practitioner, community organizer, Mom, Queer woman and Black daughter of New Orleans. She was raised in the Treme, the oldest Black community in the country, so her steps are rooted in the understanding of Black community. She grew up in a family of women from her Mom, Grandma Ruth, Great Grandma (Granni) No, and Great Great Grandmother Mary which taught her the profound beauty and resilience of Black women. She devotes her time to liberation and justice through her Mothering, her work as Community Coordinator at the LGBT Community Center of New Orleans, her performance and poetry on topics including Motherhood, Black womanhood and sacred sexuality. You can follow her as AmandaEmilySJW on Twitter.

Cat Sparks is a multi-award-winning Australian author, editor and artist whose former employment has included: media monitor, political and archaeological photographer, graphic designer, Fiction Editor of Cosmos Magazine and Manager of Agog! Press.

She's currently finishing a PhD in climate change fiction. Her short story collection *The Bride Price* was published in 2013. Her debut novel, *Lotus Blue*, will be published by Skyhorse in March, 2017.

Based in Johannesburg, South Africa, **Elizabeth Stephens** is an American author of science fiction and romance. Her post-apocalyptic novels *Population* and *Saltlands* were published in 2015 and 2016, respectively, and her unpublished young adult book, *The Rougarou*, was awarded the 2015 Tu Books New Vision Awards for outstanding fiction among authors of color. More on her past and upcoming works can be found at www.booksbyelizabeth.com.

Rachel Swirsky holds an MFA from the Iowa Writers Workshop. She's won the Nebula Award twice, and been nominated for the Hugo Award, the Locus Award, the Sturgeon Award, and others. She studied with Octavia Butler at Clarion West the year before Butler died.

Bogi Takács is a Hungarian Jewish agender person (e/em/eir/emself or they pronouns) currently living in the United States as a resident alien. Eir speculative fiction and poetry have been published in venues like Clarkesworld, Lightspeed, Strange Horizons and Apex. You can find Bogi at http://www.prezzey.net or as @bogiperson on Twitter and Instagram. E also blogs about books with a focus on marginalized authors at http://www.bogireadstheworld.com.

Sheree Renée Thomas, a native of Memphis, is the author of *Sleeping Under the Tree of Life* (Aqueduct Press), *Shotgun Lullabies*, and the editor of the World Fantasy Award-winning *Dark Matter* anthologies. She also served as the Guest Editor of a special double-issue of *Obsidian*, 'Speculating Futures: Black Imagination & the Arts' (February 2017). She was the Lucille Geier-Lakes Writer in Residence at Smith College and has been honored with fellowships and residencies from Cave Canem, Millay, The Wallace Foundation, VCCA, Ledig House/Writers Omi, Blue Mountain, the New York Foundation of the Arts, and the Tennessee Arts Commission. Read her short stories and poems in *Sycorax's Daughters, Stories for Chip: Tribute to Samuel R. Delany, Revise the Psalm: Writers Celebrate Gwendolyn Brooks, The Moment of Change, Mojo: Conjure Stories, An Alphabet of Embers, Strange Horizons, Mythic Delirium, Jalada, So Long Been Dreaming, 80! Memories & Reflections of Ursula K. Le Guin, Memphis Noir, Callaloo, Obsidian,* and Harvard's *Transition.* Find her @blackpotmojo or visit http://www.aqueductpress.com/authors/ShereeThomas.php

Jeffrey Allen Tucker is Associate Professor in the Department of English at the University of Rochester. He is the author of *A Sense of Wonder: Samuel R. Delany, Race, Identity, & Difference* (Wesleyan UP, 2004), editor of *Conversations with John A. Williams* (UP of Mississippi, 2018), and co-editor of *Race Consciousness: African-American Studies for the New Century* (NYU Press, 1997), as well as author of scholarly articles on writers such as Octavia E. Butler, George S. Schuyler, and Colson Whitehead.

Brenda Tyrrell is a Master's of Literature student at Iowa State University and is currently working on her thesis at the intersections of H. G. Wells's 'The Country of the Blind' and

Christina Alberta's Father, and disability studies. She teaches composition classes, as well as Honors classes involving Octavia Butler's *Parable of the Sower* and *Dawn*. Brenda has presented her work at a number of academic conferences and has recently published 'Tracing Wells's New Woman through *The Wheels of Chance* and *The War of the Worlds*' (*The Wellsian*, Vol. 39, 2016). She has also reviewed *Culture on Two Wheels: The Bicycle in Literature and Film* (ed. Jeremy Withers and Daniel P. Shea, Lincoln: U of Nebraska P, 2016). She plans to obtain her PhD with a continued focus on H. G. Wells and disability studies. She also enjoys reading science fiction in her free time and is currently exploring the representation of disability in the works of female science fiction authors.

An ex-pat New Yorker living in Minnesota, **Paul Weimer** has been reading sci-fi and fantasy for over thirty five years. An avid blogger, reviewer, and sometimes writer of fiction as well, he also podcasts, especially at the Skiffy and Fanty Show and SFF Audio. If you've spent any time reading about SFF online, you've probably read one of his reviews, blog comments or tweets (he's @PrinceJvstin).

Ben H. Winters is the New York Times bestselling author of *Underground Airlines* and the three novels of the *Last Policeman* series. He has been nominated three times for the Edgar Award from the Mystery Writers of America, and won once, and has also been given the Philip K. Dick Award for excellence in science fiction. He lives in Los Angeles with his wife and children.

K. Ceres Wright received her masters degree in Writing Popular Fiction from Seton Hill University in Greensburg, PA, and *Cog* was her thesis novel for the program. Wright's science fiction poem, 'Doomed', was a nominee for the Rhysling Award, the Science Fiction Poetry Association's highest honor. Her work has appeared in *Sycorax's Daughters*, *The Museum of All Things Awesome and That Go Boom*; *The City*; *Diner Stories: Off the Menu*; *Many Genres, One Craft*; *Dark Universe*; *Emanations: 2+2=5*; and other collections. She serves as president of Diverse Writers and Artists of Speculative Fiction and lives in Maryland. You can find her on Twitter @KCeresWright.

Hoda Zaki is the Virginia E. Lewis Professor of Political Science at Hood College, Frederick, Maryland, where she directs the African American Studies program and the Nonprofit and Civic Engagement minor. Her articles and reviews on Octavia E. Butler have appeared in *Sage*, The Women's Review of Books and Science-Fiction Studies. Hoda utilizes African and African American political theory to approach Butler's works. Her other publications include *Civil Rights* and *Politics at Hampton Institute: The Legacy of Alonzo G. Moron* and *Phoenix Renewed: The Survival and Mutation of Utopian Thought in North American Science Fiction, 1965-1982*.

COPYRIGHT INFORMATION

'Dear Kindred Teacher' copyright © 2017 by Rasha Abdulhadi

"Nationalism, Reproduction, And Hybridity In Octavia E. Butler's 'Bloodchild'"
copyright © 2017 by Raffaella Baccolini

'Dear Octavia' copyright © 2017 by Moya Bailey

'Dear Octavia' copyright © 2017 by Steven Barnes

'Dear Octavia' copyright © 2017 by Michele Tracy Berger

'Dear Octavia' copyright © 2017 by Tara Betts

'Dear Octavia' copyright © 2017 by Lisa Bennett Bolekaja

'Dear Ms. Butler' copyright © 2017 by K. Tempest Bradford

'Dear Ms. Butler' copyright © 2017 by Cassandra Brennan

'Dear Ms. Butler' copyright © 2017 by Jennifer Marie Brissett

'Dear Octavia' copyright © 2017 by Stephanie Burgis Samphire

'Dear Ms. Butler' copyright © 2017 by Mary Elizabeth Burroughs

'Dear Octavia E. Butler' copyright © 2017 by Christopher Caldwell

'Disrespecting Octavia' copyright © 2017 by Gerry Canavan

'Missives Through The Multiverse: Ephemeral Letters To Octavia Butler'
copyright © 2017 by Joyce Chng

'Dear Octavia E. Butler' copyright © 2017 by Indra Das

'A Letter To Octavia Butler' copyright © 2017 by L. Timmel Duchamp

'Dear Octavia' copyright © 2017 by Sophia Echavarria

'Dear Octavia' copyright © 2017 by Tuere T. S. Ganges

'Ms. Butler' copyright © 2017 by Stephen R. Gold

'The Final Frontier' copyright © 2017 by Jewelle Gomez

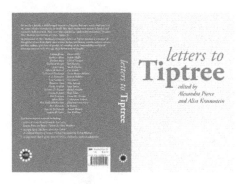

Also from multi-award winning editors
Alexandra Pierce and Alisa Krasnostein:

Letters to Tiptree

For nearly a decade, a middle-aged woman in Virginia (her own words) had much of the science fiction community in thrall. Her short stories were awarded, lauded and extremely well-reviewed. They were also regarded as 'ineluctably masculine,' because Alice Sheldon was writing as James Tiptree Jr.

In celebration of Alice Sheldon's centenary, *Letters to Tiptree* presents a selection of thoughtful letters from thirty-nine science fiction and fantasy writers, editors, critics, and fans addressing questions of gender, of sexuality, of the impossibility and joy of knowing someone only through their fiction and biography.

Winner of Locus Award, British Fantasy Award, Aurealis Convenors' Award, William Atheling Award for Criticism and Review, and Alfie Award. Nominated for British Science Fiction Award. Longlisted for Tiptree Award.

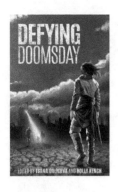

Defying Doomsday

How would you survive the apocalypse?

Teens form an all-girl band in the face of an impending comet.
A woman faces giant spiders to collect silk and protect her family.
New friends take their radio show on the road
in search of plague survivors.
A man seeks love in a fading world.

Defying Doomsday is an anthology of apocalypse fiction featuring disabled and chronically ill protagonists, proving it's not always the 'fittest' who survive – it's the most tenacious, stubborn, enduring and innovative characters who have the best chance of adapting when everything is lost.

In stories of fear, hope and survival, this anthology gives new perspectives on the end of the world, from authors Corinne Duyvis, Janet Edwards, Seanan McGuire, Tansy Rayner Roberts, Stephanie Gunn, Elinor Caiman Sands, Rivqa Rafael, Bogi Takács, John Chu, Maree Kimberley, Octavia Cade, Lauren E Mitchell, Thoraiya Dyer, Samantha Rich, and K L Evangelista.

Ditmar Winner for Best Collected Work

'Did We Break the End of the World?' by Tansy Rayner Roberts
Ditmar Winner for Best Novelette or Novella.